D0722334

Milton and Ovid

MILTON
AND OVID

Richard J. DuRocher

Cornell University Press

ITHACA AND LONDON

First published 1985 by
Cornell University Press.

International Standard Book Number
0-8014-1812-7
Library of Congress Catalog Card Number
85-47698
Printed in the United States of America
*Librarians: Library of Congress cataloging informa-
tion appears on the last page of the book.*

*The paper in this book is acid-free and meets the guide-
lines for permanence and durability of the Committee
on Production Guidelines for Book Longevity of the
Council on Library Resources.*

PR3562
.D84
1985

For Karen, my "individual solace dear"

Contents

Preface

Northrop Frye once reviewed a volume containing the complete poems of Blake and Donne by observing that the book will be useful to anyone who wants to have Blake and Donne "bound up" together. The present volume is meant for anyone willing to see that Milton and Ovid are inextricably bound up together, in more than the literal and comic senses, by Milton's thorough imitation, revaluation, and transformation of the *Metamorphoses* in *Paradise Lost*. Milton's use of Ovid's poem amounts to a profound challenge, by which the *Metamorphoses* is invoked to illuminate and support the argument of a theodicy foreign to it. Moreover, as I hope to show, Milton's extensive use of the *Metamorphoses* introduces an inventive method of presenting universal, mythic change which accounts for much of the dynamism in Milton's characterization, treatment of heroism, and epic narration.

Milton's works display something of the "plain Heroic magnitude of mind" that the poet ascribed to Samson. It may be over-dramatic to describe Milton's relation to Ovid in terms of an agon between two poetic champions, but the strenuous, open, and combative aspects of the metaphor are surely appropriate. Within *Paradise Lost,* this agon may be more accurately described as a dialogue between the two poets, an admittedly one-sided dialogue that arises during Milton's imitation of Ovid's poem. Thomas Greene has recently fused this metaphor with the Renaissance concept and practice of imitation in the phrase "dialectical imitation." Heroically and with considerable risk, Milton exposes his Christian epic to the potential contamination, fragmentation, and multivocality of

Ovid's metamorphic epic. By turning repeatedly to the *Meta-morphoses*, Milton enters into a dialogue with Ovid that not only measures the distance between their values and cultures but simultaneously spans that distance in a combative, creative interchange. From one view, Milton's dialogue with Ovid suggests the insufficiency of scripture and Judeo-Christian culture generally to supply images and material for his poem. More positively, the admixture of Ovidian elements expands and revitalizes the Christian mythos of the Fall for Milton's fit audience. Above all, Milton's dialogue with Ovid underscores the fact that both poems are epics of change: change that extends beyond the transformation of remote mythic figures to the promise of ongoing transformations throughout history; change that is reflected in a new form of the epic genre; change that involves the epic speakers themselves, who stand precariously yet prominently within their poetic worlds of change.

This study began in response to a question by a canny and reasonably skeptical reader, W. R. Johnson: "Is it possible and productive to think of an Ovidian Milton?" A more incredulous form of the question might be "How could John Milton, the high-minded Puritan revolutionary and bard, possibly have concerned himself with Publius Ovidius Naso, the author of licentious and irreverently witty Latin verse?" Because such a question about the conflicting philosophies and temperaments of Milton and Ovid is the first and most fundamental question a reader might raise on this topic, I have attempted to answer it in the first chapter. Surveying the evolution of Milton's views and uses of Ovid, Chapter 1 argues that, at a critical point in his career, Milton turned away from the amatory Ovid, the poet of the *Amores* and *Ars Amatoria,* to the epic Ovid. As he matured, moreover, Milton went beyond close, faithful imitation of Ovid's verses, as his academic training encouraged, to wide-ranging, critical transformation of Ovidian material, as his poetic genius directed him.

In light of this biographical evolution, the following chapters examine the specific ways in which Milton engages the *Meta-morphoses* in *Paradise Lost.* Chapters 2 through 4, pursuing the dialogue with Ovid from its manifestation in smaller to larger components of *Paradise Lost,* trace increasingly wider circles of Ovidian influence: on characters, on heroism, on epic structure. One brief simile, the celebrated comparison of Eden to Ovid's "fair field" of Enna, has proved so arresting and fertile that I have examined it as a model for Milton's adaptation of Ovidian figures in a preliminary section of Chapter 2. As that simile presents only the first of many Ovidian analogues for Eve, the rest of Chapter 2 considers the complete sequence and its effects on both Eve's psychology and Milton's approach to the Fall. By recombining scattered mythic figures from the *Metamorphoses*, Milton highlights distinct stages in Eve's development. The allusions alert the reader to Eve's vulnerability before the Fall and underscore her part in redemption afterward.

The same method of recombining Ovidian figures reappears in Chapter 3, which focuses on Satan. Here, figures from the *Metamorphoses* constitute only one of three Ovidian components characterizing Satan. Along with a series of mythic figures, rhetorical devices and stylistic features from the *Metamorphoses* are reembodied in Milton's most metamorphic character. These components combine to give Satan a shifting semblance of heroic grandeur which I term "counterheroism."

In opening the vexed question of heroism in terms of Ovidian poetics, Chapter 3 prepares the way for a discussion in Chapter 4 of the kind of heroic poem that can embrace the radical shifts and oppositions necessitated by counterheroism. Wittgenstein described genre as a family resemblance among literary works. Frye has aptly named the family of the *Metamorphoses* "contrast-epic," a term that, I maintain, includes *Paradise Lost* as well. In describing this family resemblance, Chapter 4 expands the inquiry from questions of characterization and heroism to those of genre and structure. The large-scale parallels speak forcefully of the poets' shared concerns: their opposition to martial, dynastic epic and their care to depict the pathos of human suffering among them. Even when he follows Ovid in shaping his epic narrative, however, Milton signals his differences from his model by revaluing Ovidian invention in terms of Christian virtues and divine inspiration.

Tracing the widest circle of all, Chapter 5 takes us outside the dialogue of Milton and Ovid to compare it with two similar dialogues: Spenser and Ovid, and Milton and Virgil. Spenser uses

Ovidian analogues generously to complicate the moral atmosphere of *The Faerie Queene;* his tacit approach interiorizes his dialogue with Ovid. Milton uses Virgil primarily as a model for sonority and static, or background, effects, such as the "darkness visible" of Hell. On the basis of these comparisons, the chapter concludes the book by offering an estimate and evaluation of the metamorphic presence of Ovid within *Paradise Lost.*

This is, then, an account of Milton's dialogue with Ovid in *Paradise Lost,* and a study of the combative kinship between the poets exemplified by that dialogue. Although I have written primarily to scholars and students of classical and English Renaissance literature, readers concerned with issues in comparative literature and readers of poetry in general may find the relationship of Milton and Ovid a valuable test case of literary influence, intertextuality, and imitation. Those primarily interested in literary theory will find in the Introduction a brief theory of influence and in Chapter 4 material bearing on narrative and genre theory. For those wishing to trace a particular passage in *Paradise Lost* to its counterpart in the *Metamorphoses,* a list of parallel passages appears in the Appendix.

Milton has Satan say that "a grateful mind /By owing owes not, but still pays, at once / Indebted and discharg'd." Satan could not accept this mystical economy; I cannot forget it. I owe a great debt of guidance, encouragement, and support in this project to my colleagues and teachers, family and friends. M. H. Abrams, Ward Allen, Max Black, Scott Elledge, W. R. Johnson, Carol V. Kaske, David Novarr, and Joseph Wittreich, Jr., all read drafts or earlier versions of the manuscript, and all have improved me while improving my pages. Evan Radcliffe sharpened my understanding of argument and commitment as only a dedicated spirit could. Kenneth J. Knoespel sustained my commitment to Ovid and the resources of history through his words and his example. Jane Armstrong, Greg Hyde, Meridith Randall, and Carolyn Sigler helped to keep the final version free of errors. All that remain are mine. My study was initially funded by the Danforth Foundation, whose support has continued in many ways. I am grateful to the editors of *Milton Quarterly* for permission to reprint "The Wealth and Blood of Milton's Sonnet XI," *MQ* 17 (1983), 15–17, part of which appears in Chapter 1; to Columbia University Press, for permission to quote Milton from the edition of Frank A. Patterson et al. (New York, 1931–40); and to BSB B. G. Teubner Press, for permission to quote Ovid from the edition of W. S. Anderson (Leipzig, 1977). I am grateful to the three universities that have supported the project: Cornell University, where the work began; the University of Wisconsin–Madison, for a visiting appointment in 1982–83; and the Florida State University, for a Research Grant in 1983–84. I wish especially to thank the three who made it possible: Mary Ann Radzinowicz, who directed my Cornell dissertation; Sister Mary Consuella, R.S.M., who taught me Latin; and my mother, Mildred McNamara DuRocher, who read me poems. My greatest debt is expressed in the dedication.

RICHARD J. DUROCHER

Tallahassee, Florida

Abbreviations

CJ	*Classical Journal*
CL	*Comparative Literature*
CP	*Classical Philology*
CPW	*The Complete Prose Works of John Milton.* 8 vols. Ed. Don M. Wolfe et al. New Haven: Yale University Press, 1953–82.
CQ	*Classical Quarterly*
ELH	*English Literary History*
ELR	*English Literary Renaissance*
JEGP	*Journal of English and Germanic Philology*
MP	*Modern Philology*
MQ	*Milton Quarterly*
MS	*Milton Studies*
OED	*Oxford English Dictionary*
PMLA	*Publications of the Modern Language Association of America*
PQ	*Philological Quarterly*
RenQ	*Renaissance Quarterly*
SEL	*Studies in English Literature*
SP	*Studies in Philology*
TSLL	*Texas Studies in Literature and Language*
Works	*The Columbia Edition of the Works of John Milton.* 23 vols. Ed. Frank Allan Patterson et al. New York: Columbia University Press, 1931–40.

Milton and Ovid

Critical Introduction

Within a generation after the publication of *Paradise Lost* in 1667, critics and editors of the poem were already calling attention to many of its allusions to and reminiscences of Ovid's *Metamorphoses*. In his *Annotations on Milton's "Paradise Lost"* (London: J. Tonson, 1695), Patrick Hume noted several "parallel places and imitations of Ovid," among them the description of Eve's fascination with her image along the lines of Ovid's fable of Narcissus. In his idiosyncratic yet scholarly *Milton's "Paradise Lost." A New Edition* (London, 1732), Richard Bentley added to Hume's catalog of Ovidian allusions many more, including evidence of Satan's deployment of Ovidian rhetoric in his speeches to the fallen angels. William Wordsworth disparaged at least one Ovidian metamorphosis in Milton's epic, in which the devils turn into serpents when Satan announces that he has seduced mankind. Writing at approximately the same time, Thomas de Quincey celebrated the poetic union between the "festal gaiety, and the brilliant velocity of [the] *aurora borealis* intellect" of Ovid and the "mighty gloom and solemn planetary movement in the mind" of Milton. In the twentieth century, Merritt Hughes, Douglas Bush, and Alastair Fowler have all produced editions of *Paradise Lost* which evidence its overwhelming quantity of Ovidian analogues and allusions. This brief survey suggests the need for a study of *Paradise Lost* and the *Metamorphoses* that goes beyond simply listing the verbal echoes in the poems or merely intimating the creative relationship between the poets.[1] I

[1]For a list of such verbal correspondences, see Mary Campbell Brill, "Milton and Ovid," diss. Cornell University, 1935. De Quincey's statement is from *Orthographic*

have attempted to provide a study of the relationship between *Paradise Lost* and the *Metamophorses* by examining the effects of Ovidian allusions, analogues, and techniques on the style and significance of Milton's epic. "Style" in this context indicates Milton's distinctive poetic expression in such local matters as diction, imagery, and tone, as well as in larger patterns including characterization, rhetoric, and narrative structure. Rather than diminishing Milton's individual talent, the Ovidian tradition tempers the poet's putatively monolithic style with flexibility, multivocality, and wit. As I hope the subsequent chapters will show, the presence of Ovid in *Paradise Lost* can enable us to discover a greater depth of characterization (especially of Eve and Satan), a broader range of expression (including satire and domestic humor), and a wider scope of significance (in poetically fusing myth, legend, and history) than has yet been recognized.

The survey with which we began suggests also that other scholars have been concerned with this relationship. A useful precedent for my study is Davis P. Harding's *Milton and the Renaissance Ovid*, which aims, according to Harding, "to throw what new light I can on Milton's debt to Ovid by examining the Renaissance editions which Milton himself might have used."[2] Although I apply a number of Harding's findings, especially those concerning Milton's early poems, my approach to *Paradise Lost* differs from Harding's in two fundamental ways. First, Milton's proficiency as a reader of Latin verse has directed me away from translations and toward the Latin text of the *Metamorphoses*, which we know was in Milton's library.[3]

Mutineers (1847), in *The Collected Writings of Thomas De Quincey*, ed. David Masson, 14 vols. (Edinburgh, 1889–90; rpt. New York, 1968), 11:449.

[2]Davis P. Harding, *Milton and the Renaissance Ovid* (Urbana, Ill., 1946), p. 7.

[3]See Jackson C. Boswell, *Milton's Library* (New York, 1975), p. 184. We do not know exactly what edition of the *Metamorphoses* Milton used, however, because it was apparently sold (by his daughters?) along with many other of the poet's books. See J. Milton French, ed., *The Life Records of John Milton*, 5 vols. (New Brunswick, N.J., 1949–58), 4:374–75; and William R. Parker, *Milton: A Biography*, 2 vols. (Oxford, 1968), 1:607–8. In this study I have used the modern scholarly edition of the *Metamorphoses*, ed. William S. Anderson (Leipzig, 1977), which is based on the 1652 Heinsius edition, the best available text in Milton's day. I have also consulted the texts of Ovid in the Loeb Classical Library (Harvard, 1977). All translations from Ovid's poetry in my text are, unless otherwise indicated, my own.

Second, I am less concerned than Harding with the valid historical question of how a generally perceptive seventeenth-century reader, following current commentaries, might have interpreted the *Metamorphoses*. The crucial question of my study is how one fiercely independent poet, overtly skeptical of glosses and commentaries, incorporated and adapted the *Metamorphoses* within his epic.

The methodology of my book is closer to that of two works which briefly consider the relationship of Milton and Ovid within their larger surveys. Douglas Bush's chapter on Milton in *Mythology and the Renaissance Tradition in English Poetry* broke new ground fifty years ago, yet it remains unsurpassed in providing a learned overview of Milton's splendid functional uses of classical myth.[4] Bush's attempt to view Milton's handling of mythology as the culmination of the Renaissance tradition distinguishes his approach from mine,[5] but Bush's philological and comparative standards have been my aims throughout. Bush's work, moreover, summarizes the findings of J. Holly Hanford, Charles Osgood, and E. K. Rand, all of whom have made important contributions to the current store of knowledge concerning Milton's personal and literary affinities with Ovid.[6]

The most recent book dealing with Milton and Ovid, Louis Martz's *Poet of Exile*, contains three short chapters on what Martz terms "figurations of Ovid": the "anti-heroic" mode, pastoral love conventions, and the historical and prophetic conclusion.[7] Martz's treatment of these topics is highly suggestive but, given his brief survey of them, not definitive. Adapting Brooks Otis's discussion of the "epic panels" of the *Metamorphoses*, Martz argues for a greater congruence between the overall structures of the *Metamorphoses* and *Paradise Lost* than I can acknowledge. A closer analogue of the "panel" construction of the *Metamorphoses* would seem to be Spenser's *Faerie Queene*, with its interlocked episodes, cantos, and

---

[4]Douglas Bush, *Mythology and the Renaissance Tradition in English Poetry*, rev. ed. (New York, 1963), p. 285.

[5]Ibid., p. 267.

[6]See Charles Osgood, *The Classical Mythology of Milton's English Poems* (New York, 1900); E. K. Rand, "Milton in Rustication," *SP* 19 (1922), 109–35; and J. Holly Hanford, *The Youth of Milton: Studies in Shakespeare, Milton, and Donne* (New York, 1964), pp. 87–164.

[7]Louis Martz, *Poet of Exile: A Study of Milton's Poetry* (New Haven, 1980).

books. Martz offers valuable insights on mode, love conventions, and structure, but he does not consider the dynamic nature of Milton's adaptation of Ovidian characters, rhetoric, and narrative structure.

Before embarking upon an analysis of the Ovidian elements in *Paradise Lost*, however, we need to have in mind two hermeneutic guides, one historical, one theoretical. These guides may prevent us from unwarranted speculation, from seeing Ovid behind every line and figure of *Paradise Lost*. Because Ovid's *Metamorphoses* has been interpreted in various ways throughout history, we need to know how its interpreters before Milton prepared him to read it. Once we are assured of the high and unique status granted the *Metamorphoses* by authorities whom Milton knew and respected, we need to consider the kind of relationship Milton openly enters with Ovid. The extensive theoretical activity of the last decade has made available various theories or models of literary influence. Often, as we shall see, the metaphors used to describe a literary relationship are more telling than the logic of theoretical arguments. My main concern in this regard is to show that a dialectical theory or metaphor is both appropriate to the Milton–Ovid relationship and consistent with the poets' intellectual and historical backgrounds.

Ovid's Metamorphic Epic

Ovid's *Metamorphoses* has proven itself a classic in J. F. Kermode's restricted sense: "The books we call classics possess intrinsic qualities that endure, but possess also an openness to accommodation which keeps them alive under endlessly varying dispositions."[8] In the centuries preceding Milton, three major dispositions, three ways of reading the *Metamorphoses*, emerge. These ways of reading—call them allegorical, rhetorical, and epical—constitute their own dialectic, in which the final stage fuses the previous and opposed readings while preserving some of their vital insights. I antic-

---

[8]J. F. Kermode, *The Classic: Literary Images of Permanence and Change* (New York, 1975), p. 44.

ipate the final step in this process to insist on the crucial point: Milton was thus prepared to classify the *Metamorphoses,* as Ovid's contemporaries and Renaissance commentators unanimously classified it, as a distinct form of the epic poem.

The allegorical way of reading the *Metamorphoses* which flourished during the late Middle Ages is well known, and it has been well documented and discussed by Douglas Bush, D. C. Allen, and Clark Hulse.[9] Essentially, medieval interpreters treated the poem as an appealing if suspect fiction that could be expounded in support of Christian theology and morality. This allegorical move attests to at least three relevant facts: the immense popularity of the *Metamorphoses* among Christian readers, inviting the Church somehow to draw it within the circle of orthodoxy; the apparent incompatibility of the surface of the *Metamorphoses* with Christian doctrine; and the exegetical habit of reading through or beyond the surface of pagan literature (including Virgil's *Aeneid*) to discover "hidden" meanings. The principal allegorical commentaries include the anonymous, fourteenth-century *Ovide Moralisé* and Pierre Bersuire's *Metamorphosis Ovidiana moraliter,* both widely published and frequently reprinted throughout the fifteenth and sixteenth centuries. In his preface, Bersuire claims that the pagan poets who invented the fables invariably (whether intentionally or by the working of the Holy Spirit, he does not say) hid some truth under their fictions. Through these fictions, Bersuire explains, the mysteries of faith might be strengthened.[10] Coming toward the end of the allegorical tradition is Peter Lavinius, who furnished the moralized commentaries on some of the fables in Raphael Regius's standard edition of Ovid. For Lavinius, too, the fictional surface of the *Metamorphoses* is a veil for its spiritual meaning: "fabuloso . . . velamenta, variae sacrarum scriptorarum allegorico sensi teguntur

---

[9]See Bush, *Mythology and the Renaissance Tradition in English Poetry,* esp. chap. 1; D. C. Allen, *Mysteriously Meant: The Rediscovery of Pagan Symbolism and Allegorical Interpretation in the Renaissance* (Baltimore, 1970), esp. pp. 168–94; and Clark Hulse, *Metamorphic Verse: The Elizabethan Minor Epic* (Princeton, N.J., 1981), pp. 244–51. My survey is particularly indebted to Hulse, who discusses these three ways of reading the *Metamorphoses* but calls the second "humanistic."

[10]Pierre Bersuire, *Metamorphosis Ovidiana moraliter* (Paris, 1509), prologue, fol. a[1]v.

historiae" (under a fictive veil, various stories from sacred scripture are hidden by means of the allegorical sense).[11] In this way, Ovid's fables acquire a contingent kind of truth, upon which Lavinius insists in a recurrent phrase in his commentary: "veritas tamen alia [referring to his summary of the fable itself] est."[12] If the fable is not true in itself, then it is nevertheless true if interpreted in the context of sacred scripture.

What underlies such comments is a concern to accommodate the *Metamorphoses* to an established order, or in Hulse's term, an ideology external to it. Given this concern, the allegorists largely neglected or even contradicted internal evidence, for example, poetic forms and their effects, verbal and structural parallels, surface meaning, and emotional coloring. One can readily find different allegorical interpretations of the same passage which flatly contradict each other;[13] and the method of reading figures both *in bono* and *in malo*, while comprehending the extremes of moral significance, simply leaves out all intermediate possibilities, moral and otherwise.

For all its shortcomings, however, the allegorical method was not without compensations. In their desire to discover order in the *Metamorphoses*, particularly an order compatible with Christian theology, the allegorists emphasized the epic framework of the poem. They noted that the poem begins with an account of creation out of chaos, proceeds through a story of a universal flood, and concludes with the apotheosis of a great ruler in Rome: all events reconcilable with Christian salvation history. The allegorists took seriously Ovid's claim to have written a *carmen perpetuum* (perpetual song), which they read as a continuous universal history leading up to and predicting the Redeemer. One might object that this reading fails to examine the peculiar kind of "history" Ovid presents, or that the historical framework leaves out huge sections of Ovid's narrative that do not conform to the Christian order. That order, to Bersuire and others, was simply of greater significance than Ovid's poem.

In sharp contrast to the allegorists, the rhetorical or humanistic

---

[11]Peter Lavinius, in *P. Ovidii Nasonis poete ingeniosissimi Metamorphoseos Libri XV* (Venice, 1527), fol. 19^r–19^v.

[12]Ibid., fol. 14^r.

[13]See Allen, *Mysteriously Meant*, pp. 177–78, for examples.

interpreters asserted that the verbal surface of Ovid's text was of primary importance. Hulse dates the rise of this new way of reading in the early sixteenth century, and he finds its manifesto in the edition of the *Metamorphoses* by Raphael Regius (Milan, 1493). An Italian humanist and philologist, Regius attacked the practice of theological allegoresis as inappropriate to Ovid's historical and cultural moment. For example, Regius finds Ovid's creation account indebted not only to Genesis but to Hesiod, Plato, and the Stoics as well. Throughout his edition, Regius documents Ovid's classical forebears and identifies his rhetorical figures. While attending closely to Ovid's literary and rhetorical contexts, however, Regius loses sight of the larger unity of the *Metamorphoses*. In Hulse's phrase, Regius "disintegrates it into an encyclopaedia of classical culture and a series of elegant rhetorical figures."[14]

The so-called disintegration of Ovid's text can be more usefully understood as its reapplication to another purpose, namely, the widespread use of the *Metamorphoses* in Renaissance education, especially for rhetorical training. Milton's initial encounter with the poem no doubt took place in this context, as I shall argue in Chapter 1. Regius's emphasis on the rhetorical figures of Ovid is writ large in the proliferation of encyclopedic handbooks of rhetoric in the sixteenth and seventeenth centuries. A glance through the popular rhetorics of Abraham Fraunce, George Puttenham, and Thomas Wilson reveals how the *Metamorphoses* was fragmented and desiccated for rhetorical training and amplification. At the same time, such widely used commentaries as the gloss of Lactantius Placidus and Robert Schuler's *Fabularum Ovidii interpretatio* (Cambridge, 1584) continued the rhetoricians' fragmentation of Ovid by breaking down the *Metamorphoses* into separable episodes—232, according to Lactantius. The "episodic" editions and commentaries obscure some of the most distinctive features of the poem: its witty transitions, multilayered narrative, and irrepressible narrative voice. In exchange for the ideological Ovid of the allegorists, the rhetorical interpreters deliver an episodic Ovid, a poem of fragments.

Before proceeding to the epical readings of the *Metamorphoses*,

[14]Hulse, p. 247.

we do well to observe that the previous two approaches continue throughout the sixteenth and seventeenth centuries. The rhetorically oriented commentaries and editions do not drive out the allegories; rather, hybrid interpretations and editions flourish. For example, Arthur Golding's English translation of 1567 somewhat awkwardly mingles allegorical and rhetorical commentary. As do John Brinsley and others, Golding gives Christian analogues for the first twelve fables of Book 1, because Ovid must (it is assumed) have received these accounts from those who knew sacred scripture. In Golding's words: "What man is he but would suppose the author of this booke / The first foundation of his woorke from Moyses wryghtings tooke?"[15] Even more syncretic, Jacob Spanmueller's scholarly *Metamorphoseon libris XV* (Antwerp, 1610) incorporates the best—or at least the most appealing—allegorical readings of his predecessors, including Moltzer, Ciofani, Tritonius, and Schuler. At no point before Milton, moreover, does Ovid become wholly unallegorical. The magnificent translation of Ovid with an allegorical commentary by George Sandys (London, 1632) was reprinted in almost every decade until the end of the seventeenth century. In one sense the high-water mark of Renaissance humanism, Sandys's edition nevertheless reverts to the medieval habit of accepting multiple layers of allegory for single passages, "so [long] as the principall parts of application resemble the grounde worke" of Ovid's text.[16]

While allegorical and rhetorical versions of the *Metamorphoses* continued to appear, toward the end of the sixteenth century a new spirit entered English literary criticism, a spirit that both radically devalued those approaches and prompted a reconsideration of the poem's unity. This new spirit was Aristotelianism. Its two greatest exponents in Elizabethan England were no doubt Sir Philip Sidney and Ben Jonson. Sidney's Aristotelian definition of poetry in his *Defense of Poetry* (1595) is almost too familiar to require quotation;

[15]Arthur Golding, trans., *Ovid's Metamorphoses*, ed. W. H. D. Rouse (Carbondale, Ill., 1962), pp. 7–8.

[16]*Ovid's "Metamorphosis" Englished, Mythologized, and Represented in Figures*, by George Sandys, ed. Karl K. Hulley and Stanley T. Vandersall, with foreword by Douglas Bush (Lincoln, Neb., 1970), p. 4.

Jonson's definition in *Discoveries* (1640), although markedly similar to it, is yet more strictly Aristotelian:

> A Poet is . . . a Maker, or a fainer; His Art, an Art of imitation or faining; expressing the life of man in fit measure, numbers, and harmony, according to *Aristotle*: from the word ποιειν, which signifies to make or fayne. Hence, hee is called a *Poet*, not hee which writeth in measure only; but that fayneth and formeth a fable, and writes things like the Truth. For the fable and fiction is (as it were) the forme and Soule of any poetical worke, or *Poeme*.[17]

As we have seen, the allegorical critics regarded the "fable and fiction" of the *Metamorphoses* as an expendable husk or covering for the moral and spiritual meaning beneath. The rhetorical critics, on the other hand, concentrated on the figures and "colours" of rhetoric in individual fables so minutely that Ovid's overarching fable and fiction were scarcely seen. According to Aristotle's theory, however, which carried the weight and authority of classical antiquity, the fable (in Sidneyan terms, the "fore-conceit") is the proper measure of poetic achievement and unity, is, in Jonson's phrase, "the forme and Soule of any poetical worke."[18] Therefore, criticism that failed to treat the fable (what Milton would call the "argument") of a poem as the primary problem or object of attention quickly became null, poetically irrelevant.[19] In particular, Aristotelianism exposed allegories and rhetorical encyclopedias as nonpoetic applications, rather than interpretations, of Ovid's poem.

Historically, Aristotelianism reached England through the mediation of Italian critics and translators, who altered the philosopher even as they spread his theory. Milton's keen interest in Renaissance Italian criticism, particularly in the commentaries of

[17]Ben Jonson, *Works*, 11 vols., ed. C. H. Herford, Percy Simpson, and Evelyn Simpson (Oxford, 1925–52), 8:635.

[18]Worth comparing is Torquato Tasso's formulation of the "fable" as constituting "the first principle and soul of the poem," in his *Discourses on the Heroic Poem*, trans. Mariella Cavalchini and Irene Samuel (Oxford, 1973), p. 17.

[19]See J. E. Spingarn, *A History of Literary Criticism in the Renaissance* (New York, 1924), pp. 277–78.

Castelvetro, Mazzoni, and Torquato Tasso, is documented in his prose tracts, *The Reason of Church Government* (1642) and *Of Education* (1644) (*CPW*, 1:813–17; 2:404–5). If there is a single theoretical principle that Milton shared with these Italian critics, it must surely be that Aristotle, although commanding great respect, could be enriched or expanded in light of the successful innovations of the best modern poets.

The central problem faced by the Italian critics of Aristotle was one Milton pondered in considering the best form for his projected masterwork. While pondering in *The Reason of Church Government* whether the epic, dramatic, or lyric mode might be "found more doctrinal and exemplary to a Nation," Milton parenthetically raises the larger theoretical question, asking "whether the rules of Aristotle herein are strictly to be kept, or nature to be follow'd, which in them that know art, and use judgment is no transgression, but an enriching of art" (*CPW*, 1:813). Milton's implicit answer aligns him most closely with the Italian theorist Giraldi Cinthio.[20] In *Dei romanzi* [*On Romances*] (Venice, 1549; 1554), Giraldi had celebrated the heroic poems or romance-epics of Ariosto and Boiardo, which diverged from the model epic of a single action praised by Aristotle. In defending these poems from censure by strict Aristotelian critics, Giraldi cites Ovid's *Metamorphoses* as an example of a heroic poem among the ancients that successfully includes both multiple plot-lines and a wide variety of subject matter. Giraldi Cinthio thereby presents the first comprehensive view of the *Metamorphoses* as a non-Aristotelian epic. His view, along with that of Tasso, exemplifies the epical reading of Ovid.

Giraldi begins his defense of the non-Aristotelian epic by arguing for the appropriateness of a historically ordered fable to the epic, and particularly to the *Metamorphoses*. Thus he recovers the historical framework of the poem which the allegorists had grasped and the rhetoricians had virtually ignored. Conscious both of Aristotle's objection to historical coverage and of Ovid's sweeping treatment of history in the epic, Giraldi maintains that a poetic innovation can temper Aristotle's rules: "In his *Metamorphoses*, Ovid has shown what is fitting for the ingenious poet to do, for abandoning

---

[20]According to the editors of *CPW*, 1:813n.

Aristotle's laws of art with admirable mastery, he commenced the work at the beginning of the world and treated in marvelous sequence a great variety of matters; nevertheless he managed to do so in a fewer number of books than Homer did in the *Iliad* and the *Odyssey*, even though both of these embrace a single action."[21] The unity of the *Metamorphoses*, Giraldi perceives, lies in its "marvelous sequence," held together by Ovid's ingenuity. Thus Giraldi finds in the *Metamorphoses* the epic norms he isolated in Boiardo and Ariosto, namely, a single proposition (though one containing diverse matter) and a unified narrative voice. The unity of Ovid's proposition is deftly summarized in the opening words of A. E. Watts's translation: "Change is my theme."[22] And it is the ubiquitous presence of the narrator that carries the poem through its wide-ranging sequence of changes.

Giraldi goes on to cite approvingly many of the devices by which Ovid moves effectively through history. He notes Ovid's use of predictions made by diviners or prophets, his glancing or summary coverage of certain historical epochs, his un-Virgilian, antidynastic approach to Roman history. Giraldi can be fairly credited with this anti-Augustan interpretation, which has only recently been revived by Brooks Otis and others.[23]

Torquato Tasso continued and developed Giraldi's celebration of the *Metamorphoses* as an original form of the heroic poem. In *Discourses on the Heroic Poem* (1594), Tasso observes that Ovid departed from historical accuracy at the end of his poem, "where the Italian philosopher Pythagoras instructs the Roman king Numa, although the more reliable account has Pythagoras born centuries later." For Tasso this practice is excusable, however, not only because it follows the example of Homer and Virgil in altering chronology but especially because it satisfies the poet's essential purpose. The historian must be accurate; the poet aims at delightful teaching, often at the expense of historical veracity. Despite the superficial framework of historical progression in the *Meta-*

---

[21]Giraldi Cinthio, *On Romances*, trans. Henry L. Snuggs (Lexington, Ky., 1968), p. 20.

[22]A. E. Watts, trans., *The "Metamorphoses" of Ovid* (San Francisco, 1980), p. 1.

[23]Brooks Otis, *Ovid as an Epic Poet*, 2d rev. ed. (Cambridge, Mass., 1970), esp. pp. vii–x.

morphoses, Ovid's "history," Tasso points out, is not much concerned with historical chronology. What Ovid is concerned to create, according to Tasso, is wonder. The spectacular theme of metamorphosis itself incites wonder, yet Ovid intensifies the effect through his narrative mode. Ovid's mannered narration leads readers to create their own images of the transformations, whereas dramatizing such changes would supply a deficient spectacle. Ovid's poem thus generates wonder, and "to move wonder," Tasso writes, "fits no kind of poetry so much as epic."[24] In particular, Tasso commends the transformation of Cadmus, which, as I shall argue in Chapter 3, Milton incorporates into his depiction of Satan.

If we combine the insights of Aristotle, Giraldi Cinthio, and Tasso, we have a body of theory that upholds Ovid's *Metamorphoses* as worthy of imitation by the Renaissance epic poet. First of all, the *Metamorphoses* is seen as Ovid's contemporaries saw it: as an epic poem. Its departures from Aristotelian canons—its multiple plot, historical framework, and prominent narrator—are recognized as successful innovations, as variations conducive to the proper epic effect of wonder. Its proximity to Italian epic and romance, along with its perceived opposition to Virgilian epic, makes the *Metamorphoses* the most forward-looking of the classical models, an epic demonstrably suited to adaptation to new languages and cultures. These synchronic and diachronic features may be summarized in the term "contrast-epic," as Chapter 4 will explain. What makes Ovid's *Metamorphoses* crucial to an understanding of Milton's epic are two of its essential properties: a nonlinear narrative structure, punctuated and arranged by an irrepressible narrator; and a universal argument, not of battles and empires, but of fundamental changes, at once mythic and psychological. The narrative voice focuses and fuses these properties, for the poet who unfolds, juxtaposes, and comments on the mythic changes also reflects the theme of change in his mercurial narrative presence.

None of these Ovidian strategies were lost on Milton. Moreover, the series of revaluations of the *Metamorphoses* traced here suggests a variety of ways in which Milton could use Ovid's poem. Its history of allegorical adaptation to Christian doctrine could point Milton to

[24]Tasso, pp. 59, 16.

his own adaptation, even transformation of Ovid. Its formal features could serve as a model for Milton's imitation or emulation in his narrative of change. Its unique epic status could direct Milton to a similar revaluation of the epic tradition. There is a further possibility. Ovid boasts at the end of the *Metamorphoses* that through this work his fame shall live. The rhetorical vitality of Ovid should alert us to Ovid's use of Milton, that is, to Ovid's effect on *Paradise Lost*. To paraphrase Hulse: so adaptable a poem as the *Metamorphoses* is as likely to transform its new environment as to be transformed by it.

Some Versions of Influence

My suggestion in the foregoing discussion of a degree of mutuality between Milton and Ovid may raise objections among some historically minded readers; at the same time, my attempt to view the *Metamorphoses* as a developing cultural artifact may strike more formalist readers as extrinsic to formal analysis. Sound historical (including philological) understanding and accurate analysis of formal structures are, I believe, mutually illuminating tools in studying literary influence. By the same token, approaches that neglect either of these tools do so to their detriment. Literary "history" without critical or aesthetic acumen is as facile as Crocean "appreciation" or evaluation without historical grounding. Source or influence study pursued in the nineteenth-century tradition of mechanically historical (positivistic) philology, pursued, that is, as an end in itself, stands as a frequently sterile and regrettable example. The errors of uncritical source study should not, however, lead us to abandon studying literary relationships in light of historical data and formal structures. Rejecting the critical complacency of Positivism as well as the antihistorical bias of New Criticism, a "new historicism" has emerged in the work of, among others, Hans Robert Jauss, Robert Weimann, and Stephen Greenblatt.[25] One of

[25]See the articles by Hans Robert Jauss and Robert Weimann in *New Directions in Literary History*, ed. Ralph Cohen (London, 1974). Stephen Greenblatt's introduction to *The Forms of Power and the Power of Forms in the Renaissance*, Special Topics Issue # 7, *Genre* 15 (1982), 3–6, is a virtual manifesto of "new historicism."

the shared tenets of these scholars is the notion that literary history (and its subspecies, accounts of literary relations) can be created and recreated, actively shaped within literary works and by literary critics. Literary history thus becomes a function of both historical data and current understanding. The new historicists warn, moreover, that our shaping of the literary past is never disinterested, that in shaping literary traditions according to present values our own ideological and methodological assumptions need to be brought to light.[26]

Yet present assumptions are themselves partly shaped by past ones. Perhaps, then, the best exposition of my version of literary influence may emerge against the background of the major theoretical approaches during the recent past. Among the relevant theories may be discerned three broad groups, distinguished primarily by their chief metaphors for influence: influence as anxiety (Bloom); influence as illumination (Wittreich); influence as dialogue (Greene). Represented thus schematically, these groups may seem distinct and independent; actually, the colloquy among their members constitutes an on-going debate.

To paraphrase (and, appropriately, to revise) one of the critic's most influential pronouncements, Bloom—not Milton—is the central problem in any modern theory of poetic influence. In *The Anxiety of Influence* (1973) Harold Bloom attacked the standard, comfortable notion that influence consists of a more or less direct "borrowing" of a previous poet's work. Rejecting this economic metaphor, with its suggestions of neighborly benignity and faithful continuity, Bloom defines influence as inherently anxious, antagonistic, and revisionary: "Poetic Influence—when it involves two strong, authentic poets—always proceeds by a misreading of the prior poet, an act of creative correction that is actually and necessarily a misinterpretation. The history of fruitful poetic influence, which is to say the main tradition of Western poetry since the Renaissance, is a history of anxiety and self-saving caricature, of distortion, of perverse, wilful revisionism without which modern poetry as such could not exist."[27]

[26]Greenblatt, pp. 5–6.
[27]Harold Bloom, *The Anxiety of Influence: A Theory of Poetry* (New York, 1973), p. 30.

To clarify the anxiety postulated on the part of the later poet toward his authentic precursor, Bloom adduces Freud's analysis of the Oedipal anxiety of a son toward his father. Accordingly, Bloom identifies a set of distortive processes, which he calls "revisionary ratios," modeled on Freud's defense mechanisms (though also equated with both the interpretive schemes of the Hebrew Kabbalists and the rhetorical tropes of classical antiquity). Bloom's subsequent criticism puckishly yet consistently practices what he calls "antithetical criticism," which he sees as a series of misreadings anxiously opposed to the standard misreadings of his precursor critics. In fairness to Bloom, he exempts Milton from the filial anxiety that riddles later poets in English. The unfortunate effect of this exemption, however, is to present an inflexible, authoritarian, fatherly Milton. In *Paradise Lost,* Milton uses the relationship of Father and Son to express an ideal, harmonious relationship, though one of creative tension. As Joseph Wittreich suggests, this harmonious image of sonship is a more appropriate model for Milton's prophetic heirs than Bloom's anxious one.[28] Moreover, Bloom's isolation of six rhetorical tropes to match his "revisionary ratios" seems highly arbitrary when applied to Ovid and Milton. These two poets employed the entire repertoire of rhetorical tropes, and employed them primarily for self-expression, not for revision of an earlier poet.

Nevertheless, a number of Bloom's colleagues have rallied around one of these tropes, transumption or metalepsis, as the master trope for diachronic allusion in general.[29] There is a metaphoric sense in which this identification is appropriate. Puttenham called metalepsis "the farfet, as when we had rather fetch a word a great way off then to use one nearer hand to express the matter aswel & plainer."[30] Certainly allusion works by seeking something distant (or at least absent) to compare to something described as if

[28]See Joseph Wittreich, Jr., *Angel of Apocalypse: Blake's Idea of Milton* (Madison, Wisc., 1975), p. 226.

[29]Angus Fletcher, *Allegory: The Theory of a Symbolic Mode* (Ithaca, N.Y., 1964), p. 241n.; John Hollander, *The Figure of Echo: A Mode of Allusion in Milton and After* (Berkeley, Calif., 1981), pp. 133–49; John Guillory, *Poetic Authority: Spenser, Milton, and Literary History* (New York, 1983), pp. 131–45.

[30]George Puttenham, *The Arte of English Poesie* (1589), ed. Gladys Doidge Willcock and Alice Walker (Cambridge, 1936), p. 183.

present. But seeking a remote name for allusion and preferring it to current terminology is itself farfetched. John Hollander's survey of the history of transumption in *The Figure of Echo* reveals his resourcefulness in expounding the term's metaphoric potential, to wit: "The whole Renaissance is in a sense a transumption of antique culture."[31] Yet Hollander's survey shows primarily that, from antiquity through the Renaissance, transumption was regarded as a trope of syntax providing a transition between single words. Quintilian's discussion, which Hollander quotes, remains standard for the Renaissance:

> It is the nature of *metalepsis* to form a kind of intermediate step between the term transferred and the thing to which it is transferred, having no meaning in itself, but merely providing a transition. It is a *trope* with which to claim acquaintance, rather than one which we are ever likely to require to use. The commonest example is the following: *cano* is a synonym for *canto* and *canto* for *dico*, therefore *cano* is a synonym for *dico*, the intermediate step being provided by *canto*. We need not waste any more time over it. (Loeb, trans. H. E. Butler)

I see no reason to read a rhetorical term allegorically in order to support an ideological meaning unrecognized by its practitioners. Moreover, a conceptually rich and historically current term for diachronic allusion already exists in "imitation."

Having excluded its Oedipal and rhetorical implications, let us return to Bloom's still useful definition of influence. Bloom's general sense of antagonism in literary relations is surely appropriate to Milton's stance toward his pagan precursors. The reason for Milton's antagonism is easily understood. As a Christian poet, he takes pains to point out the dependent epistemological status of pagan literature, always subordinate for Milton to the truth of sacred scripture or divine revelation. Paradoxically, he makes this critique even as he incorporates elements of pagan poetry into what on the title page of *Paradise Lost* he calls a poem, so that his own poetic enterprise is subjected to the same critique. If there is anxiety involved in this stance, it is the anxiety of a witness for the

[31]Hollander, p. 147.

transcendent who can express his vision only in the language of a fallen world.

To take only one example (explored more fully in Chapter 2), Milton compares Adam and Eve, in prayer after the Fall, to Ovid's Deucalion and Pyrrha, in prayer after a worldwide flood. The comparison involves an antagonistic yet ambivalent correction. Adam and Eve pray humbly:

> yet thir port
> Not of mean suiters, nor important less
> Seem'd thir Petition, then when th'ancient Pair
> In Fables old, less ancient yet then these,
> *Deucalion* and chaste *Pyrrha* to restore
> The Race of Mankind drownd, before the Shrine
> Of *Themis* stood devout.
>
> (XI, 8–14)[32]

At first glance, Milton seems to diminish the status of the pagan myth by insisting that the petition of Adam and Eve is at least as important as that of Deucalion and Pyrrha. Yet the word "Seem'd" opens that insistence to doubt. Within the comparison, Milton apparently claims superiority for Adam and Eve because of their chronological priority to the Ovidian suitors. The priority is based, of course, on the absolute primacy and authority of scripture in describing Adam and Eve as the first man and woman. Throughout *Paradise Lost* Milton repeats the claim to the temporal and hence authoritative primacy of his argument ("Of Man's *First* Disobedience"; my emphasis here, and in the following) and of his source ("Thou from the *first* / Wast present").

Yet in formulating this particular claim to primacy, Milton makes an unexpected concession to the authority of Ovid. In Milton's verses, Deucalion and Pyrrha, "th'ancient Pair / In Fables old" are "less ancient yet then these." The ambiguity of "these" allows its meaning to drift from the more remote "suiters" to the nearer, but

---

[32]All quotations from Milton's poetry in my text are reproduced from *The Columbia Edition of the Works of John Milton*, 23 vols., ed. Frank A. Patterson et al. (New York, 1931–40). Hereafter cited as *Works*.

surprising antecedent "Fables." One reading implies that Ovid's mythic suitors are less ancient than their Christian counterparts; the other that Ovid's fables are less ancient than these Christian fables. Read in the latter way, Milton's lines afford the same literary status to pagan and Christian poems ("Fables") while still affirming the priority of the Christian originals.

Nor is this an anomalous example. Milton describes the Garden of Eden as the Christian original that verifies, rather than explodes, Ovid's fables of the dragon-guarded apples of the Hesperides: "*Hesperian* Fables true, / If true, here only, and of delicious taste" (IV, 250–51). The truth of the fables is questioned as soon as it is affirmed: "*If* true." Milton's syntax, however, makes the "Fables," rather than the expected fruit, the immediate source of "delicious taste." Milton's fascination with Ovid's fables is interwoven inextricably with his judgment of their subordination to higher truth. The struggle in Milton's allusions might well lead a reader, with Andrew Marvell, to "misdoubt" that Milton "would ruin . . . / The sacred Truths to Fable and old Song." Bloom's sense of anxiety alerts us to see Milton's allusions to his pagan predecessors as arenas in which the ontological status of *Paradise Lost* is to be fought for, not without dust and heat.

Bloom's metaphor of influence as antagonism, then, becomes one component of my sense of the Milton–Ovid relationship. What Bloom and the Bloomians leave out is any indication of the positive aspect of literary relationships. Hatred, Aldous Huxley noted, pays a high dividend in emotional excitement; it may be that admiration, if not love, underlies the economy of long-term literary relations. Certainly every allusion to a precursor is a valorization in some sense, for even if the later poet corrects the precursor he or she endorses the earlier poet's authority or felicity of expression. In his *Apology for Smectymnuus* (1642) Milton tells how he found the poets (including Ovid) taught to him in school "agreeable" and "alluring"; in the same tract, Milton identifies the method of expressing his sympathetic response as "imitation." Accordingly, in describing the influence of Milton on Blake, Joseph Wittreich has advanced a more positive theory of influence than Bloom's. Wittreich finds a metaphor of illumination presented in Blake's poetry but undeveloped in Bloom's theory. When Blake verbalizes and depicts his relationship with Milton, he chooses the image of a star, an image steeped in prophetic and apocalyptic tradition.[33] Thus Milton stands to Blake as one prophet illuminating the way for the next.

Positive illumination is a second crucial component of the Milton–Ovid relationship, though I hasten to add that such spiritual union and illumination as prophets share is not to be expected between pagan and Christian epic poets. At the close of his most personal proem in Book III of *Paradise Lost,* Milton prays for "Celestial Light" to "shine inward," but for the poet to express that internal illumination requires that it be accommodated to readers in simpler, more sensuous, and more passionate forms. Milton pondered the various kinds of poetic forms available to him in *The Reason of Church Government* and elsewhere, I believe, because he realized that some combination of them would necessarily provide that essential accommodation to his readers. My concern to identify the epic genre of the *Metamorphoses* in the previous section stems from this conviction. "The familiar forms art supplies," in Barbara Lewalski's phrase, are Milton's *only* means to "tell / Of things invisible to human sight."[34] It is in this sense that Ovid's *Metamorphoses* provides partial but necessary illumination for Milton and his readers.

Thus far I have argued that a spirit of admiring antagonism and a means of partial illumination are essential aspects of the Milton–Ovid relationship. Essentially these terms express how and why Milton turns to Ovid: What we need to see finally is what kind of relationship Milton establishes with Ovid in *Paradise Lost.* An indirect approach, telling what kind of relationship it is not, may prepare the way for an eventual answer. We can begin by rejecting the applicability of the concept of influence to this case. With its root metaphor of flowing liquid and its secondary suggestion of astral

[33]Wittreich, *Angel of Apocalypse,* pp. 223–24. "Longinus," whom Milton mentions approvingly in *Areopagitica,* also spoke of a master poet lighting the way for a disciple. See Longinus, *On the Sublime,* trans. W. Rhys Roberts (Cambridge, 1907), pp. 82–83.

[34]Barbara Lewalski, "The Genres of *Paradise Lost:* Literary Genre as a Means of Accommodation," in *Composite Orders: The Genres of Milton's Last Poems,* ed. Richard S. Ide and Joseph Wittreich, Jr., *MS* 17 (1983), 78.

operation, "influence" implies either passive or unconscious reception. These suggestions are on the one hand patently inappropriate to the Milton–Ovid relationship and on the other simply unprovable on poetic grounds. Moreover, in his dealings with other poets Milton is the least passive, most deliberate and overt poet one may hope to encounter. Although the vogue initiated by Waldock of pursuing unconscious meanings in Milton's works has yielded some interesting possibilities, Milton has provided ample (and debatable) evidence concerning his literary relationships in his critical writings and in his poems.

What, then, do those prose works and poems show the Milton–Ovid relationship to be? Simply to glance through Milton's overt allusions to Ovid, more than three hundred of which are noted in the Index to the Columbia *Works,* is to realize the pervasive nature of the relationship—no less, the difficulty of easily summarizing it. Nevertheless, this pervasive and various relationship may best be understood as it is constituted within *Paradise Lost,* as a dialogue. In this dialogue, Milton repeatedly invokes yet criticizes Ovid while inviting the earlier poet to act upon, even to transform his epic argument.[35] Renaissance writers including Pico, Petrarch, and Erasmus described this process as *aemulatio,* a subspecies of *imitatio,* or imitation.[36] Thomas Greene labels this type of imitation "dialectical." According to Greene, dialectical imitation "required the writer both to assume the vulnerabilities of his own specific moment and to reach out for the specificity of his subtext" in its own, far distant place and time.[37] Milton's dialogue with Ovid meets

[35]Without using the terms "dialogue" or "dialectical," Donald Pease, in "Blake, Crane, Whitman, and Modernism: A Poetics of Pure Possibility," *PMLA* 96 (1981), 66–67, speaks of a poet's relation to a predecessor as one "in which the earlier poet ceases to remain past and suddenly beckons the later poet from the position of the future to partake in the power of what can still be said in the earlier poetry." John Guillory, p. 68, speaks of Milton's "dialogue" with earlier English poets in *Comus,* but this usage is subordinate to his concern with transumption.

[36]See G. W. Pigman, "Versions of Imitation in the Renaissance," *RenQ* 33 (1980), 1–32. The most comprehensive work on imitation in the Renaissance is Hermann Gmelin's "Das Prinzip der Imitatio in den romanischen Literaturen der Renaissance," *Romanische Forschungen* 46 (1932), 82–360.

[37]Thomas Greene, *The Light in Troy: Imitation and Discovery in Renaissance Poetry* (New Haven, 1982), p. 48. Greene's entire discussion of imitation, especially his breakdown of imitation into four distinct types (pp. 37–48) is relevant and in-

these criteria, while it adds the extra, distinguishing dynamic of the confrontation between a metamorphic pagan subtext and a fallen yet faithful Christian poet. In reaching out for the *Metamorphoses* in *Paradise Lost,* Milton exposes his blindness, isolation, and possibly contaminated humanistic learning, but he stands to recover the vision, power, and wonder of the fables by which Ovid, transformed, continues to live.

Milton's dialogue with Ovid in *Paradise Lost* is part of a larger dialogue with Ovid that extends throughout Milton's career. Aware that my reconstruction of that history is not disinterested, I propose in the following chapter to survey Milton's lifelong relationship with Ovid as a way of approaching the poets' confrontation in *Paradise Lost.* Given the various views of Ovid's epic that preceded Milton, it is fitting that in his career Milton's approaches should recall those views while submitting Ovid to unprecedented transformations.

---

sightful. It should be noted that Greene regards *Paradise Lost* as a case of not dialectical but "heuristic" imitation, in which a poem underscores the historicity of its sources but proceeds to distance its cultural moment from that of the subtexts, forcing the reader to "recognize the poetic distance traversed" (p. 40). Greene notes that heuristic imitation shades off into the dialectical variety; as I hope to show, *Paradise Lost* grows out of heuristic imitation toward the more combative, confrontative condition of dialectical imitation. Milton himself defines "dialectic" in its strict sense as "the art of questioning and answering, that is, of debating" in the *Art of Logic* (*CPW,* 8:218). "Dialectical" imitation is not discordant with this definition.

– 1 –

From Imitation to Transformation: The Development of Milton's Uses of the *Metamorphoses*

To trace Milton's creative encounter with Ovid's work requires that we first establish the biographical and textual grounds for that literary relationship. In this chapter, therefore, I intend to show that Milton read the *Metamorphoses* in Latin repeatedly throughout his life, and certainly during the composition of *Paradise Lost,* and that the *Metamorphoses* pervades Milton's poetry from its beginnings through *Paradise Regained.* Moreover, Milton's use of the *Metamorphoses* undergoes a remarkable development, from a fairly simple procedure of imitating Ovid's poetry to a more complex technique of associating Ovidian diction, imagery, and rhetoric with figures of his own creation whom he regards as emotionally wavering or ethically suspect. During this development, Milton tends increasingly to transform and transvalue episodes from Ovid's fables, a strategy that heightens the dramatic and moral conflicts in Milton's poetry. These technical developments in Milton's allusions point toward his creative dialogue with Ovid in *Paradise Lost,* in which these strategies occur cumulatively.

To see how Milton assimilated and transformed the *Metamorphoses* in *Paradise Lost* is to meet the poet in the full maturity of his poetic technique and career. In order to gauge the extent and development of Milton's uses of Ovidian material through *Paradise Lost,* one must begin with earlier manifestations of those uses. Beyond his youthful imitation of Ovid according to contemporary grammar-school methods, Milton's response to the *Metamorphoses* is manifested repeatedly, forcefully, and imaginatively in *Comus,* in later works, and in the figure of Orpheus, which recurs at pivotal junctures in Milton's career.

"Most easie . . . and most agreeable": Youthful Imitation

At St. Paul's School in London, where Milton was a day student, Ovid's *Metamorphoses* was read in Latin in the fourth form. Milton would thus have first studied Ovid's epic around 1620, that is, when he was twelve.[1] Ample research has documented Milton's extensive early apprenticeship to the amatory Ovid of the elegies, the metrical form of the *Amores, Tristia, Epistulae ex Ponto, Heroides, Ars Amatoria, Remedia Amoris, Fasti,* and *Ibis.* Milton's seven Latin elegies in imitation of Ovid are, as various scholars have observed, the strongest proof of this apprenticeship.[2] Two questions arising from Milton's grammar-school study of Ovid, however, need to be clarified for a full understanding of Milton's uses of Ovid. In what manner did Milton learn to read the *Metamorphoses?* And how, precisely, did he respond to it as a young poet?

Thanks to the work of T. W. Baldwin, D. P. Harding, and D. L. Clark, among others, we know a considerable amount about the curricula and methods of Milton's grammar-school education.[3] According to the earliest surviving curriculum of St. Paul's, students read Ovid's *Tristia* in Form III, then proceeded in Form IV to the *Metamorphoses.* In other words, students devoted roughly a half-year of study to Ovid's epic. Harding's examination of the extant curricula of St. Paul's, moreover, makes it clear that not only did pupils learn Latin grammar and poetry through the primary model of Ovid, but that they were taught to write their own verses in imitation of Ovid.[4]

---

[1]According to Donald L. Clark, *John Milton at St. Paul's School* (New York, 1948), p. 206.

[2]In addition to Brill, Bush, Harding, Osgood, and Rand, op. cit., see Merritt Y. Hughes et al., gen. eds., *A Variorum Commentary on the Poems of John Milton*, 3 vols. (New York, 1970–), vol. 1.

[3]T. W. Baldwin, *William Shakespeare's Small Latine & Lesse Greek* (Urbana, Ill., 1944), quoted in Harding, *Milton*, p. 28. I am particularly indebted to Harding, pp. 28–33, for the account of the educational background. See also Harris F. Fletcher, *The Intellectual Development of John Milton*, 2 vols. (Urbana, Ill., 1956).

[4]See Harding, pp. 29–30.

Although Milton's teachers left no account of their methods, two eminent schoolmasters in the early seventeenth century corroborate Harding's emphasis on the importance of imitation in the mastery of Ovid's poetry. Charles Hoole, master of the grammar school at Rotherham in Yorkshire, wrote in the 1630s what amounts to a teacher's guide to Latin and English composition. Toward the end of this guide, entitled *A New Discovery of the Old Art of Teaching Schoole,* Hoole insists that his methods and subjects, tested by years of his personal experience, are typical of other grammar schools of the day: "In the meantime you may observe that the Method I have here discovered, is for the most part contrived according to what is commonly practised in England and foraign countries. . . . The subject matter which is taught is the same with that which is generally used by Grammars, Authors, and Exercises."[5]

In a historical survey of classical education in Britain, M. L. Clarke observes that Hoole's educational aims and practices were essentially the standard ones of the seventeenth-century grammar school.[6] However representative, Hoole's method of introducing grammarians to the *Metamorphoses* is remarkable for its systematic movement from grammatical comprehension to poetic imitation. Hoole's half-year plan aims to secure a technical mastery of the work and a "fanciful" (in the Renaissance sense of "imaginative") response to it in English prose and verse:

> To enable your Scholars yet more to write good Latine in prose, and to prepare them further for verses by reading Poetical books, which abound with rich expressions of fansie, I would have them spend the next halfe year in Ovids *Metamorphoses.* . . .
>
> Let them repeat four or six verses (which you judge most worthy to be committed to memory) by heart.
>
> Let them construe the whole lesson *verbatim*, minding the proprietie of the words, and the elegancie of every phrase.
>
> Let them parse every word Grammatically, as they have used to do in other Authours.

[5]Charles Hoole, *A New Discovery of the Old Art of Teaching Schoole* (London, 1660), pp. 204–5.

[6]M. L. Clarke, *Classical Education in Britain: 1500–1900* (Cambridge, 1959), p. 38.

Let them give you the Tropes and Figures, the Derivations and
Differences of some words, and relate such Histories as the proper
names will hint at, which they may peruse before hand in their
Dictionarie.

Let them strive (who can best) to turn the Fable into English prose,
and to adorn and amplifie it with fit Epithetes, choice Phrases, acute
Sentences, wittie Apothegmes, livelie similitudes, apt examples, and
Proverbial Speeches, all agreeing to the matter of moralitie therein
couched . . . .

Let them exercise their wits a little in trying who can turn the same
into most varietie of English verses.[7]

Memorizing, construing, etymologizing, translating, amplifying,
and versing the *Metamorphoses* constitute the sequence of Hoole's
comprehensive plan for teaching Latin composition and, simultaneously, for teaching Ovid. Harding takes the most interesting
feature of Hoole's account to be the "statement regarding the moral interpretation of the fables."[8] What Hoole mentions of "the
matter of moralitie" in Ovid's fables, however, seems to be a given
with which the students' compositions ought simply to agree. The
schoolmaster's method emphasizes and encourages the students'
invention (in "choice Phrases, wittie Apothegmes, livelie similitudes") during a process of close imitation.

Milton's own account of his study of the "smooth Elegiack Poets"
(including Ovid) whom he had read in grammar school and at
Cambridge stresses the role of imitation in mastering these poets.
Milton's nostalgic account of his youthful reading comes in *An
Apology for Smectymnuus* (1642):

I had my time Readers, as others have, who have good learning
bestow'd upon them, to be sent to those places, where the opinion was
it might be soonest attain'd: and as the manner is, was not unstudied
in those authors which are most commended: whereof some were
grave Orators & Historians; whose matter methought I lov'd indeed,
but as my age then was, so I understood them; others were the
smooth Elegiack Poets, whereof the Schooles are not scarce. Whom
both for the pleasing sound of their numerous writing, which in

[7]Hoole, pp. 161–62.
[8]Harding, p. 31.

imitation I found most easie; and most agreeable to natures part in me, and for their matter which what it is, there be few who know not, I was so allur'd to read, that no recreation came to me better welcome. (*CPW*, 1:889–90)

Rhetorically, there is a measure of defensiveness in Milton's account: He suggests that his studies were normal ones ("as others have," "as the manner is," "in those authors which are most commended"), and he refrains from specifying the names or matter of the poets lest, in the cross fire of religious controversy, he be tainted by their reputation for lasciviousness. Yet his defensive posture cannot conceal the sensuous "allure" the poets held for him. More important for present purposes, Milton specifies "imitation" as the process by which he became acquainted with "the pleasing sound of their numerous writing," that is, their sound, rhythm, and metrics.

Milton's statement that he found imitation of classical authors "easie" and "agreeable" to his nature is in harmony with the theory of imitation set forth in 1612 by John Brinsley, master of the school at Ashby-de-la-Zouch, Leicestershire. Brinsley specifically advocates imitation of Ovid and Virgil as the best means of teaching students how to write Latin verse:

> In this matter of versifying, as in all the former exercises, I take this Imitation of the most excellent patterns, to be the surest rule, both for phrase and whatsoever: And therefore I would have the chiefest labor to make these purest Authors our owne, as Tully for prose, so Ovid and Virgil for verse, so to speake and write in Latine for the phrase, as they did.[9]

Brinsley's statement raises an apparent contradiction or paradox in imitation; that is, its dual aspiration to preserve the ancient models while developing new writers. If young poets truly make the "purest Authors" their "owne" through imitation, how in the process can they develop their individual styles? A way to resolve this paradox is to realize that "mak[ing] these purest Authors our owne" actually *requires* the later poet to transform the ancient models while absorb-

[9]John Brinsley, *Ludus Literarius* (London, 1612), p. 195.

ing them. Simply copying the predecessor neither preserves him nor produces an original work. Instead, the creative imitator must, in a ubiquitous Renaissance metaphor, "digest" the predecessor's work and thus give it new life in his own.

Perhaps the best evidence for the creative results of young John Milton's digestion of Ovid according to grammar-school imitation remains the Latin poems he wrote as an undergraduate at Cambridge. The editors of these poems have uncovered an abundance of both direct and adapted borrowings from the *Metamorphoses* which follow the methods outlined by Brinsley and Hoole. Summarizing the findings of these editors, Harding concludes that the poems written between 1625 and 1629 consist of an intricate network of phrases borrowed from Ovid and other classical models.[10] Harding's exhaustive analysis lends support to E. K. Rand's conclusion that "our young poet had simply absorbed all the niceties of Ovid's art without cataloguing them."[11] The epitome of the young poet's surprising absorption of Ovid is Milton's Third Elegy, which transforms one of Ovid's erotic dream-visions of his mistress Corinna into an ecstatic vision of the lately deceased Bishop of Winchester's entry into Heaven! In this radical if ludicrous transformation of Ovid lies a prototype of the dialectical imitation in *Paradise Lost,* for Ovid's eroticism breaks through Milton's academic panegyric to Bishop Andrewes.

Toward the end of Milton's undergraduate career, a major advance occurs in his conception of himself as a poet, and with it, a major change in his view and use of Ovid. Late in 1629 or early in 1630, during his last year at Cambridge, Milton wrote a Latin verse letter to Charles Diodati which we know as the Sixth Elegy. The letter is remarkable because it implies Milton's bold hope of becoming an epic poet. For elegiac poets—and Milton specifies Ovid, Anacreon, Pindar, and Horace—the inspiration of wine is helpful and welcome. The epic poet, Milton claims, must draw inspiration from only pure water and equally pure living:

> At qui bella refert, & adulto sub Jove caelum,
> Heroasque pios, semideosque duces,

[10]Harding, p. 43.
[11]Rand, "Milton in Rustication," p. 110.

Et nunc sancta canit superum consulta deorum,
Nunc latrata fero regna profunda cane,
Ille quidem parcè Samii pro more magistri
Vivat, & innocuous praebeat herba cibos.

(55–60)

But he whose theme is wars and heaven under mature Jove, and pious heroes and leaders half-divine, and he who sings now of the sacred counsels of the gods on high, and now of the infernal realms where the fierce dog howls, let him live sparingly, like the Samian teacher [Pythagoras]; and let herbs furnish his innocent diet.[12]

One ought to hesitate before drawing conclusions about Milton's epic practice on the basis of a playful elegy written decades earlier. The purity of the epic poet's life described in this passage emerges in sharp contrast to the convivial life of the wine-poet that Milton has extensively urged upon Diodati in the preceding lines (13–54). The hyperbolic language of both descriptions suggests an ironic tone. A further irony is that Milton's apparent denigration of elegiac poets is itself couched in the form of an Ovidian elegy. My point is that the passage by no means constitutes a complete rejection of Ovid, and certainly not of the epic Ovid. As Martz suggests, Milton aspires to the higher matter of epic, but he is far from reaching it here.[13]

That Milton has dedicated himself to the severe demands of epic poetry is no longer in question some twelve years later, however, when, in *The Reason of Church Government* (1642), he publicly announces his unshakable intention to produce "a work not to be rays'd from the heat of youth, or the vapours of wine" (*CPW*, 1:820). Before the dedicated youth metamorphosed into the purified epic poet, however, he fed upon virtually every available source of knowledge, however sullied or intemperate, pertinent to his Muse. In his biographical reminiscences of the poet, Edward

---

[12]Unless otherwise indicated, all translations of Milton's Latin in my text are my own.

[13]See Louis Martz, "The Rising Poet," in *The Lyric and Dramatic Milton*, ed. Joseph Summers (New York, 1965), pp. 3–33.

Phillips, Milton's nephew and private pupil, gives us a glimpse of his teacher's extensive reading:

> And here by the way, I judge it not impertinent to mention the many authors both of the Latin and Greek, which through his excellent judgment and way of teaching . . . were run over within no greater compass of time, than from ten to fifteen or sixteen years of age. Of the Latin, the four grand authors *De Re Rustica*, Cato, Varro, Columella and Palladius; Cornelius Celsus, an ancient physician of the Romans; a great part of Pliny's *Natural History;* Vitruvius his *Architecture;* Frontinus his *Stratagems;* with the two egregious poets, Lucretius and Manilius. Of the Greek, Hesiod, a poet equal with Homer; Aratus his *Phaenomena*, and *Diosemeia;* Dionysius Afer *De Situ Orbis;* Oppian's *Cynegetics* and *Halieutics;* Quintus Calaber his *Poem of the Trojan War* continued after Homer; Apollonius Rhodius his *Argonautica* . . . . Thus by teaching he in some measure increased his own knowledge, having the reading of all these authors as it were by proxy. (Hughes ed., pp. 1029–30)

Certainly Milton's extensive coverage of Latin and Greek authors increased the scope of his epic, as Phillips implies. As I shall argue in Chapter 4, the encyclopedic quality of the *Metamorphoses*, encompassing Greek and Roman legend and lore from the beginning to Ovid's time, was distinctive among classical epics and exemplary for Milton's encyclopedic epic.

The transition from Milton as schoolboy to Milton as teacher predicts in many ways the final emergence of Milton's comprehensive epic of man's first disobedience of God and eventual recovery of Paradise. The spiritual aim of "schoolmaster" Milton's ideal education, as set forth in the pamphlet *Of Education* (1644), is "to repair the ruins of our first parents by regaining to know God aright, and out of that knowledge to love him, to imitate him, to be like him, as we may the neerest by possessing our souls of true vertue, which being united to the heavenly grace of faith makes up the highest perfection" (*CPW*, 2:366–67). The loftiness of this ideal education in virtue, nevertheless, did not deter Milton from constructing a program of reading that would move through practical studies—including grammar, arithmetic, geometry, agriculture, and geography—and arrive at poetry only at the end of the curriculum Despite his early mastery of the Latin poets such as Ovid by imitation, Milton attacked as "preposterous exaction" the contemporary practice of "forcing invention" out of ignorant schoolchildren. Studying poetry only after being thoroughly girded with knowledge of the world, Milton argues, would enable older students to see "what Religious, what glorious and magnificent use might be made of Poetry, both in divine and humane things" (*CPW*, 2:405–406). To Milton, poetry is inevitably pragmatic: It instills spiritual and moral virtue in its listeners, and so works to repair the ignorance and discord caused by the sin of Adam and Eve. An epic poem on the Fall could be expected to touch the common memory of Milton's Christian audience and, through its "simple, sensuous, and passionate" art, help to rejoin the fragments of human knowledge to the knowledge of God.

But what of the pagan poets whose art Milton had long imitated? Could their works, often sensuous and passionate in a way contrary to Christian "vertue," be employed so as to lead ultimately to greater knowledge of God? Although Milton would eventually so employ pagan poetry in his major poems, his immediate reaction was to renounce the erroneous, impure tendency of his Latin elegies in a formal retraction. The retraction comes at a critical point in Milton's career: the publication of his first volume of poems in 1645. In that volume Milton appended a postscript to the Ovidian Latin elegies in which he condemns the "flames" of love in these verses and opposes them with his breast of "ice":

> Haec ego mente olim laevâ, studioque supino
>   Nequitiae posui vana trophaea meae.
> Scilicet abreptum sic me malus impulit error,
>   Indocilisque aetas prava magistra fuit.
> Donec Socraticos umbrosa Academia rivos
>   Praebuit, admissum dedocuitque jugum.
> Protinus extinctis ex illo tempore flammis,
>   Cincta rigent multo pectora nostra gelu.
> Unde suis frigus metuit puer ipse Sagittis
>   Et Diomedéam vim timet ipsa Venus.

These are the monuments to my wantonness that with a perverse spirit and a trifling purpose I once erected. Obviously, mischievous error led me astray and my undisciplined youth was a vicious teacher until the shady Academy offered its Socratic streams and taught me how to escape from the yoke to which I had submitted. From that hour those flames were extinct and thenceforward my breast has been rigid under a thick case of ice, of which Cupid himself fears the frost for his arrows, and Venus herself is afraid of my Diomedean strength.

The splitting of the traditional Petrarchan imagery (renouncing the fire; investing the ice) serves as a fitting envoi to the amatory poems of a hopeful epic poet dedicated to purity. Having extinguished "those flames" of errant passion in his Latin elegies, Milton henceforth turns away from their primary source, the elegiac poems of Ovid, especially the *Amores* and *Ars Amatoria*. Milton's poems written after this postscript (possibly as early as 1635, certainly no later than 1645) contain only rare and relatively insubstantial reminiscences of the amatory Ovid. To take Milton's rejection of his erotic elegies as a complete rejection of Ovid's art, however, is unwarranted. Milton's imitation of Ovid continues unabated after the elegies, but henceforth it turns almost exclusively to the epic Ovid, the poet of the *Metamorphoses*. Given the Renaissance theory of imitation that we have seen in outline, an indirect way appeared by which the fragments of knowledge in Ovid's epic might be applied toward the goal of "know[ing] God aright." Given the Christian poet's skill and delight in imitating Ovid's verses, it seems likely that, despite the attendant risk, Milton would remain in dialogue with this brilliant yet morally suspect teacher of the poetic art.

The conflict between the teachings of the intellect and those of the senses, between the "divine Philosophy" of chastity and the seductive wantonness of indulgence, reappears frequently in Milton's works. The conflict is set forth in considerable length and detail in *Comus, or A Mask Presented at Ludlow Castle* (1634). In that work the Ovidian poetics that Milton abandoned as a source of direct illumination of Christian themes will reappear indirectly in the language and characters of the masque, as forces that virtuous agents must in some way escape or control.

"Eternal restless change": Ovid and *Comus*

The central ethical principle of *Comus*, one that threatens to dissolve the dramatic conflict in the masque before it begins, is asserted by the Elder Brother to the Younger during the search for their missing sister:

> Vertue may be assail'd, but never hurt,
> Surpriz'd by unjust force, but not enthrall'd,
> Yea even that which mischief meant most harm,
> Shall in the happy trial prove most glory.
>
> (588–91)

Corollary to this belief in the "happy trial" of virtue, itself a dim precursor of the *felix culpa* that Adam expresses in Book XII of *Paradise Lost*, is a conception of evil as perpetually self-defeating:

> But evil on it self shall back recoyl,
> And mix no more with goodness, when at last
> Gather'd like scum, and setl'd to it self
> It shall be in eternal restless change
> Self-fed, and self-consum'd.
>
> (592–96)

Early in the masque the Elder Brother's notion of evil is, for all its boldness, radically ambiguous: It is either a naive sign of youthful optimism or a confident prophecy of Christian eschatology. In either case, underlying the depiction of evil as "Self-fed and self-consum'd" is Ovid's depiction of Scylla, whose loins Circe transformed into ravenous beasts:

> Scylla venit mediaque tenus descenderat alvo,
> cum sua foedari latrantibus inguina monstris
> adspicit; ac primo credens non corporis illas
> esse sui partes refugitque abigitque timetque

ora proterva canum, sed, quos fugit, attrahit una
et corpus quaerens femorum crurumque pedumque
Cerbereos rictus pro partibus invenit illis . . .

$$(14.59-65)$$

Scylla came and had waded waist-deep into the water, when all at once she sees her loins disfigured with barking monsters. At first, not believing that these are parts of her own body, she flees and pushes out and fears the loud, barking mouths, but what she flees, she drags along with her. And feeling for her thighs, her legs, her feet, she finds in their place only gaping mouths, such as Cerberus might have had . . .

Whereas Ovid explores the pathos of Scylla's discovery of her self-consumption, Milton takes such consumption as the morally appropriate result of evil. For Milton the "restless" circularity of the process—to flee, but drag along what one flees; to be self-fed and self-consumed—is both the condition and the horror of evil. In *Paradise Lost* (II, 653–800) Milton expands Ovid's figure into an allegorical personification of Sin, who is fully conscious of the consuming horrors of evil. For that development, the example of Spenser's representation of Scylla as Error in *The Faerie Queene* (1.1.14–25) must have been stimulating, if not essential.

In the masque Milton relies on Ovid's fable of Scylla chiefly to provide a mythic pedigree for the moral perversion of Comus. In the *Metamorphoses* it is Circe who out of jealousy causes Scylla's horrible transformation; in Milton's masque, it is Circe who gives Comus the power to so transform others. The Attendant Spirit relates the parentage of Comus, which Milton had invented, in the opening speech. Comus is the offspring of Bacchus and Circe, specifically the Circe "[w]hose charmed Cup / Whoever tasted, lost his upright shape, / And downward fell into a groveling Swine" (51–53). Just as Ovid's Circe excels in causing degenerate transformations, Milton's Comus excels even his mother in producing metamorphic regression in human beings:

> their human count'nance,
> Th'express resemblance of the gods, is chang'd
> Into som brutish form of Woolf, or Bear,

Or Ounce, or Tiger, Hog, or bearded Goat,
All other parts remaining as they were,
And they, so perfect is their misery,
Not once perceive their foul disfigurement,
But boast themselves more comely then before
And all their friends, and native home forget
To roule with pleasure in a sensual stie.

(68–77)

When the Elder Brother characterizes evil as being "in eternal restless change," the audience has been prepared to recognize Comus as the proponent of such evil change, specifically, of the degenerate variety of change that Circe had inflicted on Scylla. Despite the clarity of this moral framework, an unresolved problem in the masque is that Milton allows virtually no interchange between virtue and vice, between the Lady and Comus. Although Comus confines in his chair the Lady's body, which in accordance with Puritan thought she calls her "corporal rinde," he remains powerless to "touch the freedom of her mind," as she points out (662–63). A dense pattern of Ovidian metamorphoses in the masque supplements this lack of contact or tension, because it presents in varied forms the possibility that virtuous human beings may degenerate below human status if they (we?) embrace excess or sensuality.

Editors and critics of *Comus* have discerned a total of twenty-eight analogues of or allusions to the *Metamorphoses* in the masque.[14] Though the majority of these are what one might call Ovidian trappings, that is, minor parallels of diction and imagery, at least five passages incorporate substantial features of the *Metamorphoses*. The Lady's Song, the first of these passages after the Ovidian account of the parentage of Comus, conflates two of Ovid's myths of spurned lovers—Echo and Philomela—and thus doubly suggests the isolation of the singer. The conclusion of Ovid's myth of Echo, in which the nymph fades until only her voice remains (*Met.* 3.399–401), may have suggested Milton's conceit of Echo's "airy shell":

[14]See John Carey, ed., *John Milton: Complete Shorter Poems* (London, 1978).

Sweet Echo, sweetest Nymph that liv'st unseen
Within thy airy shell
By slow *Meander*'s margent green,
And in the violet imbroider'd vale
Where the love-lorn Nightingale
Nightly to thee her sad Song mourneth well.

(229–34)

By describing the nightingale as "mourning" to Echo, Milton subtly prepares for the seduction of the Lady, for in the *Metamorphoses* Philomela sings in mourning after Tereus had raped and abandoned her and cut out her tongue. The Lady's Song concludes a scene that is characteristically Ovidian, in which an isolated female character reveals her wavering personality through a long, tortuous soliloquy (169–228), as do Myrrha, Bibylis, Medea, among others.[15]

The rest of the substantive adaptations of the *Metamorphoses* in Milton's masque cluster around Comus himself. In his attempt to seduce the Lady, Comus uses mythic figures, imagery, and arguments that derive from Ovid's work. Even the pivotal action, or plot element, involving Comus, the reversing of his rod in order to free the Lady (816–18), derives from Ovid's account of Circe (*Met.* 14.299–301), as Harding points out.[16] By using ironically truncated and altered Ovidian situations, Comus reveals his depth of imaginative power and ethical perversion. In perhaps his most significant use of Ovidian figures, Comus compares himself and the Lady to Apollo and Daphne in order to remind her of his magical power over her:

Nay Lady sit; if I but wave this wand,
Your nerves are all chain'd up in Alablaster,
And you a statue, or as *Daphne* was
Root-bound, that fled *Apollo.*

(658–61)

To anyone familiar with Ovid's myth, however, Comus's attempt to heighten his putative mastery over the Lady by the comparison

---

[15]A full discussion of this stylistic and psychological parallel of Ovid and Milton appears in Chapter 2.

[16]Harding, pp. 64–65.

must seem vain, if not ludicrous. Daphne actually avoided Apollo's seduction precisely by becoming "root-bound," and her transformation into the laurel, though unwelcome, was not a result of Apollo's power. Daphne's transformation actually improves her would-be seducer: Apollo's lust for Daphne changes to a pious and patriotic devotion to laurel, thus maintaining a chaste unconsummated union. Comus, in contrast, remains unedified by the Lady's philosophy. By ascribing to Comus this and other perverse uses of Ovidian myth, Milton undercuts the power of the seducer while channeling the Ovidian material so that it contaminates only Comus.

Imagery from the *Metamorphoses* also amplifies the speeches of Comus, but again the rhetorical effect of these devices becomes double-edged when one sees that he is using them perversely. Comus initiates the "rites" of his nocturnal band by affirming the utility of darkness:

> Com let us our rites begin,
> 'Tis onely day-light that makes Sin
> Which these dun shades will ne're report.
> (125–27)

Upon close examination, this argument is dubious at best. Comus knows that what he does at night is sin, but because his sin cannot then be seen without daylight, daylight, he concludes, must cause the sin: the fallacy of post hoc, propter hoc. Comus may think that he is reinforcing his position by blaming Aurora, the "nice" (affectedly modest) Morn for revealing his solemn nightly gatherings. He invokes the nocturnal goddess Cotytto to stay:

> Ere the blabbing Eastern scout,
> The nice Morn on th'*Indian* steep
> From her cabin'd loop-hole peep.
> (138–40)

Even by fairly generous standards of sexual conduct, however, Aurora can hardly be considered modest, for, as Ovid tells the story, she openly carried off the youth Cephalus against his will (*Met.* 7.700–713). In Ovid's Weltanschauung, both legendary and natural figures (such as Aurora and Envy) feel the passion and pathos of love. In Comus's world view, such allegorical personifications as Morn, Rigour, and Severity (107–9), who do not feel the attractiveness of his midnight sport, must, he concludes, be waiting to entrap or destroy him. His view is partial and, in psychological terms, paranoid.

The argumentation from the *Metamorphoses* that Comus adapts is similarly partial, given the larger context of Ovid's passage. The main, and probably the strongest, argument that Comus uses against the Lady's refusal to taste his refreshing banquet and liquor is that to so refuse is to neglect the service of Nature:

> Wherefore did Nature powre her bounties forth,
> With such a full and unwithdrawing hand,
> Covering the earth with odours, fruits, and flocks,
> Thronging the Seas with spawn innumerable,
> But all to please, and sate the curious taste?
> . . . and that no corner might
> Be vacant of her plenty, in her own loyns
> She hutch't th'all-worshipt ore, and precious gems
> To store her children with.
>
> (709–13; 716–19)

In Ovid's description of the Four Ages of the world, the earth in like manner yields its possessions for the consumption of humanity:

> communemque prius ceu lumina solis et auras
> cautus humum longo signavit limite mensor.
> nec tantum segetes alimentaque debita dives
> poscebatur humus, sed itum est in viscera terrae,
> quasque recondiderat Stygiisque admoverat umbris,
> effondiuntur opes, inritamenta malorum;
>
> (1.135–40)

And the ground, which hitherto had been a common possession like the sunlight and the air, the careful surveyor now marked out with long-drawn boundary-line. Not only did men demand of the rich fields the crops and sustenance they owed, but they dug as well into the very bowels of the earth; and the wealth which the creator had hidden away and buried deep amid the Stygian shades was brought to light, wealth that spurs men on to crimes.

The balanced halves of line 140 reflect the problem with such exploration, for this is the Age of Bronze, and what appears to be an argument for the rightful use of nature is actually evidence of its exploitation, as the continuing conflicts which Ovid deftly sketches in the next lines show:

> iamque nocens ferrum ferroque nocentius aurum
> prodierat; prodit bellum, quod pugnat utroque,
> sanguineaque manu crepitantia concutit arma.
> vivitur ex rapto; non hospes ab hospite tutus,
> non socer a genero, fratrum quoque gratia rara est.
>
> (1.141–45)

And now deadly iron had come, and gold more deadly than iron; war came, which fights with both, and brandished in its bloody hands the clashing arms. Men lived on plunder. Guest was not safe from host, father-in-law from son-in-law; even among brothers affection was rare.

The high epic style of Ovid's passage, parodically recalling Virgil's account of the Golden Age in *Aeneid* 8, clashes with the short-sighted motives of men and so undermines the value of their explorations. The similarly magniloquent, generalized diction of Comus's depiction of Nature, her "unwithdrawing hand," her "all-worship't" ore, conceals his desire for a particular natural beauty. The Lady's no less magniloquent yet sincere counterargument to Comus, that were it not for "lewdly-pamper'd Luxury" on the part of the few, "Natures full blessings would be well dispenc't / In unsuperfluous eeven proportion" (771–72), exposes his misrepresentation of what is "natural."

The Ovidian patterns in Comus's attempted seduction of the Lady raise issues of genre in addition to those of character. The many allusions to the *Metamorphoses* in the masque provide evidence of both generic mixing and stylistic experimentation. These aspects anticipate the unqualifiedly successful achievements of *Par-*

adise Lost, but their simple, unilateral manifestation in *Comus* reveals Milton's difficulty, unresolved in 1634, in using the *Metamorphoses* decorously yet dynamically.

When, for instance, Comus dismisses the attractions of sunlight
and dawn by recalling the pretense of Ovid's Phaethon and the
cupidity of Aurora for Cephalus, his discourse strongly resembles
one-half of a dialogue, or debate. More specifically, it resembles the
"nocturnal" argument of Milton's "Il Penseroso." One might say
that Comus's argument takes a position directly opposed to that
Milton held in the First Prolusion, in which he argues that Day is
more excellent than Night. Assuming a negative position need not
condemn a speaker, as the case of the pensive man shows. Whereas
this present speech reflects the perverse, night-loving psychology
of Comus, there is no accompanying counterstatement in the masque, so that this opportunity for fruitful complication by generic
mixing leaves only a trace of discordant generic signals.

Although motivation for Comus's opposition to sunlight does not
emerge in the masque, in Book IV of *Paradise Lost* Satan states his
grounds for just such a position. He excoriates the Sun for exposing his fall from Heaven:

> to thee I call,
> But with no friendly voice, and add thy name
> O Sun, to tell thee how I hate thy beams
> That bring to my remembrance from what state
> I fell, how glorious once above thy Spheare;
> Till Pride and worse Ambition threw me down
> Warring in Heav'n against Heav'ns matchless King:
>
> (IV, 35–41)

Harding maintains that the parallel between Ovid's story of
Phaethon's journey and Milton's story of Satan's flight to the Orb
of the Sun is "marked and intentional."[17] Without speculating on
what the poet had in mind, one can notice how far Milton's technique has advanced from Comus's speech to Satan's soliloquy. The
advance may be measured in two ways: in terms of the greater
density, or depth, of allusion, by which in Satan's words reminis-

[17]Ibid., p. 89.

cences of Ovid resonate along with those of Aeschylus, Marlowe, and the Book of the Revelation; and in terms of the greater intensity, or drama, of self-revelation, by which we see Satan struggling with his guilt and wavering commitment to evil. The dramatic power of Satan's soliloquy derives in part from its generic register, for, according to Edward Phillips, it was the very beginning of a tragedy Milton planned to write on the fall of Adam.

When Comus soliloquizes, he employs a less passionate yet more lyrical sensual mode. The mixture of lyric and dramatic elements in his response to the Lady's Song is fully appropriate to the encompassing genre of the masque:

> Can any mortal mixture of Earths mould
> Breath such Divine inchanting ravishment?
> Sure something holy lodges in that brest,
> And with these raptures moves the vocal air
> To testifie his hidd'n residence.
>
> (243–47)

By acknowledging the divine presence in the Lady's Song, Comus implicitly admits the weakness of his enchantments, which are far from divine. His discovery of "something holy" in the chaste Lady contradicts and works against any tension one might feel when he has the Lady in captivity. His alliterative lyricism does not counter the moral philosophy that the Lady, her brothers, and the Attendant Spirit assert: Comus seems to move on a different, mythic plane from them, seems only to border on, not to challenge the order of the dramatized Egerton family. The occasional nature of the masque may have forced the mythic and social orders together abruptly. Lady Egerton at fifteen, one supposes, need not be involved with lust as intimately as, say, Amoret in Book 4 of *The Faerie Queene.*

Milton's masque departs finally from both Spenser's and Ovid's treatments of chastity and seduction, although Milton turns to Ovid for an essential unit of myth in the conclusion of *Comus.* Because the boys, in attempting to rescue their sister, break the tempter's enchanted wand, they must enlist the aid of Sabrina, the goddess of the Severn river, to break the spell. Like Comus,

Sabrina has a metamorphic parentage of Milton's invention. Formerly a "virgin pure" (825), she has undergone "a quick immortal change" into a tutelary goddess while fleeing her enraged stepmother. Sabrina's perpetuity, residence in nature, and nurturing of innocents after her change recall similar aspects of Ovid's metamorphosed Arethusa (5.487–647) and Scylla (13.749). After Sabrina's change, the Attendant Spirit summarizes her mythic function.

> still she retains
> Her maid'n gentlenes, and oft at Eeve
> Visits the herds along the twilight meadows,
> Helping all urchin blasts, and ill luck signes
> That the shrewd medling Elfe delights to make,
> Which she with pretious viold liquors heals.
>
> (841–46)

The specific, realistic description of Sabrina's habits ("and oft at Eeve / Visits the herds") mingles with the general, symbolic statement of her power ("all urchin blasts . . . she with pretious viold liquors heals") in order to form a myth of chastity preserved in nature. As in many of Ovid's tales of changed bodies, notably those of Daphne and Hermaphroditus, Sabrina performs her protective duty only if "she be right invok't in warbled Song" (853), that is, in the music and poetry of the masque.

The similarities between Sabrina and Scylla on the one hand, and Comus and Scylla on the other, suggest how close and fertile the relationship between Ovidian and Miltonic mythmaking is in *A Mask Presented at Ludlow Castle*. In representing the mythic antidote to Comus, whose restless concupiscence shows figural parallels to Ovid's Scylla, Milton draws upon the other side of Scylla: Scylla as violated woman turned river-goddess, protectress of chastity. The masque keeps these two sides essentially separate; Comus and Sabrina never appear together, never speak to each other, and seem completely unaware of the other's existence. It is most fitting, most decorous, in Milton's usage, that the two mythic characters should be brought together in the audience's mind by the combined power of poetry and music, in the Attendant Spirit's lyric invocation. He is best suited to resolve the conflict between Comus and the Lady because he understands that the beauty and power behind metamorphosis belong not to Comus but to nature infused by grace. From the opening scene, it is the Attendant Spirit, putting off his heavenly robes and putting on the guise of a servant-shepherd, "Who with his soft Pipe and smooth-dittied Song / Well knows to still the wild winds when they roar, / And hush the waving Woods" (86–88). It is the Attendant Spirit, commanding the beauty and power of Orphic song, who now recalls the metamorphic relationship between the Severn and Sabrina which he learned from the shepherd Meliboeus. The Attendant Spirit commands a final metamorphosis to free the Lady from Comus's unnatural enchantment, and by so doing redeems Ovid as well:

> Goddess dear
> We implore thy powerful hand
> To undo the charmed band
> Of true Virgin here distrest,
> Through the force, and through the wile
> Of unblest inchanter vile.
>
> (901–6)

More than the "divine Philosophy" that the Younger Brother extols, this song is charming. In the masque, its charm is more lasting than the enchantments of Comus, for it leads to the undoing of his "charmed band" (903). In Milton's subsequent works, the charm of the masque shall give way to the conflict and pathos of tragedy and epic. But the imaginative utility of Ovidian myth, like the protective chastity of Sabrina, remains when the pageantry of the masque is over.

Condemning and Commending: Reforming Ovid for the Muse

In a letter to Thomas Birch in 1738, John Ward reported what he had learned about Milton's reading from an interview with Milton's daughter Deborah: "Isaiah, Homer, and Ovid's *Meta-*

morphoses were books, which they were often called to read to their father; and at my desire she repeated a considerable number of verses from the beginning of both those poets with great readiness."[18] Were there no other evidence, this testimony of Milton's daughter might fail to persuade a skeptical critic that Ovid remained one of the poet's favorites during the period of the composition of *Paradise Lost.* When Deborah reportedly read Isaiah, Homer, and Ovid to her father, she could have been as young as eight but no older than twenty-two, the last seven years of this span being after the publication of *Paradise Lost.* At the time of Ward's interview, Deborah was seventy-six years of age. At no time in her life, moreover, did she learn the Latin language in which she mouthed verses to her father. How much of the *Metamorphoses* she actually read, how reliable her memory was (she makes no mention of any reading of Virgil, for instance),[19] and when she actually read Ovid to Milton are questions that admit of no certain answers.

Besides Deborah's testimony, however, there is abundant additional evidence to show that the *Metamorphoses* retained its high place in Milton's imagination beyond his youth and through the production of *Paradise Lost.* We might classify this evidence into three broad headings: contextual, theoretical, and poetic. The appearance of Latin verses from the *Metamorphoses* in the late prose works, the *Artis Logicae* and *Accedence Commenc't Grammar,* testifies to Milton's willingness to use Ovid as a model in arts contextually related to poetry. In the *Artis Logicae,* which was among the last of Milton's published works (1672), there are at least three allusions to figures from the *Metamorphoses.*[20] Seven of Ovid's verses, two of them from the *Metamorphoses,* illustrate the principles of Latin composition in the *Grammar* (1669).[21] Of the two verses from Ovid's epic, the first shows Milton alluding to Ovid's Medea, which, as I shall argue in Chapter 2, he associates with the Eve of Book IX.

---

[18]French, ed., *Life Records of John Milton,* 5:110, 327–28. See also Martz, *Poet of Exile,* p. 203.

[19]See Martz, *Poet of Exile,* p. 331, no. 2. The argument offered by Martz, that Milton had Virgil by heart and so needed no reading to refresh him, assumes that Milton sought independence from the poem he upheld elsewhere (in the headnote on "The Verse" to *Paradise Lost*) as one of his principal models for epic verse.

[20]Cf. *Artis Logicae,* VI, 212, and *Met.* 2.1–5; VI, 236 / 1.144–48; VI, 273 / 1.70–80.

[21]See *Grammar, CPW,* 8:114 (2 allusions); 116; 117; 121; 123; 124.

Theoretical arguments in Milton's works suggest a variety of ways in which a Christian poet could legitimately imitate pagan literature. Milton's beginning principle for admitting secular literature into sacred contexts takes shape as early as 1634 in *Comus*. The Attendant Spirit advances the principle that even the most fantastic creations of pagan poets may be inspired by the Christian Muse:

> Ile tell ye, 'tis not vain or fabulous,
> (Though so esteem'd by shallow ignorance)
> What the sage Poets taught by th' heav'nly Muse,
> Storied of old in high immortal vers
> Of dire *Chimera*'s and inchanted Iles,
> And rifted Rocks whose entrance leads to Hell,
> For such there be, but unbelief is blind.
>
> (512–18)

This principle, a slight but significant variant of the allegorical belief in "undermeanings" in the *Metamorphoses,* allows a Christian poet to recover from pagan poetry whatever the heavenly Muse has inspired. The obvious problem with such a principle is an epistemological one: How can one know precisely what among the works of the pagan poets the heavenly Muse has inspired? The Attendant Spirit does place two conditions on the inspired pagan works. If the poet be "sage" and the verse "immortal," conditions that would certainly admit Ovid's *Metamorphoses,* readers who neglect such pagan poets will remain unenlightened ("blind") disbelievers.

This principle stands with little qualification in Milton's treatment of pagan poetry until he adopts the ascetic style of *Paradise Regained.* The paucity of allusions to secular literature in Milton's "brief" epic is consistent with Christ's thorough-going rejection of classical art in favor of purely Christian forms and expression (IV, 286–364). Even in *Paradise Regained,* however, Milton continues to turn to the *Metamorphoses* in order to enliven and moralize an exchange between Satan and Belial. Satan energetically rejects Belial's suggestion of tempting Christ in the desert by placing fair women before him. Belial's plan is suited not to Christ's weakness but to his own, Satan argues:

> Have we not seen, or by relation heard,
> In Courts and Regal Chambers how thou lurk'st,
> In Wood or Grove by mossie Fountain side,
> In Valley or Green Meadow to way-lay
> Some beauty rare, *Calisto*, *Clymene*,
> *Daphne*, or *Semele*, *Antiopa*,
> Or *Amymone*, *Syrinx*, many more
> Too long, then lay'st thy scapes on names ador'd,
> *Apollo*, *Neptune*, *Jupiter*, or *Pan*,
> Satyr, or Fawn, or Silvan?
>
> (II, 182–91)

Not only are the stories of these nymphs' seductions all told by Ovid,[22] but the natural scenery of Belial's haunts (184–85) recalls the typical *locus amoenus* in which Ovid locates these stories. Satan's dismissal of Belial's plan is somewhat paradoxical, as Satan had engaged in a seduction of Eve under like circumstances and had boasted of that deception earlier in the poem (I, 51–52). By disapproving of the use of such means on Christ, Satan expresses the superior nature of this "greater man." Yet Milton's allusion shows that the *Metamorphoses* remains late in his poetic career as a powerful force for revealing the dissimulation of various characters.[23]

Before the radical shift in aesthetic of *Paradise Regained*, though, Milton outlines two theoretical means of salvaging pagan poetry such as Ovid's which, if lacking in spiritual inspiration or significance, nevertheless retains artistic merit or moral instruction. After describing his apprenticeship to Ovid and the other "smooth Elegiack Poets" in his *Apology for Smectymnuus* in 1642, Milton adds that he came to test those authors against high moral standards:

> For by the firme setling of these perswasions I became, to my best memory, so much a proficient, that if I found those authors any where speaking unworthy things of themselves; or unchaste of those names which before they had extoll'd, this effect it wrought with me, from that time forward their art I still applauded, but the men I deplor'd. (*CPW*, 1:890)

[22]Calisto in *Met.* 2.409; Clymene, in *Met.* 1.757; Daphne, in *Met.* 1.452; Semele, in *Met.* 3.253; Antiopa, in *Met.* 6.110; Syrinx, in *Met.* 1.690; Amymone, in *Am.* 1.10.5.
[23]For Satan's Ovidian "dissimulation" in *Paradise Regained*, see David Novarr, "Gray Dissimulation: Ford and Milton," *PQ* 41 (1962), 500–504.

By thus distinguishing between deplorable men and praiseworthy poems, Milton could celebrate the life of the Christian poet while he aligned his poetry with the best products of the classical tradition.

In *De Doctrina Christiana* some twenty years later, the former elegist is an accomplished epic poet. Moreover, he is a self-styled interpreter of scripture who is eager to call together a community of true believers. In this semipastoral role, Milton gives a rationale for salvaging good persons who happen to be heathens, and good works by those who are nominally unbelievers. Spiritual death, Milton explains, "is the loss of that divine grace and innate righteousness by which, in the beginning, man lived with God." He concludes, "However, it cannot be denied that some traces of the divine image still remain in us, which are not wholly extinguished by this spiritual death. This is quite clear, . . . from the holiness and wisdom in both word and deed of many of the heathens" (*CPW*, 6:396). A hint of the continuing presence of the divine image in the works of exemplary pagans is reason enough for the Christian poet to turn to secular authors. Again, however, Milton places strict conditions of his approval of heathen poets. It is only by reflecting "holiness" and "wisdom," not by displaying invention and knowledge, that pagan poets become worthy of attention. Moreover, Milton's resolution "not to make verbal curiosities the end" of his literary works put further restrictions on which pagan works he would approve (*CPW*, 1:811).

From these two theoretical principles on pagan art, two apparently opposite stances toward Ovid's *Metamorphoses* follow for Milton. As an apologist for pagan art in its morally useful role, Milton could adopt the form and style of Ovid's fables but condemn their pagan author. As an explicator of Christian doctrine, on the other hand, Milton could relate the occasional manifestations of holiness in Ovid's stories. Although Milton's sanction of Ovidian myth is always contingent on its agreement with—or at least its lack of contradiction of—scripture, his range of possible uses of the *Metamorphoses* according to these stances is wide. The presence of these two options in Milton's poetics also suggests a degree of uncertainty in his sense of his role as a poet, an uncertainty that he expresses repeatedly in his major poems. Milton's roles as humanist poet and Christian teacher are merged in his resolution to be "an interpreter & relater of the best and sagest things" (*CPW*, 1:811), but even here there was still room for him to maneuver between priestly interpretation and poetic narration.

Nor are these opposed stances irreconcilable, as two applications of fables from the *Metamorphoses* in Milton's sonnets show. Milton's sonnet to Mr. H. Lawes (1646) distinguishes the musician's subtle scansion from that done "with *Midas* ears," as described in *Met.* 11.146–79. Midas earned his ears by preferring the music of Pan when all other judges approved his competitor, Apollo. Accordingly, Milton matches Midas's ears with bad musicians and poetasters who cannot discern the harmony between music and verse as did Lawes.

In Sonnet XI ("On the Detraction which followed upon my Writing Certain Treatises"), dated 1646, the example of Latona's twins from the *Metamorphoses* offers an alternative to the degeneration his detractors have, in Milton's view, brought upon themselves. The brutish detractors have made such a "barbarous noise"

> As when those Hinds that were transform'd to Froggs
> Raild at *Latona's* twin-born progenie
> Which after held the Sun and Moon in fee.

The point of the allusion is initially satiric, but by the end of the simile the satire has modulated into exhortation. The satiric strain is dominant in Ovid's fable, in which the Lycian peasants who deny the common right of water to Latona and her twins (Apollo and Diana) become forever quarrelsome, mindless frogs:

> sed nunc quoque turpes
> litibus exercent linguas pulsoque pudore,
> quamvis sint sub aqua, sub aqua maledicere temptant.
> (6.374–76)

> But even now, as then, they exercise their foul tongues in quarrel, and, without shame, though they may be under water, even under water they try to curse.

Delicately and instructively, Milton's simile moves from a satiric attack using Ovid's fable to a presentation of a positive model of behavior for the detractors. Milton offers a contrasting pair of transformations: the degenerate one of the Hinds, a metamorphic regression down the scale of nature, against the natural, upward-tending one of Apollo and Diana, who grow into their proper offices of the sun and moon. The deft representation of both the offending and offended parties from Ovid's myth displays a more subtle and comprehensive mode of allusion than that revealed in *Comus*. Milton's technique of drawing upon dual aspects of mythical figures from the *Metamorphoses* to both indict and improve his audience is essential to the even more complex artistry of the similes of *Paradise Lost*, with their weighty balancing of condemnation and commendation, of warning and exhortation, of nostalgia and prolepsis.

The sheer number of allusions to the *Metamorphoses* in Milton's mature poetry calls into question the schematically comfortable conclusion of E. K. Rand that Ovid's influence fades after Milton's thirtieth year and that the influence of Virgil increases thereafter.[24] The metaphors of light, equipoise, and marriage which Thomas De Quincey used to describe the relationship between Ovid and Milton are more deeply rooted in the poets' works themselves: "Ovid was the great poetic favourite of Milton; and not without a philosophic ground: his festal gaiety, and the brilliant velocity of his *aurora borealis* intellect, forming a deep natural equipoise to the mighty gloom and solemn planetary movement in the mind of the other—like the wedding of male and female counterparts."[25]

A Choice of Muses: Orpheus in Ovid and Milton

One need not turn to the Romantics, however, for apt descriptions of Milton's literary relationship to Ovid. Perhaps the best measure of the relationship as it unfolds is Milton's repeated use of the Orpheus story as told in *Metamorphoses* 10–11. The pattern of allusions to Orpheus in Milton's poetry not only illustrates the persistence but also epitomizes the development of Milton's respon-

[24]Rand, "Milton in Rustication," p. 121.
[25]De Quincey, *Collected Writings*, ed. David Masson, 11:449.

siveness to the *Metamorphoses*. Because Orpheus is not only a lyric poet but in some sense the figure of Ovid in his work, Milton's comparisons of himself to Orpheus are especially suggestive and resonant.[26] Because Milton's audience is called upon to witness the poet's emulation of, striving with, and conquest of the mythological bard, readers of these allusions, following Milton's example, can internalize their search for both purification and legitimate power.

Early in Milton's oeuvre, Orpheus appears as a figure of the rhetorician rather than the poet. Arguing for the merits of sportive exercises, the Miltonic speaker of the Sixth Prolusion (1628) playfully claims that his situation is superior to that of Orpheus in many ways:

> And by heaven, I cannot help flattering myself a little that I am, as I think, far more fortunate than Orpheus or Amphion; for they did but supply the trained and skilful touch to make the strings give forth their sweet harmony, and the exquisite music was due as much to the instrument itself as to their apt and dexterous handling of it. But if I win praise here to-day, it will be entirely and truly my own, and the more glorious in proportion as the creations of the intellect are superior to manual skill. Besides, Orpheus and Amphion used to attract an audience consisting only of rocks and wild beasts and trees, and if any human beings came, they were at best but rude and rustic folk; but *I* find the most learned men altogether engrossed in listening to my words and hanging on my lips. (*CPW*, 1:268–69)

Ovid had connected Orpheus and Amphion in *Ars Amatoria* 3.321; Milton seems to be using the two interchangeably in this prolusion. Hereafter Amphion, perhaps because he wreaked violent retribution on his mother's captors (rather than, like Orpheus, enduring violence himself), drops out of Milton's comparisons. After differentiating between the manual achievement of Orpheus and the intellectual achievement of the rhetorician, Milton here bases his two major claims of superiority to Orpheus on the whimsically

---

[26]My examination of these allusions is indebted to Bush's fine survey of them in *Mythology and the Renaissance: Tradition in English Poetry*, pp. 296 ff. For a comparison of Virgil's and Ovid's treatments of Orpheus, see W. S. Anderson, "The Orpheus of Virgil and Ovid: *flebile nescio quid*," pp. 25–50, in *Orpheus: The Metamorphosis of a Myth*, ed. John Warden (Toronto, 1982).

alleged superiority of his audience. The speaker gives no credit to the music or the arguments of Orpheus as set forth in *Metamorphoses* 10.17–39. The fulsomeness of Milton's praise of his audience should warn against an overly rigorous scrutiny of the speaker's claims. Nevertheless, the reticence of Milton at twenty to compare his rhetorical power directly to that of Orpheus seems to indicate a mute humility in respect of the famed lyric poet.

By the end of Milton's undergraduate career at Cambridge, his allusions to Orpheus become more earnest, more positive, and more particular. Both "L'Allegro" and "Il Penseroso" (1632?) contain ample and specific references to Ovid's Orpheus. The paired allusions in these poems are further proof that Milton habitually saw ethical and aesthetic issues from two sides before moving toward a resolution.[27] The reference to Orpheus in "L'Allegro" both invokes and celebrates Mirth's gift of immortal music and verse:

> That *Orpheus* self may heave his head
> From golden slumber on a bed
> Of heapt *Elysian* flowres, and hear
> Such streins as would have won the ear
> Of *Pluto*, to have quite set free
> His half regain'd *Eurydice*.
>
> (145–50)

Again, as in the Sixth Prolusion, the Miltonic speaker imaginatively claims superiority over Orpheus: the music L'Allegro hears, or wants to hear, would have "quite [completely, *OED*, 1] set free / His half regain'd *Eurydice*." By playing on Eurydice's double death and momentary recovery, Ovid had amplified the pathos in the fable that Milton distills into the epithet "half regain'd":

> hanc simul et legem Rhodopeius accipit Orpheus,
> ne flectat retro sua lumina, donec Avernas
> exierit valles; aut irrita dona futura . . . .
> nec procul abfuerant telluris margine summae:
> hic, ne deficeret, metuens avidusque videndi

---

[27]Mary Ann Radzinowicz, *Toward "Samson Agonistes": The Growth of Milton's Mind* (Princeton, N.J., 1978), p. 5.

flexit amans oculos: et protinus illa relapsa est . . . .
iamque iterum moriens non est de coniuge quicquam
questa suo (quid enim nisi se quereretur amatam?)
supremumque "vale," quod iam vix auribus ille
acciperet, dixit revolutaque rursus eodem est.
non aliter stupuit gemina nece coniugis Orpheus, . . .

(10.50–64)

Rhodopean Orpheus then received Eurydice, and with her this condition: that he not turn his eyes backward until he had left the vale of
Avernus, or else the gift would be in vain . . . . And now they ap-
proached the margin of the upper earth, when he, fearing that she
might fail him and longing for a glimpse, turned back his eyes, then
instantly she fell back into the depths . . . . And now, dying a second
time, she made no complaint against her husband (for what could she
complain of save that she was loved?). She uttered a final "farewell"
which scarcely reached her husband's ears, and fell back again to the
infernal depths.

By his wife's double death Orpheus was astonished, . . .

In *Metamorphoses* 11.61–66 Orpheus and Eurydice are ultimately
rejoined in the Elysian Fields. Milton's revisionary lines focus on
the visionary liberation of Eurydice by song surpassing the persuasive—but only partially effective—power of Orpheus.

In "Il Penseroso" the speaker begs to hear not music that would
have rivaled that of Orpheus, but rather the very music and words
of the bard himself:

> Or bid the soul of *Orpheus* sing
> Such notes as warbled to the string,
> Drew Iron tears down *Pluto*'s cheek,
> And made Hell grant what Love did seek.

(105–8)

The revisionary impulse of the allusion in "L'Allegro" here gives
way to a more searching inquiry into the bard's method and affective power. Orpheus had evoked Pluto's tears, according to Ovid,
by cleverly protesting his weakness in dealing with love: a weakness
to which Pluto, his judge, is also prone. Thus Orpheus to Pluto:

vicit Amor. supera deus hic bene notus in ora est;
an sit et hic, dubito. sed et hic tamen augoror esse,
famaque si veteris non est mentita rapinae,
vos quoque iunxit Amor.

(10.26–29)

Love has conquered me. In the upper world that god is well known,
but whether here or not I do not know. Yet I surmise that he is known
here, for if the rumor of that ancient ravishment is not a fiction, Love
also joined you.

Il Penseroso's solemn invocation of Orpheus contains a desire to
emulate both the bard's understanding of motives (Amor) and his
mastery of harmony ("warbled" notes), both his rhetorical power
and his craft.

In "Ad Patrem" (1632?) Milton again refers twice to Orpheus.
These new allusions represent Orpheus as not only a master of
soothing music, but for the first time as a model for the aspiring
poet. The first allusion cites the authority of the gods, won over by
Orpheus, as a sign of the divine power of poetry:

Nec tu vatis opus divinum despice carmen, . . .
Carmen amant superi, tremebundaque Tartara carmen
Ima ciere valet, divosque ligare profundos,
Et triplici duros Manes adamante coercet.

(17, 21–23)

Do not despise divine poetry, the poet's creation, . . . The gods love
poetry: poetry has power to stir the trembling depths of Tartarus and
to bind the deities of hell: it grips the cruel shades with triple ada-
mant.

Ovid had similarly described the power of Orpheus to melt the
stern deities of the underworld through his plaintive song:

talia dicentem nervosque ad verba moventem
exsangues flebant animae: nec Tantalus undam
captavit refugam stupuitque Ixionis orbis,
nec carpsere iecur volucres, urnisque vacarunt

Belides, inque tuo sedisti, Sisyphe, saxo.
tunc primum lacrimis victarum carmine fama est
Eumenidum maduisse genas, nec regia coniunx
sustinet oranti nec, qui regit ima, negare.

(10.40–47)

As he spoke, accompanying his words with the music of his lyre, the bloodless spirits wept: Tantalus did not grasp at the receding wave; Ixion's wheel stopped in wonder; the vultures did not pluck at the liver [of Prometheus]; the Belides rested from their urns, and you, Sisyphus, sat upon your stone. Then for the first time, tradition has it, the cheeks of the Eumenides, who were conquered by your song, were wet with tears; nor could the queen nor he who rules the underworld deny the suppliant.

By winning the attention and hearts of these perpetually preoccupied mythic figures, Orpheus takes on the role in the *Metamorphoses* of a master of myth. The tableau of awkwardly frozen mythic figures displays Ovid's characteristically mannered rendering of a story familiar in its basic outlines from earlier accounts. Milton's allusion to Orpheus in "Ad Patrem" works in this same vein of mannered, self-conscious treatment. Perhaps Milton's knowing, mannered tone in the allusion derives from a playful superiority to pagan poetry that he could expect his father to share. Poetry that "stirs the trembling depth of Tartarus" and rivets the attention of the damned may be powerful, but it is inadequate when compared with the power to bring back Paradise that Milton had celebrated in the "Nativity Ode" some three years earlier.

Later in "Ad Patrem" Milton returns to the Orpheus myth, this time to distinguish pure melody from the more expressive, and distinctively human, mode of poetic song:

Denique quid vocis modulamen inane juvabit,
Verborum sensusque vacans, numerique loquacis?
Silvestras decet iste choros, non Orphea cantus,
Qui tenuit fluvios & quercubus addidit aures
Carmine, non citharâ, simulachraque functa canendo
Compulit in lacrymas; habet has à carmine laudes.

(50–55)

And after all, what use is the voice if it merely hums an inane tune, without words, meaning, or the rhythm of speech? That kind of song is good enough for the woodland choristers, but not for Orpheus, who with his singing, not his lyre, held streams spellbound and gave ears to the oak trees and moved lifeless spirits to tears. It is to his singing that he owes his high praise.

Orpheus merits the favorable comparison by the logic, sense, and rhythm of his songs, not, Milton points out, by some magical power of his instrument. Given this context, the allusion to Orpheus is particularly subtle and appropriate, for logical, meaningful, and rhythmic speech applies equally well to the songs of John Milton, Sr., the composer of a number of religious lyrics, and to John Milton, Jr., the young but already accomplished lyric poet. The density of Ovidian echoes in "Ad Patrem" strengthens the possibility that the allusions to Orpheus also recommend Ovid himself as a poetic model. Of the seven echoes of Ovid that John Carey notes,[28] the two that link Milton's Orpheus with Ovid's may have reached the English poet by various means. Virgil's account in *Georgics* 4.510, for example, also includes oak trees gathering to hear the songs of Orpheus. Such multiplicity of allusion is integral to a poem that displays a vast array of classical learning to its immediate audience (Milton's father) and begins by demanding a drink of "every drop" of the Pierian stream.

In "Lycidas" (1637) Orpheus again provides a model of the poet's powers, but now Milton examines closely the range and limits of that power. Despite the persuasive rhetoric of Orpheus in Hell, and despite the attraction of his music for everyone from Thracian women to shade trees (*Met.* 10.79–82; 86–105), neither he nor his mother Calliope could prevent his death. The uncouth swain observes:

> What could the Muse her self that *Orpheus* bore,
> The Muse her self for her inchanting son
> Whom Universal nature did lament,
> When by the rout that made the hideous roar,

[28]See Carey, notes to "Ad Patrem," 11.48, 52–55(2), 71, 79, 93, 98, pp. 150–52.

His goary visage down the stream was sent,
Down the swift *Hebrus* to the *Lesbian* shore.
(58–63)

The "rout that made the hideous roar" recalls the "ingens / clamor" of the Bacchantes which drowned out the music of Orpheus (*Met.* 11.15–16). Milton's arresting image of the "goary visage" of Orpheus develops Ovid's description of the dismembering of the bard:

> membra iacent diversa locis, caput, Hebre, lyramque
> excipis: et (mirum!) medio dum labitur amne,
> flebile nescio quid queritur lyra.
>
> (11.50–52)

> They hurled the poet's limbs in many places, but his head and lyre, O Hebrus, you received: and (a marvel!) while it floated in mid-stream, the lyre made a mournful plaint unknown to me.

As in the Sixth Prolusion, Milton discounts the alleged magical effect of the lyre, and he now describes the head ("caput") of Orpheus as his "visage." The gain is not simply one of more precise vision, but of emotional intensity, because Milton's uncouth swain is now confronting that part of Orpheus in which his personal identity resides. The surge of anxiety engendered by thus confronting the inevitable death of Orpheus, King, and himself leads directly to the plaintive questioning of identity and vocation by the Miltonic singer:

> Alas! What boots it with uncessant care
> To tend the homely slighted Shepherds trade,
> And strictly meditate the thankless Muse.
>
> (64–66)

These lines, which at least one commentator numbers among the most wistful in all literature,[29] develop the allusion to Orpheus in two ways. They transform the sense of helplessness of Calliope

<hr />

[29]Edward Le Comte, *Milton and Sex* (New York, 1975), p. 19.

toward Orpheus to the reflexive sense of uselessness on the part of Milton's shepherd-singer. Moreover, they question the efficacy of appealing to a transcendent pagan Muse. This tension in "Lycidas" will not be resolved until the swain gains his apocalyptic vision of the new, resurrected face of his fellow shepherd which replaces the "goary" Orphean visage.

It is in the context of these uses of the Orpheus myth that the redoubled allusion in *Paradise Lost* deserves consideration. The two appearances of the myth in Milton's epic form a dialectic that points to an unparalleled mode of allusion, a mode characterized both by a fullness of correspondence between vehicle and tenor of comparison, and by a voice that vigorously attempts to set the limits of the comparison. The first allusion to Orpheus immediately follows the invocation of "holy Light" that opens Book III:

> Thee I re-visit now with bolder wing,
> Escap't the *Stygian* Pool, though long detain'd
> In that obscure sojourn, while in my flight
> Through utter and through middle darkness borne
> With other notes then to th'*Orphean* Lyre
> I sung of *Chaos* and *Eternal Night*,
> Taught by the heav'nly Muse to venture down
> The dark descent, and up to reascend,
> Though hard and rare.
>
> (III, 13–21)

The similarity in structure between the reascent of Orpheus from the Underworld in the *Metamorphoses* and Milton's reascent from Hell to the realm of light at this point in his epic is certain, and seems to have occasioned the comparison. While making the comparison, however, the Miltonic narrator distinguishes his situation from that of Orpheus in two crucial regards. First, the "notes" of Milton's song are "other" than those of Orpheus, and the otherness may derive from either the absence of a lost Eurydice in Milton's fable, or the generically different modulation of epic versus lyric utterance, or the thematic difference of notes made for romantic love versus notes made for a Christian theodicy. Reflection on these differences in narrative, genre, and purpose reinforces one's awareness of the isolated, yet faithful Christian bard shaping this poem. Second, this Christian poet has recovered from the doubt of inspiration by the Muse as set forth in "Lycidas": the "thankless" Muse of the elegy has been replaced by the "heavenly" Muse of the epic. A further sign of confidence is that here the Muse's teaching, not the Virgilian or Orphean model of a descent to the Underworld, becomes the acknowledged guide for Milton's excursus through Hell and Chaos.

Confidence in the heavenly Muse remains in Milton's final allusion to Orpheus, but this trust in inspiration now is held in great tension with a fear of reception, a fear that a senseless audience will destroy both the poet and his song. The allusion follows Milton's prayer that Urania will "fit audience find, though few":

> But drive farr off the barbarous dissonance
> Of *Bacchus* and his revellers, the Race
> Of that wilde Rout that tore the *Thracian* Bard
> In *Rhodope*, where Woods and Rocks had Eares
> To rapture, till the savage clamor dround
> Both Harp and Voice; nor could the Muse defend
> Her Son.
>
> (VII, 32–38)

Although Milton is invoking the Muse, his implicit dialogue is with Ovid. For it is Ovid who provides Milton with the terms to express the danger of poetic rapture. In Rhodope, Orpheus remained in solitude, and there charmed all of nature with his song: "Carmine dum tali silvas animosque ferarum / Threicius vates et saxa sequentia ducit" (Meanwhile with such songs the Thracian bard entranced trees, the spirits of beasts, and stones to follow him, *Met.* 11.1–2). Milton's phrase, "where Woods and Rocks had Eares / To rapture," follows Ovid's account closely, but heightens it by synecdoche. There is an implicit but palpable parallel between Orpheus surrounded by "that wilde Rout" and Milton surrounded by the "savage clamor" of his no less dangerous audience. Despite these similarities between the audience, power, and isolation of the two poets, Milton ultimately shatters the allusion by insisting on the efficacy of his Muse: "So fail not thou, who thee implores: / For thou art Heav'nlie, shee an empty dreame" (38–39).

Even this overt dismissal of the Muse of Orpheus does not cancel either the analogy of Milton to Orpheus or the fear and urgency that the analogy conveys. These lines do, however, establish in *Paradise Lost* a crucial difference between poets such as Orpheus (and by implication, Ovid) and Milton. Whereas Orpheus claims the personal power to enrapture universal nature, and Ovid the authority to sing a *carmen perpetuum* from creation to his own day, Milton raises a song of universal scope, but he locates the authority and power of his epic argument outside his fallen self. Milton's reliance on the heavenly Muse enables him, paradoxically, to pour Ovid's fables of mythological change into *Paradise Lost* abundantly, without anxiety that they might destroy his comprehensive Christian epic.

Because the *Metamorphoses* embraces a host of timeless characters well known to Milton's contemporaries, a ready and easy way for him to develop the characters in his epic while guiding the reader's response to them was by aligning them at crucial points with Ovid's mythic figures. The following chapter examines the Ovidian figures that Milton associates with Eve, whose behavior we must understand if we are to grasp the logic of the temptation and the Fall.

—2—

From Proserpina to Pyrrha: Ovidian
Faces of Eve in *Paradise Lost*

Milton's allusions to Ovid's Narcissus and Echo, Pomona, Medea, and Pyrrha epitomize distinct stages of Eve's development in *Paradise Lost*. By "development" I mean neither the segmented presentation of a Beowulf who matures from young kinsman to adult warrior to aged king, nor the series of decisions and discoveries that characterize a Lady Macbeth, though both heroic and tragic methods contribute much to Milton's syncretic epic. "Development" here indicates a continuity in Milton's presentation of Eve which reveals potentialities and weaknesses through a series of incremental changes. Before the Fall, the various increments of a developing Eve are consistent with the divinely sanctioned plan for human progress that Milton builds into the poem. Individual progress, though, becomes increasingly hazardous in Milton's Paradise, for it brings Eve to a confrontation with Satan in which she must choose between advancing her selfhood or obeying God's sole command. Raphael tells Adam and Eve that God made them "perfect, not immutable" (V, 524). Raphael, too, offers them a teleological model for human progress:

> time may come when men
> With Angels may participate, and find
> No inconvenient Diet, nor too light Fare:
> And from these corporal nutriments perhaps
> Your bodies may at last turn all to Spirit,
> Improv'd by tract of time, and wingd ascend

Ethereal, as wee, or may at choice
Here or in Heav'nly Paradises dwell.
(V, 493–500)

Within the briefer duration of Milton's description of Eden, this teleological development may be discerned in Eve's character before the Fall. Milton's dialogue with Ovid, which rearranges scattered mythic figures into a new order, reveals and emphasizes this development in Eve.

How Milton presents Adam and Eve as sinless, much less improving, while in some way preparing for their Fall is an artistic problem that has generated much critical debate in recent years. Modern interpretations of this problem, Irene Samuel remarks,[1] have a sure starting point in C. S. Lewis's *A Preface to "Paradise Lost."* For Lewis, Milton's view of unfallen sexuality was disturbing, in part because of the inequality between male and female, but more so because of a basic inconsistency in Milton's design: "His Eve exhibits modesty too exclusively in sexual contexts, and his Adam does not exhibit it at all. There is even a strong and (in the circumstances) a most offensive suggestion of female bodily shame as an incentive to male desire. I do not mean that Milton's love-passages are objectionable by normal human standards; but they are not consistent with what he himself believes about the world before the Fall."[2]

Lewis met ready opposition from A. J. A. Waldock, who responded to Lewis's qualms about Eve's modesty by pointing out Milton's frankness and consistency regarding sexuality in angels as well as human beings. Waldock minimized the alleged offensiveness of Milton's celebration of Eve's "sweet reluctant amorous delay" by comparing it with her sudden descent into voracious sensuality after the Fall. Waldock's solution, however, introduced what he regarded as a logical impossibility, that of making a believable transition from innocence to experience: "It is obvious that Adam and Eve must already have contracted human weaknesses before they can start on the course of conduct that leads to their

[1]Irene Samuel, *"Paradise Lost,"* in *Critical Approaches to Six Major English Works,* ed. R. M. Lumiansky and Herschel Baker (Philadelphia, 1968), p. 212.
[2]C. S. Lewis, *A Preface to "Paradise Lost"* (New York, 1961), p. 124.

fall: to put it another way, they must already be fallen (technically) before they can begin to fall. Nor, again, is it possible to see just how the change from love to lust came about, or what was in the act of disobedience that necessitated it."[3] Stanley Fish seems to circumvent this putative impossibility, which harks back to Dr. Johnson's critique of the poem in *Lives of the Poets,* by concentrating on the Fall of the reader instead of the characters in the poem. Fish argues that "Milton's method is to re-create in the mind of the reader (which is, finally, the poem's scene) the drama of the Fall, to make him fall again as Adam did and with Adam's troubled clarity, that is to say, 'not deceived.' "[4] An immediate limitation on this argument is its overtly masculine bias: the reader is said to fall as Adam, not as Eve or (most appropriately) as "our first parents," the entire human community, did. The crucial test of Fish's argument is how fully his emphasis on the "harassed reader" recovers each real reader's full sense of the poem. From another perspective, Fish's stress on the reader's fall begs the question of how the design of *Paradise Lost* brings Adam and Eve from innocence to sin.

In *Milton: A Structural Reading,* Donald F. Bouchard discusses the problem of the Fall as a linguistic problem, a problem of unfallen language. In the prefallen state, Bouchard claims, "word and thing are consonant, as illustrated by the 'Morning Prayer' of Book V, where worship resounds the creation, where voice is echoed in things, and in the innate ability of Adam to name the animals." Even in the Garden, however, as he points out, the perfect coincidence of words and things is already vastly complicated. First of all, our entry into Eden is along the path of Satan, whose linguistic "project" is to defeat "the Word" with his own, self-styled words, to become, in short, his own author. Moreover, our sense of tranquillity in Paradise is shaken by the operation of Fancy, which "misjoins" words to things, and so produces a language, in Bouchard's terms, that falsifies God's version of creation as the perfect expression of "the Word" incarnate (a looser meaning of "the Word" than that of John 1.1). If Milton believes he is in control of the transition from unfallen to fallen language,

[3] A. J. A. Waldock, *"Paradise Lost" and Its Critics* (Cambridge, 1947), p. 61.
[4] Stanley Fish, *Surprised by Sin: The Reader in "Paradise Lost"* (London, 1967), p. 1.

Bouchard suggests, language itself prevents Milton from retrieving true Paradise, because language is, in Edward Said's definition, "a sequel to or supplement of the beginning event, man's fall: language is one of the events which succeeds the lost Origin." Bouchard reminds us, then, that whereas Milton describes Adam and Eve as first sinless, then fallen, the language he is forced to use for this pivotal change is always already fallen.[5]

Milton frequently calls attention in *Paradise Lost* to the fallen nature of his world, which includes fallen language. The paradox of describing heavenly subjects in earthly language is one Milton embraces and struggles with at many points, from the proems to Books I, III, VII, and IX to Raphael's account of the War in Heaven. Bouchard's claim that the only evidence of true bliss in Paradise in the poem is "Eve's narcissistic origin which recreates the bliss found in Heaven before the origin of the disturbing image" seems implausible. On the contrary, my reading will maintain that this origin, understood in its Ovidian and Miltonic contexts, depicts a limited and incomplete moment in Eve's development.[6]

By comparing the appearances of Narcissus and Echo, Pomona, Medea, and Pyrrha in *Paradise Lost* with the Ovidian passages to which Milton alludes, I hope to show that these allusions help maintain the balance between Eve's innocence and the audience's knowledge of the imminence of the Fall. Milton uses these Ovidian figures both as aesthetic emblems which Eve in Paradise nevertheless surpasses and as proleptic indicators of the moral dangers in Eve's individual development. Before considering these sets of parallels and their significance, however, I propose to examine an earlier allusion to Ovid's *Metamorphoses* which will serve as a model

[5]Donald F. Bouchard, *Milton: A Structural Reading* (Montreal, 1974), p. 75.

[6]Ibid., p. 79. In terms of this general problem, this chapter is particularly indebted to three studies: W. B. C. Watkins's *An Anatomy of Milton's Verse* (Baton Rouge, La., 1955), pp. 127–29 for the notion that Milton creates a network of circumstances which makes the argument of the Fall intelligible and persuasive; Christopher Ricks's *Milton's Grand Style* (Oxford, 1963), pp. 137–50, for my sense of the "balance" which the Ovidian figures support; and Barbara Kiefer Lewalski's "Innocence and Experience in Eden," in *New Essays on "Paradise Lost,"* ed. Thomas Kranidas (Berkeley, Calif., 1969), pp. 86–117, for her discussion of "process" and "perilous exposure" in Eden. Diane K. McColley's *Milton's Eve* (Urbana, Ill., 1983) takes an iconographic approach, stressing Eve's role as a full partner and spiritual equal with Adam, which complements my comparative study of Eve's development.

for Milton's adaptation of Ovid's mythic figures to his teleological epic.

Disavowal and Pursuit: The Example of Enna

According to Louis Martz,[7] perhaps the most significant mythological reference in the whole of *Paradise Lost* is the famous comparison of Eden to the paradises of antiquity:

> Not that faire field
> Of *Enna*, where *Proserpin* gathering flours
> Her self a fairer Floure by gloomie *Dis*
> Was gatherd, which cost *Ceres* all that pain
> To seek her through the world.
>
> (IV, 268–72)

That Ovid was the first to locate the rape of Proserpina in Enna suggests that Milton is recalling his description, yet more telling than a recall of geography are the many correspondences in expression between Ovid's account of Enna and Milton's simile. In the half-line preceding the simile, "Led on th'Eternal Spring," Milton translates Ovid's "perpetuum ver est" (5.391), which had preceded Proserpina's appearance in the *Metamorphoses*. The closeness of Milton's English to Ovid's Latin verses here reveals further parallels:

> Haud procul Hennaeis lacus est a moenibus altae,
> nomine Pergus, aquae; non illo plura Caystros
> carmina cygnorum labentibus edit in undis.
> silva coronat aquas cingens latus omne suisque
> frondibus ut velo Phoebeos submovet ictus.
> frigora dant rami, Tyrios humus umida flores:
> perpetuum ver est. quo dum Proserpina luco

---

[7]Martz, *Poet of Exile*, p. 227, notes inaccurately that the pain of Ceres is not described in the *Metamorphoses* but in the *Fasti* 4.420–620. Ovid tells the story in both works, though the language of Milton's simile is not reminiscent of the *Fasti*. This is the only inaccuracy I know of in the most comprehensive critical account of Milton's use of Ovidian material to date.

ludit et aut violas aut candida lilia carpit,
dumque puellari studio calathosque sinumque
inplet et aequales certat superare legendo,
paene simul visa est dilectaque raptaque Diti.

(5.385–95)

Not far from the high walls of Enna there is a pool named Pergus: not Cayster on its flowing waters puts forth more songs of swans than does this pool. A wood crowns the waters, binding the whole shoreline, and with its leaves keeps off the burning sun. The branches afford coolness, and the wet earth bears splendid flowers. There spring is eternal. Within this place Prosperpina is playing, and she picks now violets, now white lilies. And while with girlish eagerness she fills her basket and her bosom, and vying to surpass her peers in gathering, almost at once she has been seen and desired and taken by Dis.

The negative form of Ovid's syntax approximates Milton's repetition of negatives: "Not that . . . nor that . . . nor that" (268–80). The synesthetic imagery ("frigora . . . rami"; "humus umida flores") recurs in the lines preceding Milton's simile: "aires, vernal aires, / Breathing the smell of field and grove, attune / The trembling leaves." "Aires" and "attune" connote harmonies of sound and motion along with pleasing smell and sensation.[8] The progression of verb tenses describing the rape ("carpit," she picks; "legendo," gathering; "rapta," she has been taken) informs Milton's lines, in which Proserpin, "gathering flours . . . Was gatherd."[9] Even Milton's sense of the magnitude of Ceres' labors to retrieve her child may be found in the response of Arethusa, the water nymph, to Proserpina's rape. She turns to Ceres:

atque ait: "o toto quaesitae virginis orbe
et frugum genetrix, inmensos siste labores,
neve tibi fidae violenta irascere terrae!"

(5.489–91)

[8]See Ricks, pp. 104–6.
[9]The two major English translations of Ovid that Milton may have known both translate the perfect passive participle "rapta . . . est" actively. Milton seems not to be following a translation but responding to the original. See *Shakespeare's Ovid,*

And she cried: "O mother of the maiden sought through the whole world, and mother of grains, cease now your immense labors and do not be angry and violent toward the faithful earth."

Like the response of Arethusa, Milton's response to the plight of Ceres begins with aesthetic appreciation ("that *faire* field," my emphasis) and sympathetically arrives at a moral judgment. Milton offers a dynamic vision of that fair field in which the violent event that occurred there and the suffering that followed become more important than the beauty of the place, which was the starting point for the simile.

Milton's and Ovid's passages differ radically, however, in their scopes of reference and in their tones. Within its narrative context, Ovid's fable suggests that the suffering of both Proserpina and Ceres is extensive, and that Arethusa's response to their suffering is an implicit measure of the pathos the scene may evoke. Moreover, Arethusa's invocation of Ceres as "frugum genetrix" (mother of grains) emphasizes the etiological aspect of the myth. Ovid attributes our partial growing season to the disturbance in natural fecundity by violent passion, which Ceres, Dis, and Proserpina reenact. The episodic progression of the *Metamorphoses*, finally, shifts attention rapidly from story to story, so that neither the episode of Proserpina and Ceres nor any other episode continues to call attention to itself far beyond its place in the collection of myth and history.

In Milton's allusion to the myth, in contrast, prolepsis achieves a widening signification. C. S. Lewis explained this feature of Milton's style as a physical principle, "the power of action at a distance."[10] In the Enna simile, he noted, "Paradise is compared to the field of Enna—one beautiful landscape with another (IV, 268). But, of course, the deeper value of the simile lies in the resemblance which is not explicitly noted as a resemblance at all, the fact that in both these places the young and the beautiful while gathering flowers was ravished by a dark power risen up from the

---

Being Arthur Golding's Translation of the "Metamorphoses," (London, 1904), p. 111, and George Sandys, *Ovid's "Metamorphosis" Englished, Mythologized, and Represented in Figures*, p. 237.
[10]Lewis, *Preface*, p. 43.

underworld." Refining Lewis's reading, Christopher Ricks adds that as the simile continues precise parallels give way to a "looser suggestiveness." We know that "Ceres cannot be Christ, in the sense in which Eve is Proserpin; the most obvious thing is that the sexes are wrong, and the correspondence would be intolerable in any case, since Eve is herself later explicitly compared to Ceres."[11] The looser suggestiveness of "which cost *Ceres* all that pain," though, Ricks continues, may include a hint (in "cost") of the suffering of Christ and a hint (in "pain") of the results of the Fall. The faint but clear echo in "all that pain" of "all our woe," the metrically equivalent consequence announced in the opening invocation, reinforces the latter, more general suggestion. Milton makes Ovid's passage partly clarify his immediate context and partly predict that his vision of Eden will transvalue earlier, external representations of heroic struggles by internalizing the possibility of heroism.

The particularly negative formulation of this and other Miltonic similes echoes yet redirects the characteristically incredulous tone of Ovid's narrator toward his sources. In Book 10 of the *Metamorphoses*, Orpheus, whose power to persuade and soothe suggests that he is in some sense a figure of the poet, sings to Proserpina. He deduces from her fate that love (Amor) must reign even in the Netherworld: "famaque si veteris non est mentita rapinae" (if the rumor of your ancient ravishment is not fictitious, *Met.* 10.28). The comic scene of one of Ovid's mythical figures questioning a story that the poet himself (through Calliope, the Muse of history) has earlier presented at length explodes the potential seriousness of this line as a challenge to the status of myth. E. K. Rand has called this moment "a fling at skepticism."[12] The humor and pathos of many such moments in the *Metamorphoses* lend weight to Rand's less cryptic remark that Ovid stops short of ultimate skepticism. Ovid believed in the enduring power of his poetry, which he seems to have regarded as coextensive with imperial Rome. Speaking in his own voice in the epilogue to the *Metamorphoses*, he celebrates his poetic immortality wherever Rome rules, for, he concludes wryly, "siquid habent veri vatum praesagia, vivam" (if the prophecies of bards have any truth to them, I shall live).

[11]Ricks, p. 125.
[12]Rand, *Ovid and His Influence* (New York, 1963), p. 74.

From Proserpina to Pyrrha

The allusions to classical literature in *Paradise Lost* recall Ovid's wry skepticism; they nevertheless rely on the works of that pagan bard for characterization, narrative devices, and structural patterns. Milton relies on classical poetry throughout this epic, and not simply for formulations he will abandon in his attempt to make his "adventrous Song" soar "Above th'*Aonian* mount." Classical matter has its place in *Paradise Lost* when it points to a spiritual correlative that makes it "true," as in this description of the Garden:

> Thus was this place,
> A happy rural seat of various view;
> Groves whose rich Trees wept odorous Gumms and Balme,
> Others whose fruit burnisht with Golden Rinde
> Hung amiable, *Hesperian* Fables true,
> If true, here only, and of delicious taste.
>
> (IV, 246–51)

As noted earlier, Milton's syntax, itself derived from the loose periodic models of Virgil and Ovid, allows the "delicious taste" to modify both the fruit and the fables. For Milton, writing *Of Education* in 1644, poetry was by definition "simple, sensuous, and passionate," more so than rhetoric, and his recommended educational program outlined in that epistle culminates with the reading of epic, dramatic, and lyric poetry. As we have seen, Ovid's work was certainly a part of the mature as well as the young Milton's reading. Milton's extensive familiarity with the *Metamorphoses* suggests that Ovid's poem was no less valuable to him for its simple and passionate presentation of a variety of human situations than for its purely sensuous appeal. By reaching out to Ovid to supply specific, sensuous metaphors for his story, Milton allows Ovid's fables a share in the "truth" as well as the "delicious taste" of Edenic fruit. In this sense, Milton's use of Ovid constitutes a dialogue between two shapers and relaters of myth.

Yet the proems of *Paradise Lost* indicate that Milton was ultimately skeptical about classical poetry, beyond the witty, self-referential way of Ovid, insofar as it contradicted or was inconsistent with scriptural authority. Milton's approach to classical literature is not that of Juvencus, the earliest Christian epic poet, who inveighs against the pagan poets and replaces the Muses and Helicon in his poem with the Holy Spirit and the river Jordan.[13] Nor is his way that of Dante, whose Christian epic, although subsuming a great deal of pagan poetry, nevertheless places Ovid, Lucan, Statius, and Homer in Limbo. Milton's way is encompassing and essentialist: At the center of his epic he calls the classical name of Urania, his "Heav'nly Muse," but he announces that he is invoking the Christian meaning, not the name.

Along with clarifying Milton's method of making Ovidian matter both illuminate his subjects and suggest the consequences of the Fall, this comparison of the Enna simile with its analogue in the *Metamorphoses* may have the additional merit of suggesting Milton's flexibility in the tradition of Renaissance humanism. Milton made an additional, more personal application of Ovid's account of Ceres and Proserpina. In a Latin letter to Charles Diodati in 1637, the year of *Lycidas,* Milton found Ceres' labors to recover Proserpin a fit analogy of his continuous search for manifestations of Platonic ideal beauty:

Nec tanto Ceres labore, ut in Fabulis est, Liberam fertur quaesivisse filiam, quanto ego hanc τοῦ καλοῦ ιδέαν, veluti pulcherrimam quandam imaginem, per omnes rerum formas & facies: (πολλαὶ γὰρ μορφαὶ τῶν Δαὶμονίων) dies noctesque indagere soleo, & quasi certis quibusdam vestigiis ducentem sector.

Not with so much labor, as in the Fables, is Ceres said to have sought her daughter Proserpin as it is my habit day and night to seek for this idea of the beautiful, as for a certain image of supreme beauty, through all the forms and faces of things (for many are the shapes of things Divine) and to follow it as it leads me on by some sure traces which I seem to recognize.[14]

Milton's ceaseless effort to follow ideal beauty as it leads him on predicts both how his poetic labor will surpass that of Ceres and how his vision of beauty will surpass Proserpin, her lost but freed (Liberam) daughter. By "following it on," Milton will make of the

[13]Ernst Robert Curtius, *European Literature and the Latin Middle Ages,* trans. Willard R. Trask (Princeton, 1953), p. 235.
[14]*Works,* 12:26–27. Noted by Merritt Y. Hughes, ed., *The Complete Poems and Major Prose of John Milton* (Indianapolis, 1957), p. 284.

commitment to ideal beauty a total design in the form of an encyclopedic epic.[15] By searching "through all the forms and faces of things," Milton will examine Ovid's figures who undergo radical changes, but he will analyze and recombine these figures in order to illuminate the development of gradually unfolding characters, including Eve and Satan. The reminiscences of Ovid's verses here and throughout *Paradise Lost* are evidence that Ovidian expression continued to surface in Milton's search for spiritual ideals suggested by but ultimately transcending myth.

"With unexperienc't thought": Eve, Narcissus, and Echo

The beauty and danger of the Proserpin allusion reappear in sharper focus when Eve describes to Adam her first awakening in terms that have long been noticed as an allusion to Ovid's depiction of Narcissus and Echo.[16] My concern with this allusion, beyond documenting the specific features of Milton's adaptation of Ovid's fable, is to show that the Narcissus episode contains a poetic account of what Hermann Fraenkel has called "insecure and fleeting identity,"[17] and to suggest that this phenomenon (which we shall see again in the final section of this chapter on Medea and Eve) functions as a guide to the first stage of Eve's development in *Paradise Lost*.

The suggestion that Adam and Eve have recognizable "stages" of development may seem perverse after C. S. Lewis's insight that just as "they would never, but for sin, have been old, so they were never young, never immature or undeveloped. They were created full-grown and perfect."[18] As for Eve in particular, Lewis added, "in the first half hour of her existence she understood the purport of

---

[15]According to A. S. P. Woodhouse and Douglas Bush, Milton's letter to Diodati itself shows that "obviously he is contemplating no intrusion of less than epic ambition." See *Lycidas* in *A Variorum Commentary on the Poems of John Milton*, vol. 2, part II, 545.

[16]See Patrick Hume, *Annotations on Milton's "Paradise Lost"* (London, 1695). See also Martz, *Poet of Exile*, p. 333.

[17]Hermann Fraenkel, *Ovid: A Poet between Two Worlds* (Berkeley, Calif., 1945), p. 99.

[18]Lewis, *Preface*, p. 116.

Adam's suit."[19] By human standards the perfection and intelligence of Adam and Eve are unquestionably prodigious. That first half hour, though, deserves closer examination, because Milton draws our attention to the first meeting of Adam and Eve twice (IV, 440–91 and VIII, 253–520), in two passages that both mirror each other and develop the individual perspectives of Adam and Eve on the event. Eve's perspective on that first meeting and on her first awakening is essential to our understanding of the possibility of human development in the Garden. In the context of Ovid's myth, Milton's passage shows Eve not only as a corrected Narcissus able to escape self-enclosure but also as a perfected Echo able to initiate as well as respond to discourse.

Speaking to Adam but overheard by Satan, Eve gives her account of her first awakening:

> That day I oft remember, when from sleep
> I first awak't, and found my self repos'd
> Under a shade of flours, much wondring where
> And what I was, whence thither brought, and how.
> Not distant far from thence a murmuring sound
> Of waters issu'd from a Cave and spread
> Into a liquid Plain, then stood unmov'd
> Pure as th'expanse of Heav'n; I thither went
> With unexperienc't thought, and laid me downe
> On the green bank, to look into the cleer
> Smooth Lake, that to me seemd another Skie.
>
> (IV, 449–59)

Besides the evocation of Narcissus at the pool, this scene is especially Ovidian because, in Martz's phrase, Milton locates it "in the kind of *locus amoenus* that Ovid so often presents as the scene of a metamorphosis."[20] The pool in which Narcissus sees his reflection is no less pure, isolated, and enclosed than Eve's "liquid Plain":

> fons erat inlimis, nitidis argenteus undis,
> quem neque pastores neque pastae monte capellae

---

[19]Ibid., p. 121.
[20]Martz, *Poet of Exile*, p. 219.

contigerant aliudve pecus, quem nulla volucris
nec fera turbarat nec lapsus ab arbore ramus;
gramen erat circa, quod proximus umor alebat,
silvaque sole locum passura tepescere nullo.
(3.407–12)

There was a clear pool with silvery shining water, which neither shepherds nor goats feeding on the mountainside nor any other cattle ever chanced upon, and which neither bird nor beast nor falling bough ever disturbed. Grass was on its edge, which the nearby water fed, along with a wood that would not allow the sun to warm the spot.

Dominating our response to the pool is its inviolate beauty, yet this antipastoral *locus amoenus* suggests sterility (no sunlight) and total enclosure (the wood). Milton's description avoids these implications in that the pool, in Eve's view, reflects "th'expanse of Heav'n." Reflecting no image but that of Narcissus, Ovid's pool is an emblem of the hopelessly enclosed self, whereas in Eve's pool the heavenly purity and strong light, which recall the "holy Light" of the invocation to Book III, argue that Eve's self-concern does not cut her off either from grace or from the possibility of personal growth.

Further differences between the pools appear in two passages Milton seems to have imitated closely from Ovid. In the first passage, Narcissus's approach to self-love is recalled in Eve's infatuation with her reflection:

spem mihi nescio quam vultu promittis amico,
cumque ego porrexi tibi bracchia, porrigis ultro;
cum risi, adrides; lacrimas quoque saepe notavi
me lacrimante tuas; nutu quoque signa remittis.
(3.457–60)

You promise a certain hope for me in your amiable face, and when I have reached out my arms to you, you also reach out yours. When I have smiled, you smile back. Often, too, when I am weeping I have seen tears on your cheeks. You even answer my nod with your own.

As I bent down to look, just opposite,
A Shape within the watry gleam appeerd
Bending to look on me, I started back,

> It started back, but pleas'd I soon returnd,
> Pleas'd it returnd as soon with answering looks
> Of sympathie and love; there I had fixt
> Mine eyes till now, and pin'd with vain desire,
> Had not a voice thus warnd me,
>
>   (IV, 460–67)

There is an Ovidian playfulness in Milton's rhetorical suspension and repetition of phrases. The two sketches are almost identical, but the subject is a relatively simple matter of childlike, animal movements. Arnold Stein differentiates the underlying methods of characterization in these passages by contrasting Narcissus's ignorance of his predicament with Eve's knowing and clever use of her earlier self-regard to encourage Adam's love: "The satisfaction of Narcissus requires only a simple reflecting surface. Eve provides a complex reflection; she is beautiful and loved, and she is reproducing for the recognition of her admiring audience, no doubt with grace and evident pleasure, the winning words that she has memorized." According to Stein this is "the complex narcissism of courtship carried into wedded love, but if reason is choice on a humble plane too, then no rational being would prefer the solitary, limited joys available to Narcissus."[21] Eve's manner and narrative do compliment Adam, but the allusion to Narcissus further complicates the character of Eve because, contrary to Stein's "rational being," she would clearly have preferred the self-regarding pose of Narcissus had not Adam, "less faire, / Less winning soft, less amiablie milde" than her reflection, pursued and claimed her. The hierarchy that Eve joins with Adam proves to be more fulfilling and joyful than enclosure in the self.

In the second set of passages, the voice Eve hears (the voice of God, we shortly learn) speaks in terms almost indistinguishable from those of Ovid's narrator on Narcissus:

> quod petis, est nusquam; quod amas, avertere, perdes.
> ista repercussae, quam cernis, imaginis umbra est:
> nil habet ista sui: tecum venitque manetque,
> tecum discedet, si tu discedere possis.
>
>   (3.433–36)

[21]Arnold Stein, *The Art of Presence: The Poet and "Paradise Lost"* (Berkeley, Calif., 1977), p. 95.

What you seek is nowhere; turn, and you lose what you love. What
you see is the shadow of a reflection: it has no substance of its own.
With you it comes, with you it stays, with you it goes—if you can go.

> What thou seest,
> What there thou seest fair Creature is thy self,
> With thee it came and goes: but follow me,
> And I will bring thee where no shadow staies
> Thy coming, and thy soft imbraces, hee
> Whose image thou art, him thou shall enjoy
> Inseparablie thine.
>
> (IV, 467–73)

At first glance, Milton's God and Ovid's narrator seem to be
using the same rhetorical tropes to deliver the same warning to the
characters. The correspondences between the passages reside in
syntax (the repetition of "What thou . . . What there thou" recalls
"quod . . . quod" and "tecum . . . tecum") and in diction ("staies"
translates "manetque"; "Shadow" and "image" replace "umbra"
and "imaginis"). Yet the distinct tonal qualities of these two
voices—Ovid's taunting, condescending; Milton's gracious, mag-
nanimous—register widely divergent evaluations of the situations
of Narcissus and Eve. Ovid's omniscient narrator knows that Narcissus will not turn from his reflection: The conditional "si tu dis-
cedere possis" (if you are able to leave) indicates not an open possibility, but a grim foreshadowing of his inability to escape. God's
invitation, together with Eve's subsequent response to Adam, manages to leave open the possibility that Eve may choose between the
safe posture of self-centeredness and the more productive, if more
vulnerable, turn to others and to experience. Unlike Narcissus, Eve
need not lose her fair image by leaving the pool, but may rather
choose to regenerate it in her role as lover to Adam: "to him shalt
beare / Multitudes like thy self, and thence be call'd / Mother of
human Race" (IV, 473–75).[22]

Ovid's tale of Narcissus may have appealed to Milton as much as
a seed for Eve's false development toward self-exaltation as a sign

---

[22]For an illuminating discussion of Eve's, unlike Narcissus's, education in sexuality, see Purvis E. Boyette, "Milton and the Sacred Fire: Sex Symbolism in *Paradise
Lost*," *Literary Monographs* 5 (1973), 63–138, esp. 108–9.

of the mild vanity and attractive innocence of the newly created Eve. Certainly the coincidence of vanity and innocence in Milton's Eve provides motivation for her assertion of self-sufficiency, even when such an assertion increases her vulnerability and insecurity. In his influential study, *Ovid: A Poet between Two Worlds*, Fraenkel saw Narcissus as the chief example of the phenomenon of "insecure and fleeting identity, of a self divided in itself or spilling over into another self."[23] The former case more accurately describes Narcissus; the latter, Eve at the "liquid Plain." From the start of his narrative, Ovid treats Narcissus lightly, but serious philosophical issues attach themselves to his situation. The blind soothsayer Tiresias who narrates the story introduces Narcissus by relating the Delphic oracle's prophecy concerning him: When asked if he will live long, the oracle replies "si se non noverit" (if he never know himself). The prophecy imitates perhaps the most solemn of the oracle's injunctions ("know thyself"), yet its inversion reveals Ovid's irreverent inventiveness. When Narcissus first feels himself attracted to the image in the pool, Ovid continues this technique of inversion by describing the divided self as a transcendent image of love which, ironically, leads to confusion:

> cunctaque miratur, quibus est mirabilis ipse.
> se cupit inprudens et, qui probat, ipse probatur,
> dumque petit, petitur pariterque accendit et ardet.
> (3.424–26)

He admires all the things for which he is admired himself. Unwittingly he desires himself, he commends, and is commended by himself, and while he seeks he is sought; he kindles love in the other and burns in love himself.

G. Karl Galinsky has pointed to the way Ovid's masterful sequence of juxtaposed active and passive verb forms, expressing Narcissus's confusion of subject and object, draws the reader into the narrative.[24] All the verbs, active and passive, return to "ipse"

[23]Fraenkel, p. 99. See also pp. 86–98.
[24]G. Karl Galinsky, *Ovid's "Metamorphoses": An Introduction to the Basic Aspects* (Berkeley, Calif., 1975), p. 57.

(himself). Moreover, Ovid's antiheroic epithet for Narcissus is "in-prudens": not only imprudent, but inexperienced and unwitting as well.[25] Fraenkel's summary of the psychological significance of Narcissus's desire is also relevant to Eve: "Self-love is headed for self-destruction. Its thirst can never be quenched, because love conquers only through a mutual surrender of two selves, and in self-love there are no two, and no surrender of the self."[26] Eve's turn toward a false godhead through self-exaltation may have its beginnings in her brief phase of narcissistic contemplation. The Narcissus figure adds both a sense of present beauty and grace to Eve's character while it hints more subtly at her fatal shift from self-love to self-exaltation at the crisis.

Milton's allusions to Ovid's Narcissus suggest that Ovid's Echo may also be a partial image for Eve, because in the *Metamorphoses* the fable of Echo is interwoven with that of Narcissus. Echo's passion draws her toward Narcissus, but her inability to initiate speech frustrates her desire:

> natura repugnat
> nec sinit, incipiat; sed, quod sinit, illa parata est
> exspectare sonos, ad quos sua verba remittat.
> (3.376–78)

Her nature resists, nor does it allow that she might begin, but, what it does allow, is that she is ready to await sounds to which she may send back her own words.

The unusually choppy rhythm of Ovid's lines poetically conveys Echo's awkward, constricted nature, just as her partial repetitions of Narcissus's words convey her limited speech. The incomplete-ness of Echo's responses, along with her total dependence on the object of her love, makes her an ironically fit match for the solip-sistic and self-devoted Narcissus.

Eve, in contrast, is capable both of self-initiated speech and of a highly complex echoing of others' words. Eve initiates the account

[25]Cf. Charlton T. Lewis and Charles Short, eds., *A Latin Dictionary* (Oxford, 1969; rpt. 1980), p. 909.
[26]Fraenkel, p. 84.

of her first awakening to consciousness and her subsequent yielding to Adam, in both cases expanding upon and personalizing the topics of creation and dominion Adam had previously mentioned. Besides shaping her own words into a narrative, she echoes, or more accurately, imaginatively represents the words of God and those of Adam. In Eve's narrative, God's invitation to join Adam does more than present her with a replacement for her attractive self-image, or "shadow":

> but follow me,
> And I will bring thee where no shadow staies
> Thy coming, and thy soft imbraces.
>
> (IV, 469–71)

The artful periphrasis in the invitation ("no shadow" for Adam) recalls the "umbra" of Ovid's Narcissus, but suggests that what then awaited Eve's arrival was, unlike a shadowy reflection, substantial and independent.

In her echoing of Adam's words, too, Eve appropriates another's speech and re-presents it from her own perspective. Remembering Adam's call when she initially turned away from him, Eve paraphrases what, in Genesis 2.22–23, had been Adam's definition of woman:

> Whom fli'st thou? whom thou fli'st, of him thou art,
> His flesh, his bone; to give thee being I lent
> Out of my side to thee, neerest my heart
> Substantial Life, to have thee by my side
> Henceforth an individual solace dear.
>
> (IV, 482–86)

More than repeating Adam's words, Eve improves on them by adding a description of herself as Adam's "individual solace dear," an inseparable companion yet a complete person since her creation. With the word "solace," Eve renews her marriage vows to Adam as Milton would have styled them; in his divorce tracts Milton described the ideal wife as the "expected solace" of her husband (*CPW,* 2:245). Eve's initiation of speech and responsiveness to Adam's words align her with the "fit conversing soul" that Milton described in the *Doctrine and Discipline of Divorce,* who is able to enjoy the full mysterious union of marriage. Because for Milton "a meet and happy conversation is the chiefest and the noblest end of marriage" (*CPW,* 2:246), Eve's resourceful conversation with Adam is crucial to Milton's depiction of unfallen love. "Conversation," in this context, means far more than speech: It is the foundation of conjugal society, including commerce, intercourse, and intimacy, and it provides primarily, in Milton's view, "for the solace and satisfaction of the minde" (*CPW,* 2:246). Eve's conversation in this scene demonstrates her progression beyond both the detached, inescapable narcissism and the passive, partial echoing of Ovid's figures. For both Ovid and Milton, a more productive version of love than that of Narcissus and Echo is that of Vertumnus and Pomona, to which Milton turns for the next stage of Eve's development in *Paradise Lost.*

"What to my minde first thoughts present": Eve and Pomona

In *Paradise Lost* Eve is twice compared to Pomona, first on the day of Raphael's visit (V, 377–85), and then immediately before her departure from Adam on the day of the "fatal Trespass" (IX, 393–96). Bracketing Raphael's account of the hexameron at the center of the poem, the allusions to Pomona iconographically depict the continuity of Eve's character, particularly in her role as gardener. A comparison of these bracketing images suggests that Eve's continuity in the Garden nevertheless involves variation and development. Eve's speech and behavior surrounding her two figurations as Pomona reveal a quickening of her discursive power and a movement toward virtuous autonomy which only the proleptic lamentation of the narrator and the hindsight of the fallen audience judge as a sign of error. By showing Eve subtly developing as an individual before the Fall, Milton shows that she is not sinful but vulnerable. Eve's individual progress is not at fault, but in order to advance according to divine plan it must be integrated with the development of the human community. As virtually this same argument is made by Vertumnus (but in a different context) in the *Metamorphoses,* we may begin by considering the rhetorical motives behind Ovid's and Milton's use of the argument as an emblem for harmony with nature and harmony through mutual love.

After Adam and Eve sing their exquisite morning hymn in "various style" (signifying their liberty as well as their piety) in Book V, they proceed to their pleasant and equally free labor in the Garden:

> On to thir mornings rural work they haste
> Among sweet dewes and flours; where any row
> Of Fruit-trees overwoodie reachd too farr
> Thir pamperd boughes, and needed hands to check
> Fruitless imbraces: or they led the Vine
> To wed her Elm; she spous'd about him twines
> Her mariageable arms, and with her brings
> Her dowr th'adopted Clusters, to adorn
> His barren leaves.
>
> (V, 211–19)

To say that this passage is based solely on Ovid's story of Pomona and Vertumnus would qualify as the kind of source hunting Rosemond Tuve once called the next to last infirmity of noble minds. Milton's depiction of a natural *discordia concors* in a Garden with "rows" of fruit trees with interlocking, luxuriant branches locates his Eden in the tradition of English neoclassical landscape. The figure of the tree and vine is a commonplace in both English and Latin poetry.[27] Where Ovid's fable intersects with Milton's, however, is in Vertumnus's argument that, by avoiding him, Pomona is selfishly fleeing from marriage:

> ulmus erat contra speciosa nitentibus uvis:
> quam socia postquam pariter cum vite probavit,
> "at si staret" ait "caelebs sine palmite truncus,
> nil praeter frondes, quare peteretur, haberet;

---

[27]Cf. Catullus, 61.101–4; 62.54–58; Virgil, *Georg.* 1.2–3; 2.367–68; *Ecl.* 2.70; Horace, *Carm.* 5.30; *Epode* 2.9–10; *Ode* 2.15.4; Ovid, *Trist.* 2.143; 5.34–36; *Am.* 2.16–41; *Met.* 10.100. Alastair Fowler notes English analogues in his edition of *Paradise Lost* (London, 1971), p. 269.

haec quoque, quae iuncta vitis requiescit in ulmo,
si non iuncta foret, terrae adclinata iaceret;
tu tamen exemplo non tangeris arboris huius,
concubitusque fugis nec te coniungere curas."
(14.661–68)

There was a handsome elm opposite, covered with gleaming grapes. After he had looked approvingly on the tree together with the vine, its companion, he said: "But if that trunk stood unmarried to the vine, the elm would have nothing except its leaves, for which it is sought after; and that vine, which is joined to and rests safely on the elm, if it were not thus wedded, would lie uselessly, flat on the ground. You, however, are not moved by the example of this vine, for you flee wedlock and you do not trouble to be joined to another."

In Ovid's tale the natural objects become rhetorical tools: Vertumnus makes the mutually beneficial marriage of vine and elm a moral example that he expects Pomona to apply to his suit for her. Vertumnus's complaint that Pomona, unmoved by the example of the vine, "flees" (*fugit*) marriage becomes transumed in Milton's climactic allusion to Eve as Pomona in Book IX. In its immediate context in *Paradise Lost,* the image of the united elm and vine may imply that Adam and Eve are reunited after the divisive effect of Eve's dream,[28] though whatever division the dream brings about seems to be dispelled by their orisons, which "to thir thoughts / Firm peace recoverd soon and wonted calm" (V, 209–10). The image certainly gives evidence of our first parents' harmony with nature and their control over it in a productive way.[29] In Milton's poem they are primarily guardians, not manipulators, of nature.

When Milton first overtly compares Eve to Pomona, he supplements the sketch of Eve as productive gardener with a depiction of

---

[28]Fowler, ed., *Paradise Lost,* p. 269.
[29]In "Innocence and Experience in Eden," p. 94, Lewalski traces further implications of the vine and elm image: "The implication of the analogy we have been tracing is that Adam and Eve, like the Garden, have natures capable of a prodigious growth of good things, but which require constant pruning to remove excessive or unsightly growth, constant direction of overreaching tendencies, constant propping of possible weaknesses, and also, one supposes, further cultivation through art." I find Lewalski's reading psychologically exciting, but my interpretation stops short of the paradox that Adam and Eve *must* work *constantly* to remain free in Eden.

her as an independent being who needs no covering or artful adornment:

> So to the Silvan Lodge
> They came, that like *Pomona*'s Arbour smil'd
> With flourets deck't and fragrant smells; but *Eve*
> Undeckt, save with her self more lovely fair
> Then Wood-Nymph, or the fairest Goddess feign'd
> Of three that in Mount *Ida* naked strove,
> Stood to entertain her guest from Heav'n; no vaile
> Shee needed, Vertue-proof, no thought infirme
> Alterd her cheek.
>
> (V, 377–85)

The method of celebrating, then surpassing, the classical figures recalls that of the Enna simile. In the present simile, Eve's main difference from Pomona and from her own bower ("undeckt") indicates her moral self-sufficiency. Raphael will subsequently praise Eve as "Mother of Mankind," but in this passage the narrator stresses Eve's individual qualities and finds her "Vertue-proof." The primary meaning of "Vertue-proof," invulnerable through her virtue, is crucial to our understanding of Eve's character when she comes alone to her encounter with Satan. The word's secondary suggestion of proof against a Virtue merely points to Eve's composure before Raphael, "the angelic Vertue" (V, 371). In both cases Eve's virtue shows itself in her stately, unblushing regard for Adam and Raphael. Her physical demeanor suggests her psychological state; that is, in her steady, unself-conscious regard for others, Eve has advanced beyond the self-reflective stance of Narcissus.

Between this Pomona simile and the next, Milton shifts attention from the calm interview in the Garden to the jarring conflict of the War in Heaven. Adam and Eve develop little during this interval, although they do learn the possibility of their ultimate ascent to Heaven, and they do hear a story of disobedience and creation which bears on their present state. In light of the first Pomona simile, perhaps the most significant addition to Eve's character during Raphael's account of the hexameron is her departure from the discourse, when Adam enters on the abstruse matter of Astronomy, in order to tend the Garden, "her Nurserie" (VIII, 39–65). Chaste yet supportive of life, like Pomona, she is, however, "Not unattended, for on her as Queen / A pomp of winning Graces waited still" (VIII, 60–61). No one in the poem, not the narrator, Adam, or the angel, criticizes Eve for departing from the group in this episode, a point that should check the perverse view that Eve's departure is a sign of Eve's intellectual incapacity. On the contrary, Eve's departure to tend the Garden exemplifies Raphael's admonition to Adam in response to his questions concerning astronomical theory: "joy thou / In what he gives to thee . . . be lowlie wise: / Think onely what concernes thee and thy being" (VIII, 170–74). On Eve "Graces waited still": that final word, ambiguously as an adjective (motionless; silent; *OED*, A.1; 2) or adverb (now, as formerly; now, in contrast to the future; *OED*, 4.a; b), maintains the balance between continuity in the Garden and the imminence of the Fall.

The simile containing the second allusion to Pomona actually presents a cluster of images for Eve, all of which qualify the immediate action in the narrative, namely, Eve's departure from Adam to labor apart in the Garden that morning. Among Pales (Roman goddess of pastures), Ceres (goddess of agriculture), and Proserpina, Pomona is the central figure, but the unfolding of Milton's simile suggests that each comparison is appropriate to a specific moment in each myth, and only to a specific aspect of Eve at this point:

> To *Pales*, or *Pomona* thus adornd,
> Likeliest she seemd, *Pomona* when she fled
> *Vertumnus*, or to *Ceres* in her Prime,
> Yet Virgin of *Proserpina* from *Jove*.
> (IX, 393–96)

Eve has gone out with "such Gardning Tools as Art yet rude, / Guiltless of fire had formed, or Angels brought," and in part her resemblance to these mythological deities is suggested by her accoutrements. But because the simile shifts from the method of tableau ("*Pales*, or *Pomona* thus adornd") to that of drama or cinema ("*Pomona* when she fled"), that is, from an arrested image to an image of a character in action, the resemblance of Eve's action to Pomona's is especially significant. According to Ovid, Pomona has decided to remain a virgin within her garden and so avoids men generally:

> vim tamen agrestum metuens pomaria claudit
> intus et accessus prohibet refugitque viriles.
>
> (14.635–36)

Fearing some rustic violence, she locked herself within her orchard and so avoids and prevents the approach of men.

Although Milton refers specifically to a time when Pomona fled Vertumnus (the Roman god of the changing year), this reclusiveness is the closest Pomona comes to fleeing him in the *Metamorphoses*. Rather, she stands and listens as Vertumnus, in various disguises, sings her praises and recommends himself as a fit match for her. Milton nowhere compares Adam to Vertumnus, perhaps because the god's shiftiness is inappropriate to Adam's stable character.[30]

When Milton compares Eve to Pomona *fleeing* Vertumnus, then, he depicts a moment that is not in Ovid's myth. Unless Milton had a source other than Ovid or an intermediary that suggested this flight,[31] this rewriting of myth seems to be an instance of Milton's moral imagination supplanting earlier poetry, which is comparable to his famous misprision in *Areopagitica* of the Palmer's role in Book 2 of *The Faerie Queene*. In the present case, Milton may have pieced together "*Pomona* when she fled / *Vertumnus*" from either her flight from marriage or from men, or both. In any case, the moral significance of the line is radically ambiguous. If Eve, like Pomona, is fleeing her lover unwisely, then the result may be the sterility of which Vertumnus warned. If Eve, like Pomona, is seen as morally

---

[30]Milton does, however, accuse his detractors of "Vertumnus-like" reasoning in *De Doctrina Christiana*, I, chap. 5, *Works*, 14:303.

[31]Neither the *Ovide moralisé*, ed. C. de Boer et al. (Amsterdam, 1915–38); Sandys' *Ovid;* Natalis Comes, *Mythologiae* (New York, 1979); Giraldus's *Syntagma;* nor any of the commentaries that I have seen describe Pomona as fleeing from Vertumnus. Vincent Cartari's *Images des Dieux* (Lyons, 1610), p. 351, includes a woodcut that depicts Pomona as standing, bearing fruits in her hands for reclining Vertumnus.

innocent, as Milton's phrase "Yet Virgin" suggests, then her flight would seem to enhance her moral purity. The compression of mythological lore which the Pomona similes achieve suggests that Milton's imagination was fired by his reading of Ovid, but that his judgment found moral and aesthetic uses for the material beyond those in the fables. The relationship between this Eve and the one in Book IV is continuity over experience, and she is "yet sinless" until she trusts her limited experience ahead of obedience to God's command.

"Nor was God-head from her thought": Eve and Medea

So far, clear allusions in *Paradise Lost* to mythic figures and echoes of lines from the *Metamorphoses* have been the basis not only for our approach to Eve but also for our sense of Milton's transformation of Ovidian matter. In this section, however, which compares Eve's speeches before the Tree of Knowledge with Medea's speech upon Jason's arrival in her father's kingdom, the significance of the comparison is drawn less from verbal parallels than from correspondences of mood and structure in the speeches. The one clear echo of Ovid's Medea passage in *Paradise Lost* is Adam's affirmation to Raphael concerning Eve's unsettling effect upon him: "yet still free / Approve the best, and follow what I approve" (VIII, 610–11). This affirmation sounds dubious when one recalls Medea's declaration: "video meliora proboque, / deteriora sequor" (I see the better things and approve them, but I follow the worse).[32] Although the stylistic features of Medea's soliloquy occur, in varying degrees, in a number of other soliloquies from the central books of the *Metamorphoses*,[33] Medea's fascination with her tempter, desire for glory, and ingenuous reliance on experience make her the closest analogue among Ovid's heroic characters to Eve during the temptation. As in the case of Narcissus, Ovid's represen-

---

[32]See Douglas Bush, "Ironic and Ambiguous Allusions in *Paradise Lost*," *JEGP* 60 (1961), 639. Adam's phrase seems also to be indebted indirectly to Augustine's *Confessions* and Petrarch's *Rime sparse*.

[33]Cf. Scylla (daughter of Nisus), 7.11–72; Althaea, 8.481–511; Byblis, 9.474–516; Myrrha, 10.320–55.

tation of "insecure and fleeting identity" in Medea shows strong similarities to Milton's depiction of the mental process that takes Eve from innocence to sin. To notice where the similarities break down, primarily in Eve's progress by repentance to a new model of heroism, should enable us to fix the limits of the overlap between the poets' methods of characterization.

Ovid's concentration on the young Medea's initial response to Jason goes a long way toward distinguishing his portrait of Medea in the *Metamorphoses* from other versions of the popular legend. Euripides' play of the fifth century B.C., in contrast, takes place on the day the mature Medea first discovers that her husband Jason has chosen a second wife. On that same day, Medea, banished from her new home in Greece, plans and carries out her revenge, and the revenge plot dramatizes her decision to punish her husband by murdering their young children along with Jason and his new bride. Ovid telescopes these murders into four lines late in his narrative (7.394–97) and so diminishes the revenge motive and its effect of cathartic awe and horror. Horror and frenzy are, on the other hand, precisely the aspects of Medea's situation that Seneca, in the generation after Ovid, emphasizes in his tragedy. By reversing the sympathies of the chorus in Euripides' play, an alteration that directs the audience's sympathy entirely toward Medea, Seneca brings his heroine closer at points (particularly in her speech at 11.203–51) to Ovid's than to Euripides' pattern. Seneca's extensive treatment of Medea's witchcraft and derangement, though, owes little to Ovid. The classical treatment closest to Ovid's is probably that in Book 3 of the *Argonautica* by Apollonius Rhodius, whose brief but moving version of Medea's first glimpse of Jason may have been the germ for Ovid's far fuller version.[34] Ovid's choice of an inexperienced, youthful Medea accounts also for the major differences between his earlier depiction of the character in *Heroides* 12. There, Medea's letter tallies her insufferable injuries at Jason's hands, including his new bride, and ends by promising a veiled revenge, but the letter reflects little of the analysis of motivation and anguish of decision that Ovid achieves in *Metamorphoses* 7.

[34]Medea also appears in Corneille's tragedy (1635), which Milton may have known. Ovid wrote a tragedy about Medea, now lost, which Quintilian and others considered a masterpiece of Roman drama. See *Institutio Oratoria* 10.1.98.

From Proserpina to Pyrrha

In order to comprehend the mood and structure that convey Ovid's fresh conception of Medea, we may begin with the main points of her opening speech and its context. A rather long quotation is needed to represent the varieties of metamorphosis in the passage: Ovid's shift from his high epic style to the darting Senecan style for the young woman; the shifting arguments and images employed; the rapid swings in Medea's mood and tone. The episode opens the seventh book of the *Metamorphoses:*

> And now the Argonauts were slicing through the sea in their Thessalian ships. . . . Having suffered much under their brilliant leader Jason, they reached at last the swift waters of the muddy Phasis. And when they approached King Aeetas and demanded the golden fleece of Phrisus, and the dreadful condition with its enormous labor was given to them, meanwhile the king's daughter began to burn with a powerful passion, and fought against it long, and when by reason she had not been able to subdue her frenzy, cried: "Vainly, Medea, do you resist; some god, I know not which, opposes you. And I wonder whether this, or certainly something like this, may be the thing called love. For why do my father's conditions seem too cruel? Yet they are too cruel. Why do I fear that he may perish, a man whom I have barely even seen? What could be the cause of such fear? Cut out from your breast this fire you feel if you can, unhappy girl. If I could, I would be saner, but some new power holds me against my will: reason persuades me one way, desire another. I see the better things and approve them, but I follow the worse. Why do you, a royal maiden, burn for a stranger and imagine marriage with a foreign world? This land as well can give you something to love. . . . But unless I deliver him, he will be burned by the bulls' fiery breath, and he shall go to meet an enemy of his own sowing sprung from the earth, or he shall be given as prey, like a beast, to the bloodthirsty dragon. If I permit this, then shall I reveal that I am sprung from a tiger, and that iron and stone are in my heart. Why not see him dying, and, seeing, defile my eyes with crime? Why not incite the wild bulls against him, and the earth-sprung warriors, and the unsleeping dragon? May the gods will better things. Yet that is not to be by my praying, but by my doing— Shall I then betray my father's kingdom, and shall our unknown stranger be preserved by my power to aid, so that, saved by me, he may set sail without me as a free man and become another's husband, while Medea is left behind for punishment? If he can do that, or prefer another woman to me, let him die, ingrate! But no: his face, his

noble spirit, his grace of form are such that I need not fear his deception or forgetfulness of my service. . . . Indeed my father is cruel, my country barbarous, my brother still an infant; my sister, though, vows to stand with me, and the greatest god is within me. Nor shall I be leaving great things, but going to them: the title of liberator of the Achaean youth; acquaintance with a better land; great cities, whose fame flourishes even here; the manners and arts of those places; and the man for whom I would exchange all these things, or even all that the world possesses, the son of Aeson, as whose wife I shall be spoken of as a blissful favorite of the gods, and with whom I shall rise to the stars. . . . But do you deem it marriage, Medea, and so give a splendid name to your crime?—no, rather look ahead to what a wicked thing you are approaching and, while you can, flee it!" She spoke, and before her eyes stood Righteousness, and Piety, and Modesty; and Love, vanquished, was now beginning to turn away. (7.1– 73)

The mood of this speech combines high excitement with great uncertainty. Medea's conflict, like Eve's, is between the virtues of the attractive object (*Met.* 7.27, 55–60; *Paradise Lost,* IX, 649, 745, 795–97), and its dire consequences. Jason represents an opportunity for Medea to discover foreign lands, to exercise her power by delivering him with her magical herbs, and to experience love. In a frenzied manner, Medea hangs these opportunities in the balance with their possibly disastrous consequences: losing her homeland and family ties; facing death at sea; suffering guilt for an irreparable crime. For Eve in her first speech before the Tree in Book IX, the fruit also represents vast opportunities, especially, as she sees it, the chance to gain knowledge and wisdom and thus godhead (IX, 789–90). The consequences of her act, which she begins to realize in the second speech, include losing Adam, dying herself, or facing isolation in the possession of her new knowledge. Without realizing the magnitude of her error, Eve decides that Adam shall share her lot; that is, shall if necessary die with her.[35] Ultimately, Medea's resolution to flee the crime she has envisioned so thoroughly proves to be as feeble as it appears: Upon seeing Jason again the ravaging flame burns anew ("exstinctaque flamma reluxit").

Perhaps the strongest similarity in mood between these speeches

[35]Lewis, *Preface,* p. 126.

of Medea and Eve is a sense of emerging transcendence tinged with irony. The characters declare their awareness of transcendence; the narrative voices behind them create the irony. Medea is at first deeply troubled by the workings of a god she does not know (12). In her inexperience she tries to align her feelings with what she has heard about love (13–14), and she dimly recognizes that she is being altered by some divinity (18–19). Medea's fullest recognition comes when she realizes that this "god" implies her individual transcendence: "maximus intra me deus est" (the greatest god is within me). The tone of this realization is triumphant, though this moment of *superbia* is, as usual in Ovid's poem, of short duration. In context the line can hardly be a statement of Stoic doctrine: Medea is trying, rather, to express the enlarging power of her own spirit. The pageant of allegorical virtues (72–73) suggests that to the narrator, her view of her situation is schematic and oversimplified. Certainly Medea's moral sense triumphs only briefly, for she not only succumbs to the power of love when she next sees Jason but reverts shortly to a code of vengeance even more "barbaric," in her formulation, than the values of her country.

Eve, too, is troubled by and attentive to Satan's insinuation of a self-styled divinity. She calls the fruit "divine," and the narrator adds that while she ate she expected to gain in knowledge, "nor was God-head from her thought" (IX, 790). Eve's attempt to reach "God-head" by eating the fruit, which fulfills God's prophecy that man shall fall, "affecting God-head" (III, 316), is certainly errant and "rash" in comparison with the program for gradual human evolution that Raphael had suggested. Yet Milton's account of Eve's fall gains credibility through Satan's appealing arguments for self-assertion. In the context of Eve's individual development through Ovidian stages, Satan's temptation is carefully calculated to appeal to an Eve who is able in time to reach a fuller understanding of intellectual issues. His barrage of rhetorical questions and answers, aimed at minimizing her sense of the danger of the fruit, follows the pattern of Medea's hypophora minimizing the dangers of joining Jason:

Who that is not heartless might not be moved by Jason's youth and high birth and virtue? Who would not, though the rest were lacking, be moved by his face? Certainly he has moved my heart. (7.26–28)

> ye shall not Die:
> How should ye? by the Fruit? it gives you Life
> To Knowledge. By the Threatner? Look on mee.
>
> (IX, 685–87)

Consistently, minimizing God's goodness and justice toward Eve and Adam, Satan employs further hypophora:

> Of good, how just? of evil, if what is evil
> Be real, why not known, since easier shunnd?
>
> (IX, 698–99)

The aphoristic compression of Satan's language makes his answers apparently inevitable while it conceals subtle conflations of terms, most importantly, his use of "knowledge" to include theoretical knowledge of evil (which God approves in man) and experienced knowledge of evil (which He does not).[36] Were there no higher authority in Milton's view, Satan's arguments valorizing experience would be perfectly persuasive: They are such stuff as Renaissance heroes are made on. Eve's hope to "grow mature / In knowledge, as the Gods who all things know" (IX, 803–4), recalling Medea's greatest internal god, receives a bitter answer in Adam's and Eve's actual gain in knowledge through the Fall: "since our Eyes / Op'nd we find indeed, and find we know / Both Good and Evil, Good lost, and Evil got" (IX, 1070–72).

The mood of excitement and momentary transcendence common to Medea's and Eve's speeches shifts according to similar structural and rhetorical patterns in the passages. The structure of Eve's speeches is well suited to describe the unfolding of "insecure and fleeting identity" during a personal crisis. This phenomenon is particularly appropriate to Eve at this point, as she is, in effect, becoming a new person through the Fall. In the first speech, Eve begins by addressing the fruit (745–55), then turns to an abstract consideration of good (756–59), freedom, and death in which she mimics Satan's reduction of complex issues to simplified terms:

> For good unknown, sure is not had, or had
> And yet unknown, is as not had at all.

[36]Noted by Fowler, ed., *Paradise Lost*, p. 479.

In plain then, what forbids he but to know,
Forbids us good, forbids us to be wise?
(IX, 756–59)

Eve's fascination with knowledge forbidden by God suggests a return to her stage of narcissistic fascination with self-knowledge. At the same time Eve's imitation of Satan's argument that the fruit is good and should be known shows Eve regressing to the passive dependency of Ovid's Echo. Milton's rhetoric reveals that her thinking is precipitous as well as derivative. For example, an extreme use of polysyndeton, the reduplication of conjunctions in a series of clauses, conveys Eve's perception of how Satan has changed by eating the fruit: "hee hath eat'n and lives, / And knows, and speaks, and reasons, and discerns, / Irrational till then" (IX, 764–66). Eve's perception is as tortuous and halting as Satan's course through Chaos, as he "pursues his way, / And swims or sinks, or wades, or creeps, or flyes" (II, 949–50). Eve then turns to question and dismiss her fear, as Medea had done, and finally turns to praise the fruit as a panacea ("this cure of all"), which recalls Medea's celebration of Hecate's magic herbs (*Met.* 7.194–96).[37] Overall, Eve's speech appears to be progressive but actually shows Eve circling back to her mistaken beginning: "Great are thy Vertues, doubtless, best of Fruits." The structure of the speech lacks both the concentration of the narrative style of her first awakening and the tenacity of her argumentative style applied to the division of labor in the Garden. The structure of this speech follows the misjoining of word to thing induced by Satan in Eve's dream, or, more closely, the misjoining of reason and emotion found in Medea's wavering soliloquy.

Eve's second speech shows no less wavering a character. Eve addresses, in turn, the Tree, Experience, and herself in a parody of the hymns she and Adam sang to God. Continuing the descent to mechanical echoing, Eve's address to the Tree ("O Sovran, vertuous, precious of all Trees") mimics Satan's apostrophe: "O sacred, wise, and wisdom-giving plant."[38] In a reversal of her earlier

---

[37] In *Milton and the English Revolution* (New York, 1978), p. 379, Christopher Hill discusses Milton's probable disregard for magic.

[38] Kathleen M. Swaim, in "The Art of the Maze in Book IX of *Paradise Lost*," *SEL* 12 (1972), 139–40, discusses this instance of Eve's imitation of Satan in the context of the rhetoric of the temptation.

expression of satisfaction with the hierarchy of the human sexes, Eve expresses a new sense of inadequacy:

> But to *Adam* in what sort
> Shall I appeer? shall I to him make known
> As yet my change, and give him to partake
> Full happiness with mee, or rather not,
> But keep the odds of Knowledge in my power
> Without Copartner?
>
> (IX, 816–21)

The irony of Eve's false belief that her "change" has brought her "Full happiness" has been anticipated not simply by our knowledge that the Fall is under way but also by Eve's expectation that this change is accelerating her personal development. Her speech concludes in the mordant, and bitterly ironic, resolution that "*Adam* shall share with me in bliss or woe." By the end of the speech, Eve has undergone a metamorphosis as certain as any in Ovid's poem, one reflected not in a fantastic change to a natural emblem by divine fiat, but in her own words, which to Adam reveal her, with Spenserian consonance and insistence: "Defac't, deflourd, and now to Death devote" (IX, 901).

Under these similarities of mood and structure between the speeches of Eve and Medea lies a profound disparity in poetic designs. The narrative verses that open the Medea episode, like the other opening passages of the fifteen books of the *Metamorphoses,* reflect Ovid's high epic style. Though slightly less grand, Medea's declamatory speech maintains the pace and elevation of the narrative in which it is imbedded, primarily because of its rapid exposition of Medea's rapidly changing psyche. By presenting the long speech as if in the young Medea's own words, Ovid engages the reader's sympathy. Yet the poet maintains his distance ultimately by staging a brief allegory to suggest the oversimplification and self-deception of Medea, who in retrospect we may view as an almost melodramatic figure. What Ovid is exploring through this approach is constant changeability, both in his subjects and in his poem itself. Although Medea interests him as a wavering heroic character who may be seen from various perspectives, there is for

Ovid no character or fable that stands outside flux and so organizes his entire work.[39]

Eve's speeches before the Tree of Knowledge move quickly forward, too, in their blurring of the steady aesthetic, moral, and theological stances the poem has taken. The force of Milton's cohesive narrative, long building toward the Fall though the viewpoints of Satan, God, angels, and humans, pushes the reader quickly through these speeches while Eve, responding to Satan's rhetoric, deliberates in simplified versions the complex issues—free will, providence, the end of knowledge—that the epic has labored to clarify. Eve's arguments recall Medea's passionate mental exertions as well as her sententious conclusions, through which Medea is shown to lack the narrator's sophistication. Eve's fault, however, comes from aspiring to just such sophistication when, in the world of *Paradise Lost,* the recommended course is to "be lowlie wise." Whereas Medea's predicament may engage the reader's sympathy, the pathos of Eve's predicament extends to its vast consequences in human history, to the trials of the poet, and ultimately to the situation of the fallen audience, to "all our woe."

Yet Eve's response to the loss of Eden also indicates the prospect of repairing toward "a Paradise within" the human heart through faith and virtuous action. It is Eve's repentance that moves her beyond Medea's self-centered moral sense and her wavering mental process. Despite Adam's initial rejection of Eve's "soft words" in response to his distracted outbursts after the Fall, Eve asserts her sense of conviction in sin and desire to suffer alone in order to spare Adam:

> While yet we live, scarse one short hour perhaps,
> Between us two let there be peace, both joyning,
> As joyn'd in injuries, one enmitie
> Against a Foe by doom express assign'd us,
> That cruel Serpent: On me exercise not
> Thy hatred for this miserie befall'n,
> On me alreadie lost, mee then thy self
> More miserable; both have sin'd, but thou
> Against God onely, I against God and thee,

[39]Cf. Richard Lanham, *The Motives of Eloquence* (New Haven, 1976), pp. 36, 50.

And to the place of judgement will return,
There with my cries importune Heaven, that all
The sentence from thy head remov'd may light
On me, sole cause to thee of all this woe,
Mee mee onely just object of his ire.

(X, 923–36)

Outlasting her false sense of injury by fate, Eve's remembrance of Eden's foundation on divine justice and love, in contrast to Medea's relapse to her country's barbarism, makes possible the reconcilement of our first parents, which begins the difficult journey out of the Garden and toward "a Paradise within." Although Adam reproves Eve's morbid offer to suffer all for him, her understanding of Edenic hierarchy ("both have sin'd, but thou / Against God onely, I against God and thee") and of God's concern ("[t]here with my cries importune Heaven") moves Adam to forgive her and pray with her for mercy.

While Adam and Eve begin the rebuilding of the human community by praying together, Heaven responds by mollifying their hardness of heart: "Prevenient Grace descending had remov'd / The stonie from thir hearts, & made new flesh / Regenerate grow instead" (XI, 3–5). Milton's phrasing alludes to Ezekiel 11.19: "And I will give them one heart, and I will put a new spirit within you; and I will take the stony heart out of their flesh, and will give them an heart of flesh." Yet it adds to the Old Testament verse an emphasis on regeneration through prayer. Stressing this essential change, a final Ovidian figuration recasts Adam and Eve from tragic lovers into pious supplicants. In their contrition, Adam and Eve are compared to "th'ancient Pair / In Fables old, less ancient yet then these, / *Deucalion* and chaste *Pyrrha*" (XI, 10–12). In their devotion to Themis, the non-Olympian goddess of the earth and of justice, Deucalion and Pyrrha had prayed for the restoration of mankind, of which they were the sole survivors after the universal flood. In Ovid's formulation, their prayer calls for the same mollification and restoration as do Milton's characters:

atque ita "si precibus" dixerunt "numina iustis
victa remollescunt, si flectitur ira deorum,

dic, Themi, qua generis damnum reparabile nostri
arte sit, et mersis fer opem, mitissima, rebus."
(1.377–80)

And they said: "If with just prayers deities are softened, if the wrath
of the gods is thus averted, say, Themis, by what means the loss of our
race may be repaired, and bring your aid, O most merciful, to a world
overwhelmed."

Themis answers their prayer, telling the supplicants to throw behind them "bones of your great mother" (383), whereupon they
cast from the earth stones, which become men and women. Milton's
God, too, responds to the prayers of the most ancient human supplicants, but his response calls for more than the interpretation of
an oracle. It calls for the devastating knowledge of human history,
with all its catastrophes and reversals, before Adam and Eve can
comprehend the scope of their Fall and the possibility of recovery.

For Adam, education in human history and prophecy comes
through the series of visions supplemented by Michael's guidance
in Books XI and XII. For Eve, the equivalent of this knowledge
comes through dreams inspired by God (XII, 611). It is appropriate to the metamorphic development of Eve in Milton's epic that
these dreams recall the dream Satan inspired through the ear of
Eve, but recall the start of the temptation in order to contrast it
with the promise of a Savior born of Eve: "By mee," Eve says, "the
Promis'd Seed shall all restore" (XII, 623).

The inspiration through dreams also recalls the creation of Eve,
as she comes into being during Adam's dream (VIII, 460–84).
Between these pivotal dreams Eve's character gains depth and significance from Ovid's mythic characters. By the method of comparison employed in the Enna simile, Milton associates Eve with, in
turn, the innocence of Narcissus, the responsiveness of Echo, the
chastity of Pomona, the passion of Medea, and the piety of Pyrrha.
By selecting specific moments from Ovid's fables, Milton dissoci-
ates Eve from the egregious faults of these characters, especially
the self-enclosure of Narcissus and the dependency of Echo, while
the suggestions of vulnerability and limitation in all these Ovidian
figures remain to develop suspense and pathos in *Paradise Lost*. In

Milton's design, Eve surpasses these figures in two ways: by her greater participation in ideal beauty, which makes her for Milton the embodiment of a reality Ovid had foreshadowed; and by her participation in an epic that recombines images and episodes from the *Metamorphoses* and other classical poems into a continuous narrative. Milton's literary epic aligns Ovid's mythic figures with Eve as she develops in Eden in an unexcelled attempt to demonstrate that these Ovidian elements illuminate and inform, and are finally outshone and subsumed by Milton's higher argument.

Milton regarded the "art of composition" in poetry as "critical." His composition of Eve as examined here, his arrangement of Ovidian figures into a coherent pattern of development, is vital to Milton's composition on the loss of Paradise. It is, however, a relatively simple, small part of that larger story. When Milton applies Ovidian precedents to the volatile character of Satan, his procedure goes beyond the uses of Ovidian figures to embrace Ovidian rhetorical and stylistic devices. By so doing, Milton reorients the notion of heroism in an unprecedented way.

—3—

Satan's Metamorphoses and
Ovidian Counterheroism

The journey of Satan through *Paradise Lost* ends in a scene for which Milton had no biblical precedent, and which represents the most extensive metamorphosis in the poem.[1] After tempting Eve, Satan returns from Eden to Pandaemonium, announces his success to the fallen angels, and pauses to await their applause. Unexpectedly, however, Satan and the devils feel themselves transformed into serpents, and then are led by "a great power" to a nearby grove, where they reenact the temptation by chewing the ashen fruit of counterfeit Trees of Knowledge.[2] This parodic action and Satan's

[1] In *Milton and the Christian Tradition* (Oxford, 1966), pp. 91–94, C. A. Patrides reviews the scriptural evidence for the rebellion and fall of Satan, which is essentially contained in Isa. 14.12–15 and Rev. 12.3–9, and finds it "distressingly inadequate." Taking a more comprehensive view of biblical authority than Patrides, however, Milton discusses in *De Doctrina Christiana*, I, ix (*CPW*, 6:348–50) the following passages in sequence as potentially relevant to Satan and the fallen angels: Matt. 8.29; 2 Pet. 2.4; Jude 6; 1 Cor. 6.3; Matt. 25.41; Rev. 20.10; Job 1.7; 1 Sam. 16.15; 1 Pet. 5.8; John 12.31; 2 Cor. 4.4; Matt. 12.43; Eph. 2.2; 6.12; Job 1.6; 2.1; 1 Kings 22.21; Zech. 3.1; Luke 10.18; Rev. 12.12; Luke 8.31; Mark 5.10; Rev. 20.3; Job 1.12; Matt. 8.31; Rev. 20.2; Luke 11.15; Col. 2.15; John 8.44; 1 Thess. 2.18; Acts 5.3; 1 Chron. 21.1; Rev. 12.9; Matt. 4.3; Rev. 9.11. Though not specifically related to the description of Satan's fall in *Paradise Lost*, these passages no doubt contribute to the imagery and diction of the poem. Nevertheless, given the limited biblical account of Satan, Milton was free to seek out relevant pagan myth and legend, including the *Metamorphoses*.

[2] In "Tantalus and the Dead Sea Apples," *JEGP* 64 (1965), 35–40, John M. Steadman compares this deluded consumption of dry fruit with the frustrated attempt of Tantalus to quench his thirst. The pre-Homeric Tantalus myth is retold in *Met.* 4.458–59 and 6.173–75.

accompanying ironic speech present more than a Miltonic variation on the motif of the deceiver deceived, and far more than the inartistic or merely punitive dismissal of Satan that some readers have indicated. Because the scene offers the last view of Satan in the poem, and because it recalls earlier stages in his career, it acts primarily as a synopsis of Satan's role in the epic. Because the presence of Ovid's *Metamorphoses* is especially discernible in this scene, it will also serve as a model, both of the way Ovid's poem informs the character of Satan and of the metamorphic effect this presence has on the notion of heroism in *Paradise Lost.*

The methods of characterization and corresponding effects, which, I will argue, bear a close kinship with those of the *Metamorphoses,* are threefold. By depicting Satan as an analogue of seemingly heroic but ultimately debased figures from the *Metamorphoses,* Milton repeatedly signals Satan's degeneration while he maintains the semblance of the character's heroism. By embodying in Satan rhetorical strategies and tropes from the *Metamorphoses,* Milton, without denigrating Ovidian rhetoric, creates a pattern of disjunction between Satan's language and its referents which further reveals his degeneration. By adopting stylistic features characteristic of the *Metamorphoses,* including derisive wordplay and humor, Milton enforces the counterheroic narrative that centers around Satan. Milton's dialogue with Ovid at once upholds and undermines Satan's heroism, for the same Ovidian figures, rhetoric, and style that present Satan as an appealing and powerful leader also expose Satan as a hero in a tradition valorizing brute force, willful deception, and self-assertion. To be sure, these methods and effects depend on materials other than the *Metamorphoses,* to some extent. The *Iliad,* the *Odyssey,* and the *Aeneid* contain debased figures of the classical heroic types;[3] Socratic and Ciceronian speeches display the rhetoric of disjunction;[4] *The Faerie Queene* and Italian epic made available a range of stylistic features of literary

[3]See Francis Blessington, *"Paradise Lost" and the Classical Epic* (Boston, 1979), pp. 1–73; Mario Di Cesare, *"Paradise Lost* and Epic Tradition," *MS* 1 (1969), 31–50; and K. W. Grandsen, *"Paradise Lost* and the *Aeneid," Essays in Criticism* 17 (1967), 281–303. None of these critics considers Ovid's *Metamorphoses* in their discussions of the epic tradition.

[4]See Anne Ferry, *Milton's Epic Voice: The Narrator in "Paradise Lost"* (Cambridge, 1963), esp. p. 119; J. B. Broadbent, "Milton's Rhetoric," *MP* 56 (1959), 224–42; and John Steadman, *"Ethos* and *Dianoia:* Character and Rhetoric in *Paradise Lost,"* in

epic.[5] Studies comparing Satan with various dramatic heroes and villains have improved critical understanding of the composition of Satan.[6] A strictly dramatic model, however, minimizes those aspects of character that depend on the narrative voice and the surrounding imagery and action, while it abstracts the presentation of Satan from the particular epic context that *Paradise Lost* establishes.

Although Satan's character involves various literary materials and methods, the pattern of Ovidian references and analogues is central to the presentation of Satan as a counterheroic figure.[7] "Counterheroic" describes the semblance of heroic grandeur that

---

Language and Style in Milton, ed. R. D. Emma and John T. Shawcross (New York, 1967), pp. 193–232.

[5]See A. Kent Hieatt, *Chaucer, Spenser, Milton: Mythopoeic Continuities and Transformations* (Montreal, 1975), pp. 131–71, and A. Bartlett Giamatti, *The Earthly Paradise and the Renaissance Epic* (Princeton, N.J., 1966), pp. 232–355.

[6]See Helen Gardner, "Milton's 'Satan' and the Theme of Damnation in Elizabethan Tragedy," *English Studies* n.s. 1 (1948), 46–66; and John Steadman, *Epic and Tragic Structure in "Paradise Lost"* (Chicago, 1976), esp. pp. 20–28 on "modal variation." In his preface to *Prometheus Unbound* (1820), Shelley compared Satan as dramatic hero to Prometheus. The strongest external evidence for the dramatic makeup of Satan is the series of drafts Milton wrote for a tragedy on the seduction of Adam and Eve by Lucifer. Scott Elledge reprints the Trinity manuscript in his edition of *Paradise Lost* (New York, 1975), pp. 288–90.

[7]The term "counterheroic" should be distinguished from similar formulations in contemporary criticism. In "Milton's Counterplot," *ELH* 25 (1958), 1–12, Geoffrey Hartman terms the response of the forces of creation to those of Satan the counterplot: "Milton's feeling for this divine imperturbability, for God's omnipotent knowledge that the creation will outlive death and sin, when expressed in such an indirect manner, may be characterized as the counterplot" (p. 3). Hartman's "counterplot" implies that the primary plot to which Providence is opposed must be Satan's. My term departs also from the conclusion in T. J. B. Spencer's *"Paradise Lost:* The Anti-Epic," in *Approaches to "Paradise Lost,"* ed. C. A. Patrides (London, 1968), p. 98, that Milton's poem "is the anti-epic. Wherever we turn we find the traditional epic values inverted." Spencer does not make clear what these values are or why they should be overturned by a poem that ostensibly incorporates so much of the epic genre. "Counterheroism" in this chapter is closer to Murray Roston's conception of Satan as "that vital Baroque counterforce required to demonstrate God's might," described in *Milton and the Baroque* (Pittsburgh, 1980), p. 65. Roston's imaginative study has influenced my interpretation of Satan, but my approach differs from his in two important ways. First, to accept Satan as a "near-equal" (p. 72) to God is to engage in a form of Manichaeism that the poem, in the Son's easy victory over Satan in Book VI, clearly disavows. Second, the view, also held by Stanley Fish, that there is a balance of forces between Satan's speeches and the Miltonic narrator's comments (the former showing Satan's grandeur, the latter his degradation) differs from my recognition that there are hints and patterns of degeneration within Satan's words and actions themselves.

Satan projects in his opposition to Heaven and in his assertion of individual will. By this opposition he stands counter both to the heroism of martial prowess, exemplified by Achilles and Aeneas, and to the heroism of "Patience and Heroic Martydom" and other interiorized virtues that Adam and Eve are called upon to exemplify at the end of *Paradise Lost.* Nor does the deceptiveness of Satan, at least in the early books of the poem, cast him clearly either as a villain like Archimago or a wily hero like Ulysses. Although Satan engages in parodic or, in Louis Martz's phrase, "anti-heroic" warfare,[8] neither of these terms accounts for the central motive that Satan's projection of heroism reflects. Satan's aim is essentially negative: to discredit or destroy the grandeur of God and his creation. Because he cannot conquer or equal God's absolute goodness, he takes a contrary position: "Evil by thou my Good" (IV, 110). More specifically, as Dennis Burden has suggested, Satan fabricates an epic narrative parallel but counter to Milton's and attempts to persuade us of his heroic part in this story.[9] Ovidian figures are particularly appropriate to Satan's attempted revaluation of heroism because they are involved in Ovid's revaluation of the classical epic in the *Metamorphoses.* Ovidian rhetoric is particularly appropriate to Satan in that he, like Ovid, in Richard Lanham's phrase, "could envisage no hero greater than his diffuse authorial self."[10] In the larger structure of *Paradise Lost,* however, Satan's heroic self-assertion is contained and qualified by a more subtle and authoritative stylist—the Miltonic narrator. These points will appear more clearly when we examine not only the final metamorphosis but several distinctive scenes involving Satan: his opening dialogue with Beelzebub; the devils' first entry into Pandaemonium; the Council in Hell; Satan's journey through Chaos; the temptation of Eve.[11] By comparing Satan's final metamor-

---

[8] Martz, *Poet of Exile,* pp. 205–11.

[9] Dennis Burden, *The Logical Epic: A Study of the Argument of "Paradise Lost"* (Cambridge, 1967), pp. 57–64.

[10] Lanham, *The Motives of Eloquence,* p. 36.

[11] The one major episode involving Satan not treated in this chapter is his soliloquy atop Mt. Niphates, IV, 32–113, and his subsequent spying on Adam and Eve in the Garden. This beautifully crafted soliloquy reveals much concerning Satan's motives, but little of the disjunction otherwise characteristic of his speech. For iconographic connections between Satan in this episode and Phaethon in *Met.* 1.747–2.400 see D. P. Harding, *Milton and the Renaissance Ovid,* pp. 88–93. Satan's

phosis with those in the earlier books, one can see that Milton's presentation of Satan is consistent throughout, in that the allusions to the *Metamorphoses* gradually discover the breakdown of Satan's heroic appearance.

A review of some exemplary critical analyses of Satan's final metamorphosis will show how the principles I have isolated arise in part from earlier insights but finally are distinct from them. The eighteenth-century scholar Richard Bentley denied Milton's hand in the passage, which he regarded as "overwrought."[12] Here, as elsewhere in his edition of *Paradise Lost,* Bentley credited a mischievous editor with the dilution of Milton's genius. Three such annotations are the following: Of X, 524–32: "Our Editor, who for many Pages had in vain sought where he might intrude something of his own, found here a fit opportunity: for the Devils being turn'd into *Serpents,* he whips into the Texts all the Serpents that he knew." Of X, 559–60: "Our Editor was such a lover of Fables, that he would never balk one, could he but crowd it in." Of X, 578–84: "Here our Editor does not only tap his Mythology, but explains and interprets it . . . Ophion the Serpent is Eve's Husband, and so all Mankind are descended from Satan. Let any man believe if he can, that Milton gave such wretched nonsense."[13] Despite the possibility that an amanuensis might have corrupted the text of the blind poet, the very elements to which Bentley objects—an epic catalog, a mythological fable, a pagan myth (Ophion) later exploded by the narrator—are staple features of *Paradise Lost.* Bentley's unidentified "Editor" must have been a tireless and consistent worker.

Bentley's discontent with the scene, however, won distinguished supporters. William Wordsworth found the passage "unworthy" of his great predecessor. His comment on the scene in Book X is illuminating:

Here we bid farewell to the first character perhaps ever exhibited in Poetry. And it is not a little to be lamented that, he leaves us in a

---

metamorphoses into various animal forms after the soliloquy (IV, 395–98) indicate the transition from his anthropomorphic stature in the earlier books to his serpentine proneness in Book IX.

[12]Richard Bentley, *Milton's "Paradise Lost": A New Edition* (London, 1732), p. 324.
[13]Ibid., pp. 324–27.

situation so degraded in comparison with the grandeur of his introduction. Milton's fondness for the Metamorphoses probably induced
him to draw this picture, which excellently as it [is] executed I cannot
but think unworthy of his genius. The "spattering noise" &c. are
images which can ⟨only⟩ excite disgust. The representation of the
fallen Angels wreathing [sic] their jaws filled with soot and cinders
with hatefullest disrelish contains in it nothing that can afford pleasure. Had the poet determined to inflict upon them a physical
punishment, certainly one more noble[,] more consonant to the dignity of the beings might easily [cetera desunt][14]

Three phrases from Wordworth's comment suggest the thor-
oughness, or negatively, the inflexibility of the Romantic poet's
evaluation of Satan. If the "images" only "excite disgust" in Wordsworth, a reading more distanced from Satan might regard the
overt disclosure of his corruption as more profitable and pleasur-
able. Like Archimago and Duessa, who are stripped and exposed at
the end of Book 1 of *The Faerie Queene,* Satan confronts his own
perversion in this scene, and the closure provided by that confrontation is effective whether one feels disgusted or joyful on reading
it. Wordsworth's suggestion that Milton ought to have "inflicted"
upon the devils "a physical punishment" has already been taken in
Book VI, when the faithful angels hurl mountaintops onto Satan
and his followers. The effect of that measure, though, is closer to
ridicule and fragmentation than to the preservation of heroic no-
bility. Finally, the ostensible "dignity of the beings," already said to
be "diminished" in Satan's first appearance, fades throughout the
poem, so that Wordsworth's interest in maintaining the grandeur
of Satan's introduction seems misplaced.

In this century the view of Satan as "degraded" by Milton has
persisted in several forms. Assuming a static model of heroism
similar to Wordsworth's, C. H. Herford concluded that Milton reduced Satan to a serpent lest he be thought the hero of the poem.[15]
Herford's article may offer a belated correction to Dryden's famous statement in the dedication of his translation of the *Aeneid*

[14]Quoted in Joseph A. Wittreich, Jr., ed., *The Romantics on Milton* (Cleveland,
1970), p. 106.
[15]C. H. Herford, "Dante and Milton," *Bulletin of the John Rylands Library* 8 (1924),
223.

that Satan is the real hero of *Paradise Lost*.[16] Using a more fully articulated aesthetic theory than Herford's, A. J. A. Waldock found the passage an objectionable instance of the overarching "technique of degradation" aimed at Satan: "To attempt to link such a scene as this with what happens in the first two books of *Paradise Lost* is to try to bring incommensurables together, for the kind of art exemplified in this passage and the kind of art with which the presentment of Satan began have simply no meeting-point."[17] Waldock's certainty that the Satan of the opening books is incompatible with the Satan of later books does not, however, explain why Satan is degraded instead of degenerate. A sympathetic response to Waldock comes from Harold Bloom, though Bloom seems more eager to degrade Milton for showing Satan's decline than to cast light on the poem. In Bloom's view, Satan's original project, "to rally everything that remains," allies him with the figure of the modern poet and involves a special heroism:

> This is a heroism that is exactly on the border of solipsism, neither within it, nor beyond it. Satan's later decline in the poem, as arranged by the Idiot Questioner in Milton, is that the hero retreats from this border into solipsism, and so is degraded; ceases, during his soliloquy on Mount Niphates, to be a poet and, by intoning the formula: "Evil be thou my good," becomes a mere rebel, a childish inverter of conventional moral categories, another wearisome ancestor of student non-students, the perpetual New Left.[18]

Bloom's political preoccupations aside, his championing of a precarious yet fixed kind of heroism leads him to discredit what the poem shows to be Satan's major impulse and to substitute for it a neo-Romantic concept of *poesis:* something ever more about to be solipsistic. Milton's procedure in *Paradise Lost* is to show Satan in action, and by so doing he exposes Satan's character as the poem unfolds.[19] The process is analogous to the development of Eve's character by means of Ovidian figures as discussed in Chapter 2. A

[16]*Essays of John Dryden*, 2 vols., ed. W. P. Ker (Oxford, 1900), 2:165.
[17]Waldock, *"Paradise Lost" and Its Critics*, p. 92.
[18]Bloom, *The Anxiety of Influence*, p. 22.
[19]For the concept of Satan's exposure I am indebted to Joseph A. Wittreich, Jr.

balanced judgment about both Miltonic characters ought to take into account the overall shape of their careers throughout the poem.

Along with detractors, the final scene involving Satan has found able defenders in this century. Anne Ferry regards it as the clearest expression of the "dissociation" characteristic of Satan.[20] According to John Steadman, Milton's Satan is duplicitous and degenerate from the start, and the innovation of delaying the doom reserved for Satan until Book X enabled Milton to present the devils initially in a heroic light.[21] In the last fifteen years the defense of the scene has become more cautious. Irene Samuel defends the consistency if not success of the final change in Satan, suggesting that "apparently Milton thought decorum called for such a scene if the meaning of evil was finally to be clear."[22] Samuel argues further that the punitive aspect of the transformation is owing to Dante, yet this indebtedness need not exclude Ovidian presence or style. As Kevin Brownlee and Edward Moore have shown, Dante's epic frequently corrects Ovidian characters while absorbing Ovid's manner.[23] As we saw in the previous chapter, Milton uses both corrected and unchanged Ovidian figures, and he often follows the example set by Dante's mediating Christian epic.

Christopher Grose admits that the final transformation of Satan may be inaccessible to some readers, but he warns against dismissing the scene as simply a comic ploy or doctrinal lesson.[24] Francis Blessington sees Satan's return to Hell as the completion of his "Odyssean phase" and the hissing of the devils-turned-serpents as a counterpart to the uncontrollable laughter of the suitors in *Odyssey* 20.345–49.[25] There is an Odyssean aspect to Satan's journey,

[20] Ferry, pp. 137–38.

[21]John Steadman, *Milton's Epic Characters* (Chapel Hill, N.C., 1959), p. 282. See also Steadman's essay, "Milton's Rhetoric: Satan and the 'Unjust Discourse,'" *MS* 1 (1969), 67–91.

[22]Irene Samuel, *Dante and Milton: The "Commedia" and "Paradise Lost"* (Ithaca, N.Y., 1966), p. 110.

[23]Kevin Brownlee, "Dante and Narcissus," *Dante Studies* 96 (1978), 201–6; Edward Moore, *Scripture and Classical Authors in Dante* (Oxford, 1896), pp. 206–8.

[24]Christopher Grose, *Milton's Epic Process* (New Haven, 1973), p. 232. Grose goes on to link the "devils' corporeal fate" with the "brute forms" of "this poem and of poetry," though this connection seems tenuous whether taken metaphorically or logically.

[25]Blessington, p. 18.

but his return "homeward" creates more subtle reversals than Ulysses' revenge intended. Unlike the reader of the *Odyssey*, the reader of *Paradise Lost* finds that the character of superabundant intellectual will, who has from the beginning focused our attention, who is in that fundamental sense the "hero," is the hero of an epic tradition that the poet ultimately disavows.[26] Disavows—yet reshapes, submerges, and builds upon as the foundation of a new kind of heroic poem.

Contrary Heroism: Ovid and the End of Satan

In the midst of the final transformation of the devils in Book X, Satan is figured as Python, a huge dragon that sprang up, according to legend, at the same time as the human race. The passage in which Satan appears as Python is especially Ovidian in that it immediately follows the transformation of the most eminent devils into serpents and a comparison of their number to the drops of blood from Medusa's head which, as Ovid recounts the fable (*Met.* 4.617–20), became deadly serpents. Depicted as the largest and most powerful serpent, Satan enjoys a final moment of heroic grandeur as he leads the chief devils out of Pandaemonium:

> but still greatest hee the midst,
> Now Dragon grown, larger then whom the Sun
> Ingenderd in the *Pythian* Vale on slime,
> Huge *Python*, and his Power no less he seem'd
> Above the rest still to retain.
>
> (X, 528–32)

The allusion to Python underscores the seeming power of Satan, for in Ovid's account the hugeness of Python serves ultimately to glorify Apollo's victory over him:

> illa quidem nollet, sed te quoque, maxime Python,
> tum genuit, populisque novis, incognite serpens,

---

[26]For an indispensable discussion of heroism and its involvement with the postclassical epic see Curtius, *European Literature and the Latin Middle Ages*, pp. 167–82.

terror eras: tantum spatii de monte tenebas.
hunc deus arquitenens et numquam talibus armis
ante nisi in dammis capreisque fugacibus usus
mille gravem telis, exhausta paene pharetra,
perdidit effuso per vulnera nigra veneno.

(1.438–44)

She [Themis, goddess of the earth] indeed would not have wished it, but she also then brought forth you, greatest Python, and, a serpent unknown before, you were the terror of newly created man: so large a tract of mountainside did you occupy. This creature the bow-bearing god destroyed with such arms as were never used before, except on fleeing she-goats and does, nearly emptying his quiver of its weight of a thousand arrows, until the poisonous blood of the serpent was flowing through black wounds.

Just as the destructiveness of Python is contrary to the goddess's wish, the destructiveness of Satan is contrary to the divine plan. Like Python, Satan sets in motion his eventual downfall by causing suffering to newly formed humanity. Like Python, he is by this point in the epic "greatest" only in bulk. The cyclical observance of Apollo's victory by the Pythian games, celebrated in Ovid's lifetime during the third year of every Olympiad, is refigured in the forced observance of Satan's return to serpent form. Deceived by a multitude of forbidden trees, the devils repeatedly attempt to satisfy their appetites with the fruit, but find themselves chewing "bitter Ashes" instead:

> Thus were they plagu'd
> And worn with Famin, long and ceasless hiss,
> Till thir lost shape, permitted, they resum'd,
> Yearly enjoynd, some say, to undergo
> This annual humbling certain number'd days,
> To dash thir pride, and joy for Man seduc't.

(X, 572–77)

While apparently upholding the grandeur and power of Satan, then, the allusion to Python both reminds us of his conquest by a "greater power" in the present scene and looks forward to the repetition of this humbling throughout history. The narrator's apparently casual relegation of the annual humbling of Satan to uncertain sources ("some say") is actually an integral part of his degeneration, for it implies a movement toward total indifference to the tempter on the part of the faithful. Such indifference is to be Satan's ultimate frustration, since the Redeemer shall succeed, as Michael tells Adam, "Not by destroying *Satan,* but his works / In thee and in thy Seed" (XII, 394–95).

More pervasively than in the figure of Python, Satan reveals his degeneration in this scene through his rhetoric, which contains a number of features characteristic of Ovidian rhetoric. As had the historical Ovid, Satan in *Paradise Lost* wields prodigious power as a rhetor in the classical sense, that is, one "skilled in speaking who addresses a public audience in order to make an impact upon it."[27] Seneca the Elder, Ovid's tutor in rhetoric, records his young pupil's remarkable proficiency in writing and delivering *suasoriae* (speeches recommending a particular course of action) and *ethica controversiae* (speeches arguing for or against the correctness of previous actions),[28] forms of oratory underlying the speeches in the Council at Pandaemonium in Book II as well as Satan's soliloquy atop Mt. Niphates in Book IV. Curtius and others credit Ovid with the virtual establishment of the use of rhetoric in Latin poetry.[29] The young Milton, too, was trained to deliver complex rhetorical orations, as his prolusions and other exercises at Cambridge show. As we saw in Chapter 1, much of the young Milton's education in classical rhetoric and poetry was filtered through Ovid's works. For the mature epic poet, called upon to marshal the distinctive rhetorical patterns of various speakers, rhetoric has a broader application, becoming "all the techniques by which a writer establishes rapport with his readers, and by which he elicits and guides their responses to his work."[30] Satan employs his skills as a rhetor to influence his immediate audience, but Milton has arranged Satan's discourse to reveal to the larger audience of the poem a radical conflict between his words and their referents.

[27]Peter Dixon, *Rhetoric,* in *The Critical Idiom Series,* gen. ed. John D. Jump (London, 1971), p. 2.
[28]See George A. Kennedy, *The Art of Rhetoric in the Roman World* (Princeton, N.J., 1972), pp. 406–8.
[29]Curtius, p. 66.
[30]Dixon, p. 3.

Satan's rhetorical overstatement in his final speech makes this conflict clear. He begins by invoking the honorific titles for the fallen angels: "Thrones, Dominations, Princedoms, Vertues, Powers, / For in possession such, not onely of right, / I call ye and declare ye now" (X, 460–62). This tactic wins the attention of his immediate audience, but contains a cautionary note for the reader who remembers that although the fallen angels may possess these titles in practice, the absolute right to confer them still rests with God, as V, 601–2, points out. Moreover, for the reader who recalls the series of uses of these titles Satan has made—beginning with a noble confrontation of their loss (I, 315–18), shifting to a vain assertion of their power (II, 11–16), and continuing with an insinuation of their injury when the Son is exalted (VI, 772–77)—Satan's final invocation of these honorific titles, in which he assumes the divine authority to bestow them, concludes a further pattern in his pervasive degeneration.

Through the distinctively Miltonic duplication of adjectives around a noun,[31] Satan continues his appeal to the devils by contrasting Hell with Earth, which he has gained for them:

> I call ye and declare ye now, returnd
> Successful beyond hope, to lead ye forth
> Triumphant out of this infernal Pit
> Abominable, accurst, the house of woe,
> And Dungeon of our Tyrant: Now possess,
> As Lords, a spacious World, to our native Heaven
> Little inferiour, by my adventure hard
> With peril great atchiev'd.
>
> (X, 462–69)

Satan's excoriation of Hell as the "Dungeon of our Tyrant" indicates a shifting of ground from his previous recommendation that the devils accept and improve their "home" (II, 456–62). The contrast between "abominable" Hell and the now almost heavenly Earth enables him to magnify his conquest of mankind, actually his

---

[31]See F. T. Prince, *The Italian Element in Milton's Verse* (Oxford, 1969), pp. 11–21. Prince finds that this pattern is common in Italian poetry from Petrarch onward. This frequency in Italian verse may be due to the loose syntax of Latin poetry, especially that of Virgil and Ovid.

inferiors, to heroic dimensions. In his *Tristia,* Ovid in exile repeatedly made just such a contrast between his prison on Tomi in Asia Minor and an idealized vision of Rome, as part of his appeal for the mercy of the emperor.[32] Unlike Ovid, though, Satan argues in a tone of *superbia,* or overweening pride, and ends this section of his speech with an inflated account of his personal risk in the undertaking (X, 468–69).

That such expressions of pride and self-congratulation frequently precede the transformations of characters into degenerate forms in Ovid's epic suggests that Satan's degeneration follows a general stylistic pattern from the *Metamorphoses.* Narcissus (3.354), Niobe (6.184), Jason (7.156), Peleus (11.218), and Anaxarete (14.715) are all examples of figures whose explicit *superbia* foreshadows their personal disasters. Of these Ovidian characters, Niobe is undoubtedly the closest to Satan as rhetor. That Milton was familiar with the Niobe episode in the *Metamorphoses* is certain from his sonnet, "I did but prompt the age to quit their clogs," in which he upholds Apollo and Diana, the "twin-born progeny" of Latona, as examples of rightful divinity and authority. In Ovid's narrative, Niobe is outraged when the Ismenides (Theban women) venerate Latona and her children instead of herself and her fourteen offspring. As noted in Chapter 1, Milton used Ovid's myth in Sonnet XI in a double way: both to provide a model of growth into rightful authority and to expose the folly of those who ignorantly, presumptively claim authority and divinity. Both impulses, but especially the latter one, are at work in Milton's incorporation of Ovidian rhetoric in Satan. Niobe's conflict, like Satan's, stems from a "sense of injured merit," which she vents in a long, tortuous oration (*Met.* 6.170–202).

Her speech falls into three main parts, of which the first begins boldly by challenging the piety of the Theban women on logical grounds:

> "quis furor, auditos" inquit "praeponere visis
> caelestes? aut cur colitur Latona per aras,
> numen adhuc sine ture meum est?"
>
> (6.170–72)

---

[32]See Ovid, *Trist.* 3.4.51–58; 3.8.35–42; 4.1.99–107.

What madness is this? Do you prefer purported to witnessed divinities? Or why is Latona worshipped at the altars, while my godhead goes without incense?

According to William Anderson, Niobe's claim to be a god on earth is an Ovidian invention, and one that intensifies the *superbia* of the speech.[33] Satan's flattering description of himself and the other devils as "gods" has a similar effect. The rhetorical suspension of *caelestes* (divinities) until the beginning of the following line is an Ovidian finesse that Milton so mastered and varied that J. Holly Hanford has labeled it "an authentic character of Milton's utterance and one which contributes perhaps more than any other single element to the elevation of his poetic style."[34]

Satan employs rhetorical suspension frequently in *Paradise Lost*, from his first speech in the poem (I, 84–91; quoted by Hanford as evidence of Miltonic suspension) through this last in describing his seduction of man to the fallen angels:

> Him by fraud I have seduc'd
> From his Creator, and the more to increase
> Your wonder, with an Apple.
>
> (X, 485–87)

By delaying the completion of the sense of this sentence, Satan induces a heightened emphasis on the simple means of the temptation: "with an Apple." Anne Ferry has identified the corruptness of Satan's diction at this point by noticing that God, unfallen man, and the narrator all use the biblical words "fruit" and "root" repeatedly throughout the epic; only Satan uses "Apple."[35] If Satan's rhetorical aim is to show that the divine plan can be reduced to ridicule by a thing of no value, his speech reveals his disjunction of things from their spiritual consequences, and so reveals his degeneration from a high-minded, heavenly spirit to a worldly, low-minded one.

[33]William Anderson, ed., *Ovid's "Metamorphoses," Books 6–10* (Norman, Okla., 1972), p. 175.
[34]James Holly Hanford and James G. Taaffe, *A Milton Handbook*, 5th ed. (New York, 1970), p. 248. See also Gustave Hübener, *Die Stilistische Spannung in Milton's "Paradise Lost"* (Göttingen, 1913).
[35]Ferry, p. 119.

The middle section of Niobe's speech further illuminates the rhetorical strategies of Satan's final speech. Niobe's argument for her innate superiority to Latona moves from an appeal to her celebrated ancestry to a summary of her personal achievements. The egotistical repetitions of the first-person pronoun, together with the misrepresentation of her political power, suggest that the conclusion of her speech, that she shall remain happy and powerful, is precipitate.

> me gentes metuunt Phrygiae, me regia Cadmi
> sub domina est, fidibusque mei commissa mariti
> moenia cum populis a meque viroque reguntur.
> (6.177–79)

Me the Phrygian nations fear, under me the kingdom of Cadmus is ruled, and the Theban walls, raised by my husband's [Amphion's] lyre, are ruled with their people by him and me.

The presumption of safety and the dismissal of the possibility of powers greater than herself, especially, predict Niobe's downfall.

> sum felix (quis enim neget hoc?) felixque manebo
> (hoc quoque quis dubitet?): tutam me copia fecit.
> maior sum, quam cui possit Fortuna nocere,
> multaque ut eripiat, multo mihi plura relinquet.
> (6.193–96)

I am happy (who can deny it?) and happy I shall remain. (This also who can doubt?): abundance makes me safe. I am too great for Fortune to harm: though she might take away many, many more would remain to me.

The double-edged rhetorical questions and oversimplified, aphoristic statements undermine the assertion of eternal happiness. That Niobe's attempt to persuade the Ismenides reveals to the reader both her weakness and blindness to the workings of Fortune makes her argumentation analogous to Satan's revealing attempt to persuade the devils of his victory.

In summarizing his heroic journey and its consequences, Satan amplifies his triumph and minimizes the dangers that now await the devils through patterns of repetition and aphoristic logic reminiscent of Niobe's:

> Long were to tell
> What I have don, what sufferd, with what paine
> Voyag'd th'unreal, vast, unbounded deep
> Of horrible confusion, over which
> By Sin and Death a broad way now is pav'd
> To expedite your glorious march; but I
> Toild out my uncouth passage, forc't to ride
> Th'untractable Abysse, plung'd in the womb
> Of unoriginal *Night* and *Chaos* wilde,
> That jealous of thir secrets fiercely oppos'd
> My journey strange, with clamorous uproare
> Protesting Fate supreame.
>
> (X, 469–80)

The proliferation of privative adjectives—"uncouth," "unreal," "unbounded," "untractable," "unoriginal"—suggests not so much the magnitude of his victory as that of his strain to describe it in the heroic mode. Just as Niobe had misrepresented her influence over the Phrygians and Thebans, Satan misrepresents the acquiescence of Night and Chaos to his journey as fierce opposition. Going beyond the Ovidian standard of *superbia*, Milton adds a vein of casuistry to Satan's rhetoric that enables us to see how his pride leads him to misinterpret God's judgment of him:

> True is, mee also he hath judg'd, or rather
> Mee not, but the brute Serpent in whose shape
> Man I deceav'd: that which to mee belongs,
> Is enmity, which he will put between
> Mee and Mankinde; I am to bruise his heel;
> His Seed, when is not set, shall bruise my head:
> A World who would not purchase with a bruise,
> Or much more grievous pain?
>
> (X, 494–501)

Satan is attempting to minimize his doom through the device of *correctio* ("True is . . . but"), by which he recasts Genesis 3.15 in the most favorable light possible for himself. Yet not only does this strategy fail to persuade his immediate audience, which answers him with a "dismal universal hiss," but it commits Satan to prophesying that a Savior, the descendant ("Seed") of Adam and Eve, will bruise Satan by destroying his works.[36]

Niobe's speech, like those of many characters in the *Metamorphoses*, ends with her loss of human form. Her vain boasts before her metamorphosis into stone deflect the pathos that would otherwise attend the loss of all her children. In responding to the death of Niobe's youngest child, the Ovidian narrator encourages this deflection by mocking her final words through an emotionally detached but verbally playful use of *duplicatio*:

> "unam minimamque relinque!
> de multis minimam posco" clamavit "et unam."
> dumque rogat, pro qua rogat, occidit.
>
> (6.299–301)

"Leave me but one and the last! Of all my many leave the smallest, I beg, only one," she cried. And while she prayed, she for whom she prayed, died.

The shift of the repetition ("unam . . . unam" to "rogat . . . rogat") shows the narrator mocking and thereby silencing Niobe's rhetoric.[37] The objection that such rhetorical trumping is facile and blameworthy may seem just for these three lines in isolation, but it neglects the long, boastful speech that precedes it. In much the same way, Wordsworth's objection that Satan's final metamorphosis is not consonant with his earlier dignity neglects the long preparation for the scene by the increasing disjunction between Satan's rhetoric and his deeds.

---

[36]In *De Doctrina Christiana*, I, xiv (*CPW*, 6:416) Milton clarifies what had been a traditional interpretation of Gen. 3.15: "God promised that he would raise up from the seed of the woman a man who would bruise the serpent's head, Gen. iii, 15. . . . Thus he prefaced man's condemnation with a free redemption." Cf. *Paradise Lost*, XII, 386–95.

[37] Heinrich Naumann notes the witty duplication in the Niobe passage and argues that it is peculiarly characteristic of Ovid's use of rhetoric. See "Ovid und die Rhetorik," *Altsprachliche Unterricht* 11 (1968), 86.

Other Ovidian metamorphoses suggest precedents for aspects of Satan's degenerate loss of speech and human form in this scene. Echo's partial reiterations of her beloved's words form a counterpart to the sibilant responses to Satan's invitation that the devils join with him in "full bliss":

> quotiensque puer miserabilis "eheu"
> dixerat, haec resonis iterabat vocibus "eheu."
>
> (3.495–96)

> As often as the miserable boy said "alas"
> With answering words she repeats his with "alas."

Ovid's ingenious use of reiterations and partial reiterations captures Echo's fatal dependence on the words of another speaker. In Milton's passage both the unusual concentration of echoed, or rhymed, words (after "bliss," there are five reiterations of "hiss") and the ironic fulfillment of Satan's invitation seem to be developments of Ovid's verses. The culmination of the devils' hissing in the Latinate pun on *"exploding* hiss" (to clap and hoot a speaker off the stage, *OED*, 1; to reject with scorn, *OED*, 2) indicates the complete collapse of Satan's rhetorical program.

As a number of critics have noted, the closest of Ovid's transformed bodies to Satan in this scene is Cadmus, the mythological founder of Thebes.[38] An important feature of Ovid's treatment of the change of Cadmus into a serpent is worth adding to these analyses. Remembering his careless slaughter of a sacred serpent in Illyria, Cadmus invites his transformation upon himself by his own oath:

> "quem si cura deum tam certa vindicat ira,
> ipse, precor, serpens in longam porrigar alvum."
> dixit et, ut serpens, in longam tenditur alvum.
>
> (4.574–76)

---

[38] In *Classical Myth and Legend in Renaissance Dictionaries*, DeWitt T. Starnes and Ernest W. Talbert explain Milton's use of Hermione (instead of Harmonia, as in Ovid's work) as the wife of Cadmus by noticing the same replacement in the *Dictionary* of Charles Stephanus (1638). See Starnes and Talbert (Chapel Hill, N.C., 1955), pp. 243–44. Alastair Fowler makes the more critical comment that "Milton almost certainly intends an allusion to Vulcan's fatal gift to Hermione, which made all her children impious and wicked." See Fowler's edition of *Paradise Lost*, p. 469.

"If it be this that the gods have been avenging with such unerring wrath, I pray that I, too, may be a serpent, and stretch myself in long serpentine form—" And as he spoke he was stretched out in long serpentine form.

In their spatial arrangement and rhetorical patterning, Ovid's verses are exploring the way speech transforms a speaker into a pattern of his own expressed thoughts. It is this rhetorical premise that Satan adopts when he asserts that "The mind is its own place, and in it self / Can make a Heav'n of Hell, a Hell of Heav'n" (I, 254–55). Surpassing Cadmus in rhetorical power, Satan goes on cleverly if vainly to express his delight in the literal meaning of his name: "I glorie in the name, / Antagonist of Heav'ns Almightie King" (X, 386–87). The appropriately adverse transformation he chooses is made explicit after his final speech:

> So having said, a while he stood, expecting
> Thir universal shout and high applause
> To fill his eare, when contrary he hears
> On all sides, from innumerable tongues
> A dismal universal hiss, the sound
> Of public scorn; he wonderd, but not long
> Had leasure, wondring at himself now more;
> His Visage drawn he felt to sharp and spare,
> His Armes clung to his Ribs, his Leggs entwining
> Each other, till supplanted down he fell
> A monstrous Serpent on his Belly prone,
> Reluctant, but in vaine.
>
> (X, 504–15)

The action of Satan's fall is reinforced by Milton's precise and resonant diction. In its literal, Latin sense, "supplanted" suggests that Satan as he turns into a serpent is physically tripped up; in its applied moral sense the word suggests that, having acted to supplant (to cause to fall, *OED*, 2) humanity, Satan has effected his own downfall.[39] "Reluctant" is also doubly suggestive. The *OED* cites this usage as an instance of physical "struggling" or "writhing,"

---

[39]For a detailed discussion of "supplant" and its significance, see Ricks, *Milton's Grand Style*, pp. 64–65.

which is relevant to Satan's form, while reluctant as "unwilling" (*OED*, 2) is indicative of his spirit.

The premise that one's words both reflect and affect one's moral nature, however, admits of applications other than Satan's heroism of the self. Arguing that virtuous expression would follow from a virtuous speaker, the author of *An Apology for Smectymnuus* (1642) wrote that "he who would not be frustrate of his hope to write well hereafter in laudable things, ought him selfe to bee a true Poem, that is, a composition, and patterne of the best and honourablest things" (*CPW*, 1:890). Milton's belief in an interiorized heroism of virtue opposed to the Satanic assertion of the unbridled self found fullest expression in *Paradise Lost* in Adam's realization that "suffering for Truths sake / Is fortitude to highest victorie" (XII, 569–70), and in Michael's assurance that this new kind of heroism can, with careful cultivation, result in "a paradise within."

"A mind not to be chang'd": Predictions of Counterheroism

The degenerate end of Satan in Book X examined here is implicit in the Ovidian figurations, rhetoric, and style of Books I and II. Davis Harding has carefully analyzed the association by seventeenth-century commentators of Satan both with Ovid's Typhon (once overtly, I, 199, and once by geographical connection with Aetna, I, 230–38) and with his Phaethon, whose narrative supplies parallels both to Satan's fall (I, 44–49) and to his apostrophe to the Sun (IV, 32–113).[40] By alluding in his "Nativity Ode" to Typhon (*Met.* 1.226) and Phaethon (*Met.* 11.84–85) as pagan deities humbled by the appearance of Christ, Milton had strengthened these associations. Ovidian rhetoric accelerates the revelation of Satan's degeneration in Satan's opening speech. William Kennedy has isolated the way in which Satan's first line in the poem, his address to Beelzebub ("If thou beest he; But O how fall'n!"), echoes the narrator's exclamation ("O how unlike the place from whence they fell!") and so begins the characterization of Satan as a diminished figure.[41] The next sentence of Satan's speech suggests further ruin

[40]Harding, p. 85.
[41]William J. Kennedy, *Rhetorical Norms in Renaissance Literature* (New Haven, 1978), p. 168.

while it subtly claims for the devils the sympathy usually extended to survivors of natural catastrophes, as it incorporates the words of Deucalion to Pyrrha after the universal flood described in the opening book of the *Metamorphoses:*

> If he whom mutual league,
> United thoughts and counsels, equal hope
> And hazard in the Glorious Enterprize,
> Joynd with me once, now misery hath joynd
> In equal ruin.
>
> (I, (87–91)

> "O soror, o coniunx, o femina sola superstes,
> quam commune mihi genus et patruelis origo,
> deinde torus iunxit, nunc ipsa pericula iungunt."

"O sister, O wife, O sole surviving woman, whom our common race and family, and then the marriage bed joined to me, now our self-same perils join us." (1.351–53)

The parallels of syntax ("iunxit . . . iungunt" = "Joynd . . . joynd"), diction ("ipsa pericula" = "misery . . . In equal ruin"), and dramatic situation suggest initially that Satan and Beelzebub deserve the same sympathy due the pious survivors Deucalion and Pyrrha. Yet Satan's glaring addition to Deucalion's words, the "Glorious Enterprize," is a rhetorically amplified and self-serving version of what the narrator earlier described as "impious War in Heav'n and Battel proud / With vain attempt" (I, 43–44). Unlike Deucalion, Satan quickly shifts from a concessive equality to his "neerest mate" to his assertion of his solitary opposition to divine power:

> yet not for those,
> Nor what the Potent Victor in his rage
> Can else inflict, do I repent or change,
> Though chang'd in outward lustre.
>
> (I, 94–97)

The opening outburst of Satan upon the lost brightness of Beelzebub proves here to be as much a realization of his own sad change as a response to that of his fellow. In the larger structure of *Paradise*

Lost it is Adam and Eve, figured as Deucalion and Pyrrha, whose prayers to Heaven merit the sympathy of suppliants joined in mutual loss. That Satan can imitate the moving language of the classical precursor of Adam, however, in order to advance his destructive plan against humankind shows that the subtlety and power of his rhetoric are formidable.

The relevance of the style of the *Metamorphoses* to the characterization of Satan in Book I is capable of even fuller elaboration. The first epic simile in the poem, which follows Satan's dialogue with Beelzebub, proceeds with Ovidian flexibility and wit to depict Satan's bulk:

> Thus Satan talking to his neerest Mate
> With Head up-lift above the wave, and Eyes
> That sparkling blaz'd, his other Parts besides
> Prone on the Flood, extended long and large
> Lay floating many a rood.
>
> (I, 192–96)

This introduction to the simile foreshadows Satan's adoption of serpent form, as lines 193–95 are modeled on Virgil's description of the shining-eyed serpents that swam toward Laocoön in the *Aeneid* 2.206–10.[42] Despite the Virgilian echo, the manner of the introduction to Milton's simile is far from the "haunting uncertainty" of the *Aeneid*.[43] Milton's description is precise and anatomically analytic: "With Head up-lift . . . "; "and Eyes"; "his other Parts . . . extended." Stylistically, a closer analogue than Virgil's to this passage is the condensed retelling of the *Aeneid* in the *Metamorphoses*. Ovid's spatial, anatomical overview of Aeneas produces a heavily ironic revision of Virgil's hero, as his final metamorphosis into a minor god suggests:

> hunc iubet Aeneae, quaecumque obnoxia morti,
> abluere et tacito deferre sub aequora cursu.

---

[42]Noted in Fowler, ed., *Paradise Lost*, p. 55.

[43]C. M. Bowra, in *From Virgil to Milton* (London, 1945), pp. 83–84, identifies the dominant mood of the *Aeneid* as "haunting uncertainty" and discusses the contribution of Virgil's similes to this effect.

corniger exsequitur Veneris mandata suisque,
quidquid in Aenea fuerat mortale, repurgat
et respersit aquis: pars optima restitit illi.
lustratum genetrix divino corpus odore
unxit et ambrosia cum dulci nectare mixta
contigit os fecitque deum; quem turba Quirini
nuncupat Indigetem temploque arisque recepit.

                                                     (14.600–608)

She ordered the river-god to wash away from Aeneas all his mortal part and carry it down in his silent stream into the ocean depths. The horned god obeyed Venus' command and in his waters cleansed and washed quite away whatever was mortal in Aeneas. His best part remained to him. His mother sprinkled his face with ambrosia and sweet nectar mixed, and so made him a god, whom the Roman plebeians style Indiges and honor with temple and with sacrifice.

Ovid's particular optic proceeds from "quidquid . . . mortale" to "pars optima" to "corpus" to "os," and then to the specific preparation of the dead body before the sudden apotheosis. The mannered treatment of the physical details contaminates the apparent spirituality of the transformation. The irony of the apotheosis has been carefully prepared for: Fifteen lines earlier, Aeneas is said to be "ripe" (*tempestivus*) for heaven, hardly a heroic epithet for the man Virgil celebrated for *pietas*. Along with this similar visual strategy, Ovid's means of diminishing the heroic mode are appropriate to Milton's simile in two additional ways. Any discussion of Satan's physical parts, however "sparkling," is in itself a reduction of angelic grandeur for one who "in the happy Realms of Light . . . didst out-shine / Myriads though bright" and whose "Empyreal substance cannot fail" (I, 85–87, 117). Moreover, the facile metamorphosis of Aeneas into a minor god worshipped by Roman plebeians is parallel to the facile campaign of Satan to rule in Hell. By calling the fallen angels "gods," Satan adopts a rhetorical ploy contained in Ovid's manual of seduction, the *Ars Amatoria* 1.637: "expedit, esse deos et, ut expedit, esse putemus" (if it is expedient that there be gods, when expedient, let there be gods). Because of his perverse ambition, Satan's apparent power is further removed than that of Aeneas from its spiritual source.

Christopher Grose ably describes the "dovetailing" in this simile of classical, Christian, literary, and commonplace matter of which the *Metamorphoses* provides only a fraction: "The image moves from fabled monsters warring against a patently classical diety (material from Hesiod and Ovid) to the true, and rather more complicated, situation of the biblical Leviathan, one of God's works which yet wars. against mankind."[44] Parallel to the gradual turn from classical to Christian imagery, however, is a stylistic movement, itself Ovidian, from epic elevation to the middle, or even low, style of a sea story, complete with indulgent punning, before the conclusive, earnest, and doctrinal preview of Satan's unintended evocation of "infinite goodness, grace and mercy" for humanity:

> in bulk as huge
> As whom the Fables name of monstrous size,
> *Titanian,* or *Earth-born,* that warr'd on *Jove,*
> *Briareos* or *Typhon,* whom the Den
> By ancient *Tarsus* held, or that Sea-beast
> *Leviathan,* which God of all his works
> Created hugest that swim th'Ocean stream:
> Him haply slumbring on the *Norway* foam
> The Pilot of some small night-founder'd Skiff,
> Deeming some Island, oft, as Sea-men tell,
> With fixed Anchor in his skaly rind
> Moors by his side under the Lee, while Night
> Invests the Sea, and wished Morn delayes:
> So stretcht out huge in length the Arch-fiend lay
> Chain'd on the burning Lake, nor ever thence
> Had ris'n or heav'd his head, but that the will
> And high permission of all-ruling Heaven
> Left him at large to his own dark designs.
>
> (I, 196–213)

The pun on "at large" draws together the huge size, apparent freedom, and suspect ethical status of the creature (even in Milton's day, escaped criminals were said to be "at large"[45]). In the same

---

[44]Grose, p. 151.

[45]*OED*, II, 5–6 contains four instances of "at large" in criminal contexts prior to *Paradise Lost,* though it has no separate category for escaped criminals.

line, the narrator's description of Satan's designs as "dark" superimposes the suggestions of ignorance, such as the mistaken pilot of
the skiff displays, and malice on the already darkened setting, the
"darkness visible" of Hell (I, 26–65). Rand has suggested that Ovid
had a "limbering effect" on Milton's temperament.[46] In the poetry
of *Paradise Lost*, one clear sign of this effect is the frequency of
learned, Latinate puns, many of which go toward suggesting the
low-mindedness of Satan. The puns cluster around three passages
in the poem: Satan's confrontation with Sin and Death in Book II;
the War in Heaven in Books V–VI; and Satan's accounts of his
deeds in Book X. Such puns as "pontifical" (X, 313), describing the
bridge to carry the evil spirits to Earth, align Satan with a combative
if low side of Milton reminiscent of his pamphleteering campaigns.

One pun of special importance in the *Metamorphoses* reappears in
Paradise Lost, where it has the effect of sustaining the dignity and
beauty of Satan that so appealed to the English Romantics. In *Ars
Amatoria* 2.113, Ovid had made the double meaning of the word
forma proverbial: "forma bonum est fragile" (a fine form is a fragile
good). Milton's use of "form" in describing Satan's preeminence
among the fallen angels relies on Ovid's use of *forma:*

> he above the rest
> In shape and gesture proudly eminent
> Stood like a Towr; his form had yet not lost
> All her Original brightness, nor appear'd
> Less then Arch Angel ruind, and th'excess
> Of Glory obscur'd.
>
> (I, 589–94)

The play on gender ("his form" and "her brightness") indicates
that Milton is availing himself of the Latin *forma*, which is feminine,
to highlight the suprasexual nature of the angel.[47] The Latinate
sense of "form" as beauty is also operative in Milton's passage. The
Metamorphoses had both explored and expanded the possibilities of
the significance of *forma*. The word appears ninety-four times in

[46]Rand, "Milton in Rustication," p. 133.
[47] Cf. I, 301: "Angel Forms" and I, 423–24: "For Spirits when they please / Can
either Sex assume, or both," for further signs of the double sense of *forma*.

Ovid's poem,[48] perhaps most significantly in the prologue announcing the epic subject:

> In nova fert animus mutatas dicere formas
> corpora: di, coeptis (nam vos mutastis et illas)
> adspirate meis primaque ab origine mundi
> ad mea perpetuum deducite tempora carmen.
>
> (1.1–4)

My spirit desires to tell of forms changed into new bodies: you gods (for you have changed, and those) inspire my beginnings and spin out my continuous song from the first origin of the world to my own times.

Here the sense of *formas* as "shapes" is primary, and as beauty, secondary: frequently the emphasis is reversed.[49] In a passage from the *Metamorphoses* that seems to underlie the characterization of Satan generally, it is the beauty of Lucifer, Satan's name before his fall, that is stressed. Ovid makes Lucifer's brightness the standard of comparison for human beauty:

> quanto splendidior quam cetera sidera fulget
> Lucifer et quanto quam Lucifer aurea Phoebe,
> tanto virginibus praestantior omnibus Herse
> ibat eratque decus pompae comitumque suarum.
>
> (2.722–25)

As Lucifer shines more brilliantly than all the other stars, and as the golden moon outshines Lucifer, so Herse was the loveliest of all maidens, the ornament of her train and companions.

These lines may have been the germ for Milton's rhetorically balanced and elegant, if logically impossible, celebration of the pre-eminent beauty of Adam and Eve among human beings:

---

[48] According to Roy J. Deferrari, M. I. Barry, and M. R. P. McGuire, in *A Concordance of Ovid* (Washington, D.C., 1939), pp. 710–11.

[49] For a delicately balanced instance of both possibilities, see the Apollo and Daphne episode, *Met.* 1.527–30.

Adam the goodliest man of men since borne
His Sons, the fairest of her Daughters *Eve*.
(IV, 323–24)

That Satan shares the attractive beauty of Eve is a small correspondence that Milton developed into a strong support for the verisimilitude of the temptation, as Eve is seduced by Satan in the form of a serpent lovelier than all his kind (IX, 504–5).

Stylistic correspondences between the *Metamorphoses* and *Paradise Lost* continue through the end of Book I. There Satan and the chief fallen angels assemble in Pandaemonium for the first time. Despite the objections of Voltaire, the scene is crucial to the counterheroic presentation of Satan in the poem.[50] By announcing that the fallen angels "Bru*sh*t with the hi*ss* of ru*s*tling wing*s*" (I, 768; my emphasis), Milton not only provides an onomatopoetic introduction to a recognizably epic bee simile, but especially prepares for the ultimate "hissing" of Satan by the same angels in Book X. The Miltonic narrator prefaces his description of the angels' metamorphosis into the dimensions of dwarfs with an exclamation reminiscent of the Ovidian narrator: "Behold a wonder!" Wonder, as Tasso described it in *Discourses on the Heroic Poem* (1594), is an effect particularly appropriate to transformations narrated in epic: "And so too with many other transformations [than that of Cadmus by Ovid] that we read of with wonder in many other poets, ancient and modern. We gladly read in epic about many wonders that might be unsuitable on stage, both because they are proper to epic and because the reader allows many liberties which the spectator forbids."[51] Not

---

[50]Voltaire, in *An Essay upon the Civil Wars of France, . . . And also upon the Epick Poetry of the European Nations from Homer down to Milton*, 4th ed. (London, 1731), p. 78: "Methinks the true Criterion for discerning what is really ridiculous in an *Epick* Poem, is, to examine if the same thing would not fit exactly the Mock-Heroick. Then I dare say that nothing is so adapted to that ludicrous way of Writing, as the Metamorphosis of the Devils into Dwarfs." In a mock-heroic poem such as Pope's *Rape of the Lock*, however, the style is elaborate and ceremonious, palpably grander than the subject matter (the theft of a lady's curl). The case of Milton's passage is precisely the opposite. The power and magnificence of the fallen angels exceed their human counterparts, but the devils literally reduce their own grandeur in a momentary exposure of their spiritual diminution. Voltaire's heroic/mock-heroic opposition does not address the stylistic innovation presented here.

[51]Torquato Tasso, *Discourses on the Heroic Poem*, p. 16.

only does Tasso regard the *Metamorphoses* as an epic worthy of imitation, but he also defends the effect of wonder in epic as a product of the reader's greater imaginative freedom. Relying on this freedom, the Miltonic narrator both claims that the devils' transformation is wondrous and suggests, in his summary, that this change is counterheroic in that it diminishes the grandeur of the chief devils:

> Thus incorporeal Spirits to smallest forms
> Reduc'd thir shapes immense, and were at large,
> Though without number still amidst the Hall
> Of that infernal Court.
>
> (I, 789–92)

The pun on "at large," even more striking here than in the first simile, exposes the devils' actual lack of greatness and freedom within the gilded prison of Pandaemonium. In Ricks's words: "Nothing could more effectively belittle the devils."[52] The belittlement of the devils is only momentary, however, for we learn immediately that within the assembly the chief devils retain their own dimensions. The presentation of Satan in Book I as a defeated hero whose schemes reveal his diminishing heroic status is fully compatible with his final appearance in Book X. Only the overt exposure of Satan's failure to establish himself as a heroic figure differentiates the final scene from earlier ones involving Satan, while the overtness of the dismissal makes way for the new heroism of interiorized virtue that Adam learns from his visions in Books XI and XII.

Exposure and Success: Satan's Ovidian Temptations

Between the first and the final transformation scenes in Pandaemonium, Satan continues to appropriate the rhetoric, figures, and style of the *Metamorphoses*. Building on the work of Arnold Stein, Louis Martz has analyzed two major instances of what he terms "figurations of Ovid": Satan's encounter with Sin (II, 650–814) and the War in Heaven (VI, 44–912).[53] The description of

[52]Ricks, p. 15.
[53]Martz, *Poet of Exile*, pp. 208–16.

Sin, who is both Satan's offspring and consort, relies on the *Metamorphoses* 14.40–74 for the phrase "*Cerberean* mouths" and for the picture of Sin as Scylla, the figure Spenser had presented as Error in the first book of *The Faerie Queene*, perpetually devoured by her own young. Milton's Sin is essentially an instance of Ovid allegorized. The observation of Anne Ferry that allegory in *Paradise Lost* is a fallen mode of language, used only by or of the fallen angels, supports the process of exposing Satan by means of Ovidian rhetoric. The War in Heaven, as Stein has shown, exposes Satan's descent into derisive humor and sheer physicality in the angelic combat. Martz compares the War in Heaven with Ovid's "anti-heroic" description of the battles between Perseus and Phineus (*Met.* 5.1–235) and the Lapiths and Centaurs (12.210–458). As the debased and nihilistic form of the War in Heaven suggests, Satan's opposition to Heaven serves only to diminish his own once noble nature and mind.

Three further episodes of *Paradise Lost* suggest ways in which Milton completes in Satan rhetorical, figural, and narrative patterns of counterheroism sketched in Ovid's poem. Milton's Council in Hell (II, 1–505) bears strong similarities to the most exuberant display of rhetoric in the *Metamorphoses*, the so-called Judgment of the Arms (*judicium armorum*), the debate between Ajax and Ulysses to determine who shall receive the armor of slain Achilles. The disputants seem to stand for two competing notions of heroism: Ajax, for martial prowess as described in the *Iliad;* Ulysses for cunning as in the *Odyssey*. The setting for the debate is a council of the Greek leaders reminiscent of that at the opening of the *Iliad*, but in the *Metamorphoses* what begins as a confrontation between exemplary heroes over a point of honor becomes a self-consciously rhetorical investigation of the power of language. Ajax is aware of the handicap he labors under in taking on the polished speaker Ulysses:

> sed nec mihi dicere promptum
> nec facere est isti, quantumque ego Marte feroci
> inque acie valeo, tantum valet iste loquendo.
>
> (13.10–12)

But I am not quick to speak as he is not to act, and I am just as strong in a fierce conflict in a battle-line as he is in the art of speaking.

Despite the impossibility of defeating Ulysses on his terms, Ajax speaks over a hundred more lines and produces, finally, only a murmur among the lower soldiers (*vulgi*). Ulysses, despite his lack of deeds answering to those of Ajax, speaks nearly three times as long and produces, through his rhetorical brilliance, the desired result:

> Mota manus procerum est, et, quid facundia posset,
> re patuit, fortisque viri tulit arma disertus.

> (13.382–83)

> The company of chiefs was moved, and, what eloquence might do, the contest revealed. The well-spoken man carried off the arms of the brave.

As Richard Lanham argues, the impersonal, laconic form of this statement converts the agency of the victory from Ulysses to eloquence itself.[54] Whereas Homer's Ulysses fought and suffered as well as talked his way through ten years of wandering, Ovid's Ulysses stands counter to even this kind of heroism by merely outtalking his less eloquent rival in a prearranged debate.

In its transvaluation of heroism by rhetoric, this scene from the *Metamorphoses* made available to Milton a strategy for arranging the Council in Hell which would both advance Satan's approach to heroism and discredit him for the guile and abuse of rhetoric this approach entails. Satan, sitting on a throne in Pandaemonium, begins the council by posing the question, in the words of the prose argument, "whether another battle be to be hazarded for the recovery of heaven." Only Moloc, "the strongest and fiercest Spirit / That fought in heav'n," a spokesman for the heroism of military valor, even credits the presumptuousness of this question by arguing for a direct assault on Heaven. Belial, who speaks for the heroism of eloquence, rejects all activism by counseling, in the narrator's terms, "ignoble ease, and peaceful sloth." The speech of Mammon, approved by vast applause, suggests that the devils would be delighted to mimic their former home in the negative light of Hell, "this nether Empire, which might rise . . . In emula-

[54]Lanham, p. 12.

tion opposite to Heav'n" (II, 296–98). Beelzebub advises disturbing God indirectly by tempting mankind, and he shrewdly calls for a vote to guarantee that this proposal will be carried out. Satan, silent throughout the debate, rises only to answer Beelzebub's question, which had reduced the other spirits to silence:

> But first whom shall we send
> In search of this new world, whom shall we find
> Sufficient?
>
> (II, 402–4)

Satan's sole acceptance of this challenge seems to place him in a heroic context, for he wins the unqualified admiration of the council:

> Towards him they bend
> With awful reverence prone; and as a God
> Extoll him equal to the highest in Heav'n:
> Nor fail'd they to express how much they prais'd,
> That for the general safety he despis'd
> His own.
>
> (II, 477–82)

This response indicates that Satan's heroism is a more efficient variety than that of Ovid's Ulysses: Rather than argue for his plan himself, Satan as manipulator of rhetoric arranges for others to prepare for his "Glorious Enterprize." In a less flattering sense, Satan's preparation for the success of his plan by prompting Beelzebub beforehand makes the display of rhetoric in the Council of Hell at least unnecessary and possibly ridiculous. Milton qualifies Satan's triumph even at its peak, at which the devils praise Satan "as a God . . . equal to the highest in Heav'n." In a poem in which God literally appears, this simile reveals the perversity of Satan's heroism and the partiality of his imitation of godhead.

Having accepted the sole enterprise of tempting mankind, Satan undertakes the "uncouth journey" from Hell to Earth which he strains to describe in the heroic mode in his final speech. During the journey itself, the manner in which Satan moves manages to suggest both heroic struggle and comic impotence. His entrance into Chaos shows Satan exerting himself vigorously, though his means of locomotion border on Rabelaisian, and Ovidian, drollery:

> At last his Sail-broad Vannes
> He spreads for flight, and in the surging smoak
> Uplifted spurns the ground, thence many a League
> As in a cloudy Chair ascending rides
> Audacious, but that seat soon failing, meets
> A vast vacuitie: all unawares
> Fluttring his pennons vain plumb down he drops
> Ten thousand fadom deep, and to this hour
> Down had been falling, had not by ill chance
> The strong rebuff of som tumultuous cloud
> Instinct with Fire and Nitre hurried him
> As many miles aloft.
>
> (II, 927–38)

The neologism "pennons" from the Latin *pennae*, the eager though useless flapping of wings, and the unexpected blast from "som tumultuous cloud" suggest that Milton is incorporating these details from the Phaethon episode, *Met*. 2.1–440. Thematically, Phaethon's rash theft of the chariot of the Sun and his fatal ride through the heavens reappear in Satan's presumptuousness ("Audacious") and lack of control ("all unawares"). Stylistically, Ovid's treatment of Phaethon as unequal to the epic narrative in which he appears approximates those moments in Milton's treatment of Satan when the supposed hero is overwhelmed by chance or greater powers.[55]

Satan's climactic action in the poem, the seduction of Eve, is explicitly rhetorical, as the comparison of Satan before the Tree to "som Orator renound / In *Athens* or free *Rome,* where Eloquence / Flourishd" (IX, 670–72) shows. This epic simile effectively elevates Satan in the reader's imagination to the level of a noble statesman, as it recalls the situation of the speaker at the beginning of *Areopagitica,* for whom "the very attempt of this addresse thus made, and the thought of whom it hath recourse to, hath got the power within

---

[55]On the epic manner of the Phaethon episode and its parodic significance see R. Coleman, "Structure and Intention in the *Metamorphoses,*" *CQ* 65 (1971), 475.

me to a passion, farre more welcome than incidentall to a Preface" (*CPW*, 2:487). Moreover, like Milton's argument in *Areopagitica*, Satan's speech imitates the formal arrangement of the classical oration, with *exordium* (IX, 679–84), *narratio* (685–90), *confirmatio* including *explicatio* (691–99), *partitio* (700–702), and *amplificatio* (703–15), *refutatio* (716–29), and *peroratio* (730–32).

Within this venerable framework, however, Satan's oratory displays a consciously duplicitous manipulation of rhetoric. Satan bases his appeal on Eve's demonstrated weakness (her vanity), claims an unreal experience (eating the fruit), and relies on specious arguments. The most noteworthy of these is his false enthymeme, or condensed syllogism, asserting the injustice of God:

> God therefore cannot hurt ye, and be just;
> Not just, not God; not feard then, nor obeyd:
> Your feare it self of Death removes the feare.
>
> (IX, 700–702)

The argument is flawed in two ways. It misrepresents God's command not to eat the fruit, actually the sole pledge of man's obedience (III, 95), as God's willful restriction and therefore injury of mankind. In other words, it ascribes to God Satan's own jealousy. More importantly, it simplistically contradicts the necessarily complex justification of God's ways to men which the overall argument of *Paradise Lost* asserts. Satan's counterargument gains suasiveness from its resemblance to the Miltonic argument, for although God could change the nature of Adam and Eve (which would "hurt" them in a different sense), God has announced that instead, humanity shall find grace and mercy upon its fall. Satan's persuasive unfolding of his enthymeme relies on an elegant use of *anadiplosis*, the repetition of "just" and "feare" to smooth over such logical problems. The repetition of negatives in Satan's argument reinforces the perversity of both the rhetoric and the aim of the "arch-adversary."[56]

---

[56]The perverse rhetoric of Satan's speech may recall the use of faulty enthymemes in the speech of Pythagoras, which effectively concludes the *Metamorphoses*. For example, Pythagoras's catalog of powerful cities that have fallen (Troy, Sparta, Thebes, Athens) makes a warning rather than a celebration of the

The reader may easily forget that at this moment in *Paradise Lost* Satan has assumed the form of a serpent, a fact that elicits Satan's doleful awareness of his willful degeneration:

> O foul descent! that I who erst contended
> With Gods to sit the highest, am now constraind
> Into a Beast, and mixt with bestial slime,
> This essence to incarnate and imbrute,
> That to the height of Deitie aspir'd;
> But what will not Ambition and Revenge
> Descend to?
>
> (IX, 163–69)

It is in the context of Satan's dramatic situation as orator in serpent form that the final Ovidian figuration, the comparison of Satan to both Cadmus and Aesculapius, should be understood. On the surface the comparison celebrates the unique beauty of the serpent that contains Satan:

> pleasing was his shape,
> And lovely, never since of Serpent kind
> Lovelier, not those that in *Illyria* chang'd
> *Hermione* and *Cadmus*, or the God
> In *Epidaurus*.
>
> (IX, 503–7)

Martz reads these metamorphoses of humans into serpents as evidence of the uncertainty of appearances in *Paradise Lost:* The apparently base form of entwining snakes nevertheless represents a benevolent union for Cadmus and his wife, he argues, and the same form enables the healing power of Aesculapius to reach Rome from Epidaurus in Greece.[57] More lasting than the sug-

---

oracular announcement that Rome shall become the capital of the whole world (15.428–35). What W. R. Johnson, in "The Problem of the Counter-classical Sensibility and its Critics," *California Studies in Classical Antiquity* 3 (1970), 123–52, aptly calls Ovid's "counter-classical" poetics, evidenced by such ricocheting, anti-authoritarian uses or rhetoric, is only verbally similar to Satan's "counterheroism." Pythagoras is unaware of the warning Ovid delivers through him; Satan is fully conscious of the lies he tells, and his rhetorical style reveals his debased character.

[57]Martz, *Poet of Exile*, p. 91.

gestions of beauty and beneficence in these changes, however, are suggestions of deceptiveness and mutability. We have already seen how Milton's allusion to Cadmus prepares for Satan's ultimate punishment in the same form he used for the temptation. At this moment in Milton's narrative, Satan, enclosed in the serpent, is approaching Eve, and his loveliness increases his seductiveness. If the change of Cadmus and Harmonia in the *Metamorphoses* resulted in beautiful, mild creatures, it certainly produced less noble ones from the far-sighted founders of Thebes. Moreover, as serpents only Cadmus and his mate find each other beautiful: Their transformation fills all who witness it with horror (*Met.* 4.598). Satan as serpent is attractive to Eve, but among his fellow angels he appears as one of the crowd of "ugly Serpents" (X, 539).

The allusion to Epidaurus also depicts Satan as superior in beauty to Aesculapius, a figure who, according to the *Metamorphoses*, adopted serpent form to purge Rome of a deadly pestilence.[58] Like Satan, the god of Epidaurus undertakes the metamorphosis to a snake himself, in which form he persuades his countrymen of his desire to confer his healing powers on the Romans. The pleasing shape and motion of Aesculapius described in the *Metamorphoses* are remarkably similar to those of Satan:

> vix bene desierant, cum cristis aureus altis
> in serpente deus praenuntia sibila misit . . .
> pectoribusque tenus media sublimis in aede
> constitit atque oculos circumtulit igne micantes. . . .
> inde per iniectis adopertam floribus ingens
> serpit humum flectitque sinus.
>
> (15.669–89)

Scarce had they ceased to speak when the golden god, in the form of a serpent with high crest, uttered hissing warnings of his presence. Then, raised breast-high in the temple's midst, he stood and gazed about with eyes flashing fire. . . . Thence the huge serpent wound his way along the ground covered with scattered flowers, bending and coiling as he went. (Loeb)

---

[58]According to Virgil's *Aeneid* 7.772–73, Jupiter, angry at the attempt of Aesculapius to gain immortality, hurled him down into the noxious river Styx. The allusion to "the god in Epidaurus," then, may once again indirectly depict the fall of Satan.

So spake the Enemie of Mankind, enclos'd
In Serpent, Inmate bad, and toward *Eve*
Address'd his way, not with indented wave,
Prone on the ground, as since, but on his reare,
Circular base of rising foulds, that tour'd
Fould above fould a surging Maze, his Head
Crested aloft, and Carbuncle his Eyes;
With burnisht Neck of verdant Gold, erect
Amidst his circling Spires.

(IX, 494–502)

Within the context of the temptation, Satan's resemblance to Aesculapius intensifies Eve's moral dilemma, because even as a serpent he can impersonate a wondrous, beneficient power. Above all, the resemblance of Satan as a serpent to the "god in Epidaurus" maintains the doubleness of his character, which is crucial to his function in the poem. To Eve and to himself, Satan seems already to possess "god-head." The Ovidian figures, rhetoric, and style help to make Satan's temptation as appealing to the reader as it was to Eve, but they simultaneously alert the "fit audience" to the danger of counterfeit, self-styled divinity. So far as it concerns Satan, the dialogue with Ovid thus shows Milton's willingness to let the metamorphic poet stand as one of the exemplars of Satan's heroism, even as that heroism is exposed and judged erroneous. To the "fit audience" of *Paradise Lost,* moreover, Satan's "god-head" is not only counterfeit but based on a pagan theology that had been put to flight, as Milton's "Nativity Ode" had described, by the birth of the Savior.

In *A Preface to "Paradise Lost"* C. S. Lewis summarizes the metamorphic regression of Satan in Milton's epic: "From hero to general, from general to politician, from politician to secret service agent, . . . and thence to a toad, and finally to a snake—such is the progress of Satan."[59] The pattern of counterheroism shows that beast, rhetor, and hero are all present continuously in Satan, and that the varying proportions of these roles throughout the poem enable us to chart Satan's true progress. By condensing the loose array of figures from the *Metamorphoses* into the dense multiplicity

[59]Lewis, *Preface,* p. 99.

of his single narrative, Milton insists upon the integrity and subtlety of Satan's transformations in *Paradise Lost*. The recurrent metamorphoses of Satan elicit from the Miltonic narrator a recurrent response of "wonder," in keeping with Tasso's citation of the change in Ovid's Cadmus as an effective instance of "maraviglie" (the wondrous) in epic. From his metamorphosis in the first council at Pandaemonium through his metamorphosis into a pleasing snake during the temptation, Satan maintains the illusion of his control of events, while his rhetoric, including versions of the speeches of Ovid's Deucalion, Niobe, Cadmus, Echo, and Ulysses, reveals his degeneration into pride and selfishness. Satan is committed to the rhetorical flexibility that Ovid had introduced to the epic genre. The narrative voice of that epic claims total authority in accounting for events from creation to the end of the established order. Satan claims the similar right to account for his revolt from God and seduction of humankind in his own terms. The wonder that Satan generates in Books I and II and during the temptation in Book IX fittingly ends when he can no longer maintain a counterfeit appearance or voice, when his counterheroic designs are displaced by "a greater power."

Within *Paradise Lost* the power that more immediately displaces Satan, however, is the Miltonic narrator, whose Ovidian mockery and humor reveal the stylistic corruption of Satan. The similarity between Satanic and Miltonic rhetoric suggests an unresolved difficulty, in that both speakers would seem to be subject to corruption and change. The next chapter examines how the structure of *Paradise Lost*, following the example of the *Metamorphoses*, transformed classical epic to include historic, mythic, and psychic degeneration, while it encouraged Milton to locate the source of his poetic argument outside his own fallen self.

–4–

Revaluating the Contrast-Epic: Generic and Narrative Continuities

Part of the enduring beauty and power of *Paradise Lost* lies in its massive yet intricate epic structure, reminiscent of those of Homer and Virgil.[1] Without question Milton attempted to hold *Paradise Lost* up for comparison with the acknowledged masterpieces of classical epic: the *Iliad,* the *Odyssey,* and the *Aeneid.* In so doing, he imitated not only the formal features of classical epic (for example, invocation of the Muse, catalogs of warriors, and supernatural councils) but also its structural and narrative formulas (for example, beginning *in medias res,* descent into the underworld, and lengthy flashbacks and prophecies). Through these devices, Milton's imitation creates a startling impression of continuity between the world of *Paradise Lost* and those of Homer and Virgil.

It would be a great mistake, however, to assume that those three poems were the only possible models for Milton's epic, or that *Paradise Lost* shares the same values as those classical epics.[2] Recent comparative studies have advanced the concept of revaluation, or transvaluation, to explain the process by which a later poet echoes yet redeploys generic formulas from previous works.[3] Milton's im-

[1]On the structural parallels to classical epic see Blessington, *"Paradise Lost" and the Classical Epic*; G. K. Hunter, *"Paradise Lost"* (London, 1980); and especially John T. Shawcross, *With Mortal Voice: The Creation of "Paradise Lost"* (Lexington, Ky., 1982), pp. 45–52.

[2]Barbara K. Lewalski summarizes the generic models of *Paradise Lost,* including the *Metamorphoses* among the varieties and subspecies of epic, in "The Genres of *Paradise Lost.*"

[3]See Judith A. Kates, "The Revaluation of the Classical Heroic in Tasso and

itation of Ovid's *Metamorphoses* takes the concept of revaluation a step further, to an arena where the pagan and the Christian poet's values compete for the reader's approval, and where the poetic strategies are markedly, even dangerously similar. In his dialogue with Ovid, in short, Milton imitates and revalues a metamorphic epic that had itself revalued the epics of Homer and Virgil. However rhetorically dangerous, this approach was for Milton the most economical and consistent use of the pagan author. For Milton thereby underscores and distinguishes his own changes in epic expectations, while he allows the reader to choose between Ovid's commitment to unending change and his own belief in divinely sanctioned, teleological change.

The crucial features of Ovid's revaluation of epic that Milton incorporates in *Paradise Lost* are the following: a rejection of external, martial force in favor of interiorized, psychological virtues; an expansion of the role of the narrator, who now examines the sources, comments on the action and theme, and responds to the characters of the poem; an extension of structural techniques that afford multiple perspectives over both space and time; and a resolution of the narrative in personalized, imaginative history. Approximations of these features appear, of course, in other poems before *Paradise Lost*. The *Aeneid* and Dante's *Divine Comedy* significantly altered the thematic core of Homeric epic; innovations in authorial presence and narrative technique may be found in Ariosto's *Orlando Furioso* and Spenser's *The Faerie Queene*;[4] Lucan's *Pharsalia* and Camoëns's *Lusiad* extensively adapt history to the

---

Milton," *CL* 26 (1974), 299–317; and Barbara J. Bono, *Literary Transvaluation from Vergilian Epic to Shakespeare* (Berkeley, Calif., 1984).

[4]On Ariosto's narrative innovations and their relevance to *Paradise Lost* see Joan Webber, *Milton and His Epic Tradition* (Seattle, 1979), pp. 24–26. On the narrator's presence in *The Faerie Queene* see Kathleen Williams, "Vision and Rhetoric: The Poet's Voice in *The Faerie Queene*," *ELH* 36 (1969), 131–44; Jerome S. Dees, "The Narrator of *The Faerie Queene*: Patterns of Response," *TSLL* 12 (1971), 537–68; Stan Hinton, who compares Miltonic and Spenserian narration in "The Poet and His Narrator: Spenser's Epic Voice," *ELH* 41 (1974), 168–91; and Paul Alpers, "Narration in *The Faerie Queene*," *ELH* 44 (1977), 19–39. The classic work on narrative presence in epic remains Robert M. Durling's *The Figure of the Poet in Renaissance Epic* (Cambridge, 1965), which discusses the figure of Ovid in his *Ars Amatoria* and *Remedia Amoris*, but treats neither the narrative voice of the *Metamorphoses* nor that of *Paradise Lost*.

epic. Yet the intensive combination of these features in a single work, along with Ovid's rhetorical trumpeting of them, makes the *Metamorphoses* both an original and influential variant of epic. Although these achievements were in one sense a convenience to Milton, his pervasive use and radical transformation of them amounts to a profound challenge, by which the *Metamorphoses* is invoked to support the theodicy of *Paradise Lost.*

Critical studies have well documented Milton's responses to various classical and Renaissance epics, but until recently commentators have overlooked the place of the *Metamorphoses* in the epic tradition and the relevance of Ovid's work to *Paradise Lost.*[5] The major cause of this neglect seems to be the persistence of an overly simplified, rigidly formalistic notion of epic which, deduced from the *Iliad,* the *Odyssey,* and the *Aeneid* alone, excludes most other works from the genre. To be sure, the *Metamorphoses* strains the margins of the class of poems commonly considered epic; by the same token, so does *Paradise Lost.* The problem may lie not with the poems but with the exclusively synchronic, taxonomic tendencies implicit in treating epic as a "class." By regarding epic as an evolving, mixed genre,[6] we can account more fully for the recurrence of certain formal features in epic and for the variation in their usage. To isolate two works from an evolving tradition and to investigate their relationship is, admittedly, an artificial and partial procedure. It is also an absolutely necessary one if we are to measure how persuasively Milton, imitating Ovid's mercurial, irrepressible voice and his method of unfolding perpetual change, conducts his "great Argument" of human change.

Aristotle's remarks in the *Poetics* pertain directly to the theory of classical epic, yet critics employing Aristotelian terms or interpretations often overlook their limited relevance to later developments

[5]Largely responsible for recovering the Augustan view that the *Metamorphoses* is an epic poem is Brooks Otis's *Ovid as an Epic Poet.* The only study to investigate the relationship between the *Metamorphoses* and *Paradise Lost* as epic poems is Louis Martz's *Poet of Exile.*

[6]For a stimulating but all too brief discussion of epic as a work of "genera mixta," that is, a mingling of various genres within a subsuming kind, see Rosalie Colie, *The Resources of Kind: Genre-Theory in the Renaissance,* ed. Barbara K. Lewalski (Berkeley, Calif., 1973), pp. 119–22. According to Wittreich, *Angel of Apocalypse,* p. 168, epic was from its inception a mixture of genres.

in epic poetry. Aristotle himself, by way of the concept of entelechy, or the realization of potentialities in actual forms, observed that genres could change after reaching definition. His account of tragedy, for example, traces its origins in satyr-dance and its eventual addition of multiple actors and episodes. He excludes from his account of epic, however, any discussion of evolution or formal change. Two of Aristotle's overarching conceptions, that "imitation of human beings in action" defines the art of poetry and that epic differs from other kinds of imitation in its (narrative) means, (great human) objects, and (elevated) manner, are generally applicable to epics beyond his own time and place. His notion of the proper features of epic is limited, of course, to those of the Greek epics he has examined. Certainly Aristotle in offering these observations is neither prescribing rules nor giving advice to would-be poets. By isolating particular features of epic, however, Aristotle does arouse expectations that readers will henceforth bring to works labeled "epic." Accordingly, epic poets after Aristotle must in some way fulfill, deflect, or transform these expectations, if they wish to satisfy readers and to signal the arrival of an original work within the genre.

Aristotle's discussion of epic plot and theme, in particular, reveals his commitment to a static taxonomy of the genre. Maintaining that everything in an epic "should be based on a single action, one that is a complete whole in itself, with a beginning, middle, and end,"[7] he concludes that in this respect Homer manifestly transcends the other epic poets. Explicitly, Aristotle praises Homer's selection of a single phase of the Trojan War as the main action of each of his epics and disapproves of poets who "treat of one man, or one period; or else of an action which, although one, has a multiplicity of parts in it."[8] Gerald Else contends that Aristotle's treatment of the epic is thus "skewed" from the beginning. "What it gives," Else observes, "is not really a theory of what the epic is, but of what it ought to be—or, to put the same thing in another way, it gives a *theory based on the Homeric epic*" [his italics].[9] As Else

[7]Aristotle, *On the Art of Poetry*, trans. Ingram Bywater, preface by Gilbert Murray (Oxford, 1962), p. 79.
[8]Ibid., p. 80.
[9]Else, *Aristotle's "Poetics": The Argument* (Cambridge, 1957), pp. 571–72.

points out, Aristotle's implicit standard for the unity of an epic action is the dramatic unity of Greek tragedy.[10] This standard would tend to discredit a work that recombines parts of previous epics, such as the *Aeneid*, whose twelve-book structure consists of an Odyssean half and an Iliadic half. Moreover, Aristotle admits only heroic and martial subjects as appropriate to epic. Works such as Hesiod's *Theogony*, expanding the paideutic and mythological concerns of Homeric epic while diverging from its martial center, do not fit the taxonomy and thus, in effect, are denied epic status.

The proper relationship between the epic bard and his work, according to Aristotle, is also to be found in Homer. "The poet should," Aristotle maintains, "say very little *in propria persona*, as he is no imitator when doing that."[11] Aristotle's emphasis on effecting *mimesis* by uninterrupted narration no doubt underlies this dictum. Nevertheless, Ovid and Milton will explode this notion by representing themselves as extensive commentators and thus characters within their epics, thereby extending the domain of *mimesis*.

Anticipating another feature that Ovid and Milton developed, Aristotle does celebrate the power of epic narrative, unlike drama, to represent a number of incidents as occurring simultaneously, which adds to the fullness, grandeur, and variety of epic. The similar mechanism of history, however, he excludes from epic. He demands that the plot of an epic poem must be unlike what we commonly find in histories,[12] as histories fail to offer a single or unified action.

In short, Aristotle's perception of epic as a general type of poem with certain standard features is an essential if limited first step in approaching epic. Accordingly, Milton in *Of Education* recommended that students consult Aristotle, Horace, and the Italian commentators to learn "what the laws are of a true *Epic* poem, what of a *Dramatic*, what of *Lyric* . . ." (*CPW*, 2:405).[13] As E. D. Hirsch

[10]Ibid., p. 572.
[11]Aristotle, p. 83.
[12]Ibid., p. 79.
[13]Though Milton's sense of these genres may seem at first purely formal and prescriptive, the inclusion of "a *Dramatic* [poem]" describes a conflation of "genre" and "mode." Earl Miner aptly distinguishes between these terms in the preface to *The Metaphysical Mode from Donne to Cowley* (Princeton, N.J., 1969).

argues, such broad generic notions "serve speakers in the way that pictorial schemata serve painters."[14] That is, the notion of a genre as a fixed type has a necessary heuristic function for readers and authors; it enables them to start with a basic set of shared expectations, which, in the case of each particular epic, prove to be only provisional and finally expendable. Further, as Hirsch shows, fixed generic categories such as Aristotle's epic enable us to avoid invalid readings based on false expectations.

Each new poem that readers recognize as epic and that introduces deviations from the Homeric patterns, however, alters the features and possibilities of the genre. By the first century A.D., for instance, Quintilian mentions more than thirty works in Greek and Latin, including the *Metamorphoses,* as representative of epic.[15] A comprehensive literary taxonomy of epic written after Virgil, which Quintilian does not attempt, would encounter great difficulties in defining the essential features of epic, unless it treated a few works as "correct" and others as less successful because they varied from the exemplary form. Such a hypothetical taxonomy would arguably build in evaluations of the various poems, as Aristotle's *Poetics* had done, which would interfere with its descriptive function. A comprehensive theory of epic ought to account for, rather than downplay, the variation among poems widely recognized as "epic."

In the Introduction we saw how Italian Renaissance critics, principally Giraldi Cinthio and Tasso, supplemented Aristotle's poetic theory with the successful practice of poets after him. Both Giraldi and Tasso regarded the *Metamorphoses* as epic, and both approved of its expansive epic argument, romance-epic structure, and creation of wonder—all specifically anti-Aristotelian features and effects. The strength of the Italian critics' theory was that it wedded the rules of Aristotle with poetic and historical precedents unavailable to him. In current terminology, they combined a synchronic, or formalist approach (Aristotle's) with a diachronic, or historical perspective (the growth of literary and romance-epic).[16] The mer-

---

[14]E. D. Hirsch, Jr., *Validity in Interpretation* (New Haven, 1967), p. 108.

[15]Quintilian, *Institutio Oratoria* 10.1.85–96.

[16]Thomas L. Kent, in "The Classification of Genres," *Genre* 16 (1983), 1–20, describes such a combined synchronic and diachronic model of genre as "holistic."

its of such a hybrid or holistic approach have, I hope, already suggested themselves in this study. It was by seeing both the immediate and the overall effects of Ovidian figurations of Eve that we gained a balanced view of the Fall and of Eve's development. It was by regarding Satan in this double way that the dynamic, unsettling potential of his transformations—both on the historical problem of heroism and on the reader's immediate confrontation of the fallen angel—was realized. Because it is with Satan that we first enter the narrative of *Paradise Lost,* and with Adam and Eve that we retrace the Fall, our concept of these characters ought to be consistent with our concept of the narrative overall, that is, our understanding of *Paradise Lost* as epic.

If we reapply the method of Giraldi Cinthio and Tasso, having the added perspective provided by *Paradise Lost,* we ought to be in a better position to understand the epic than could any purely formalist or purely historical critic. In an essay entitled "The Life and Death of Literary Forms," Alastair Fowler sketches out such a holistic approach to genre, and thereby offers a model of epic that he terms "evolutionary."[17] Expanding upon C. M. Bowra's useful though potentially prejudicial distinction between primary (folk, oral) and secondary (literary, written) epic,[18] Fowler identifies three stages in the evolution of epic. The Homeric poems represent the primary stage, in which the epic first takes shape. The second stage, best represented by the *Aeneid,* describes the imitation of the original form and the adaptation of it to a new cultural setting. The final stage, in which Fowler includes both *The Faerie Queene* and *Paradise Lost,* marks a shift in modality and ethical content—from high seriousness to sporadic satire and comedy, from external to interiorized heroism—which signals the death of

---

Kent discusses the "ontological contradictions" inherent in the holistic theories of Barthes, Frye, and Lotman. By alternating between synchronic and diachronic views, however, Kent suggests that a holistic theory might work toward the unification of meaning and form. With Kent, I am willing to risk ontological contradictions toward that goal.

[17]Alastair Fowler, "The Life and Death of Literary Forms," in *New Directions in Literary History,* ed. Ralph Cohen (Baltimore, 1974), pp. 77–94. Fowler has expanded and defended his evolutionary model of epic in *Kinds of Literature: An Introduction to the Theory of Genres* (Cambridge, 1982), pp. 106–67.

[18]See Bowra, *From Virgil to Milton,* pp. 1–5.

the genre. Whether the genre has "died" or whether epics after Milton need reflect three stages are ancillary and, in light of Wordsworth's *Prelude*, Melville's *Moby Dick*, and Joyce's *Ulysses*, moot questions. What seems to me most useful about Fowler's scheme is its delineation of sequential, stylistic change without neglecting the palpable, formal features of epic.

Readers rightly perceive features repeated in a number of poems as belonging to "epic," yet behind these features lies a series of revaluations. Milton expects readers to recognize Satan, for example, as the hero of the classical epic, which *Paradise Lost* ultimately is not.[19] According to Scholes and Kellogg, Virgil "imitated all of what we might call the accidentals of Homer—many of which had been in Homer the result of the exigencies of oral formulaic composition (recurring epithets, 'epic' similes, and the rhetoric of oral poetry in general)."[20] The "essentials" of Homer are, by implication, inimitable; Homer's true successor cannot copy his style and themes slavishly, but must use them creatively to discover his own. What Virgil had established as conventions of epic Ovid largely imitates in his epic, but he adapts them to his own purposes. For example, Virgil's poignant epic simile, itself derived from Homer, for the shades of Roman youths who "thick as the leaves that with the early frost / of autumn drop and fall within the forest" (*Aen.* 6.309–10)[21] reappears as Ovid's epic simile for the destruction of Pentheus by the Bacchantes:

> non citius frondes autumni frigore tactas
> iamque male haerentes alta rapit arbore ventus,
> quam sunt membra viri manibus direpta nefandis.
>
> (3.729–31)

Not more quickly are leaves, touched by the first cold of autumn and now barely hanging, whirled from the high trees by the wind than is Pentheus torn limb from limb by those impious hands.

---

[19] Fowler, *Kinds of Literature*, p. 68.
[20] Robert Scholes and Robert Kellogg, *The Nature of Narrative* (New York, 1976), p. 70.
[21] *The "Aeneid" of Virgil: A Verse Translation*, trans. Allen Mandelbaum (New York, 1972).

The form of the comparison links Ovid's story with the matter of epic; the association of the dismembered parts of Pentheus with the scattered leaves adds horror to the pathos of Virgil's lines. Part of what Ovid foregrounds as constitutive of his new, transforming epic, Milton, in turn, imitates and transforms to reflect his values as a Christian poet. Thus Milton uses a similar epic simile to characterize the fallen angels "who lay intrans't / Thick as Autumnal Leaves that strow the Brooks / In *Vallombrosa*" (I, 301–3) as insensate, practically lifeless as a result of their expulsion from Heaven. The fury of the Bacchantes in Ovid's simile gives way to the fury of the Lord in *Paradise Lost,* because Milton's simile recalls not only the classical tradition but also the scriptural accents of Isaiah 34.2–4: "For the indignation of the Lord is upon all nations, and his fury upon all their armies . . . and all their host shall fall down, as the leaf falleth off from the vine." In this way the repetition of certain features of epic may be explained as a means of revitalizing the tradition by engrafting new themes and purposes.

From their opening lines both *Metamorphoses* and *Paradise Lost* announce their revaluations of previous epic and, implicitly, their authors' adaptations of the genre beyond previous models. Even while altering the theme of epic, Ovid's prologue establishes continuity with previous epics in both its dactylic hexameter verse, the standard meter for epic since Homer, and its invocation of divine assistance for what is undoubtedly a vast, serious undertaking:

> In nova fert animus mutatas dicere formas
> corpora: di, coeptis (nam vos mutastis et illas)
> adspirate meis primaque ab origine mundi
> ad mea perpetuum deducite tempora carmen.
>
> (1.1–4)

> My spirit desires to tell of forms changed into new bodies. You gods (for you have changed and those) inspire my beginnings and spin out my continuous song from the first origin of the world to my own times.

Though brief, Ovid's proem contains a number of subtle revaluations. Ovid immediately distinguishes the novelty of his epic subject: Sandys highlighted the change in theme by beginning his translation: "Of bodies chang'd to other shapes I sing."[22] As if revising Aristotle's *Poetics*, Ovid insists that his poem can be not only continuous ("perpetuum") but comprehensive as well, both in its broadened subject matter and inclusive time scheme. The universal scope of Ovid's epic argument, describing transformations of beautiful forms regardless of location and time, transcends the national scope of epics describing the fall of Troy or the founding of Rome. Finally, the three signs of the first person (my "animus"; my "carmen"; my "tempora") indicate that the means of unifying this diverse material is to be the ubiquitous presence of the narrator.

Although Ovid uses the meter and opening formula of classical epic, he inverts the expectations these patterns initially create. Whereas previous invocations of the Muses and gods in the *Iliad*, the *Odyssey*, Lucretius' *De Rerum Natura*, and the *Aeneid* represented the poet as a pious suppliant requesting the aid of higher powers, the invocation in Ovid's prologue depicts a speaker who is critical of higher powers. The placement of "et" in the narrator's invocation ("nam vos mutastis et illas," for you have changed and [changed] those) momentarily suggests that the gods themselves have changed, while it finally increases the emphatic, demonstrative force of "illas," those beautiful forms that the gods have actively changed. As the Olympian gods, especially Jupiter and Apollo, are responsible for a series of rapes, exploitations, and devastations of human beings throughout the poem, the invocation contains a subtle condemnation of the offending deities.[23] No less subversive than this pointed invocation is the stress, by extreme syntactic suspension, on "corpora" and "nova." "Corpora" (bodies) seems to glance playfully at Virgil's epic theme of "arms and the man"; taken seriously, this wordplay indicates the greater scope of Ovid's subject in comparison with a military, heroic one. The syntax of Ovid's lines raises doubt concerning the referent of "nova" underlining the newness of Ovid's poem, which literally begins: "Into the new . . . spirit desires. . . ."

---

[22]Sandys, *Ovid's "Metamorphosis" Englished, Mythologized, and Represented in Figures*, p. 25.
[23]See John Fyler, *Chaucer and Ovid* (New Haven, 1979), p. 4.

Milton's prologue emphasizes the newness of his poetic utterance and reveals its new epic subject in ways that continue and extend Ovid's inventive manner. At the same time that Milton asserts the novelty of his epic "while it pursues / Things unattempted yet in Prose or Rhime," he ironically recalls Ariosto's similar boast in *Orlando Furioso* to treat "Cosa non detta mai in prose ne in rima" (Things undone in either prose or rhyme).[24] The originality Milton claims for *Paradise Lost* is thus overtly dependent on the standards of the epic tradition. Like Ovid's "changed bodies," Milton's announced subject both reflects and replaces previous epic subjects. "Of Mans First Disobedience" echoes the line of poems treating "man" in their announcement of subject, as in the *Odyssey:* "Tell me, Muse, of the man of many ways."[25] Instead of choosing a man with a specific national heritage, Milton chooses Adam, a man with mythic, universal significance in the Judeo-Christian tradition. When we recall that Milton long planned to write an epic about King Arthur, "Begirt with *British* and *Armoric* Knights" (I, 581), we see more clearly the deliberate shift from a national hero to a mythic representative of humanity. John Steadman astutely argues that Milton "introduced a significant variant by basing his proposition on the Pauline distinction between two men—two Adams— the 'earthy' and the heavenly—whose disobedience and obedience had brought condemnation and salvation to mankind."[26] Milton's exordium brings about human and divine contact without impugning the motives of the gods, as had Ovid, for the justification of God's ways to men requires us to reserve judgment until human, angelic, and divine motives appear clearly in the poem. When Milton twice echoes the parenthetical remark in Ovid's proem— "for Thou know'st; Thou from the first / Wast present" (19–20), and "for Heav'n hides nothing from thy view" (27)—he modulates Ovid's implicit reproach toward the gods into absolute confidence and esteem. Milton, no less than Ovid, claims for his epic the comprehensive temporal scope of a *perpetuum carmen*, beginning "from

---

[24]See the Hughes *Milton*, pp. 212 and 379. For the development of this topos in the epic tradition see Curtius, *European Literature in the Latin Middle Ages*, pp. 85–86.

[25]*The Odyssey of Homer*, trans. with intro. Richmond Lattimore (New York, 1965), p. 27.

[26]John M. Steadman, *Milton and the Renaissance Hero* (Oxford, 1967), pp. 190–91.

the first." By singing of "all *our* woe" (my emphasis), moreover, Milton extends the time frame and scope of his epic to include each generation of new readers of *Paradise Lost*. In these small but significant ways, Milton's dialectical imitation of Ovid allows the pagan poet's claims of novelty and universality to be heard even as Milton transvalues these notions in his Christian theodicy.

In the *Metamorphoses*, further, Milton could have found a clear precedent for his rejection of a martial subject: "Warrs, hitherto the onely Argument / Heroic deem'd" (IX, 28–29).[27] Milton's verse may contain a Janus-like reflection on his own poem. Judging from the demonic councils and the War in Heaven, the reader may have "deem'd" that up to this point ("hitherto") warfare constitutes heroism in *Paradise Lost*. If any readers still think so, Milton gently instructs them to change their minds. What the Miltonic narrator proclaims to be "more heroic" argument than a story of battles becomes explicit in Book IX, when he changes the notes of his song to tragic:

> foul distrust, and breach
> Disloyal on the part of Man, revolt,
> And disobedience: On the part of Heav'n
> Now alienated, distance and distaste,
> Anger and just rebuke, and judgement giv'n.
> (IX, 6–10)

The parallel units of syntax and the heavy alliteration and consonance of these tragic parts of his argument stress the interdepen-

---

[27]Milton's attitudes toward war are the focus of a number of recent critical discussions, most notably James A. Freeman's *Milton and the Martial Muse* (Princeton, N.J., 1980); Michael Lieb's *Poetics of the Holy: A Reading of "Paradise Lost"* (Chapel Hill, N.C., 1981); and Stella P. Revard's *The War in Heaven: "Paradise Lost" and the Tradition of Satan's Rebellion* (Ithaca, N.Y., 1980). Lieb grants that Milton valued peace as highly as anyone in the Renaissance, but Lieb's primary concern is to document Milton's interest in the theory and practice of just warfare. Revard brilliantly documents the traditions of warfare bearing on *Paradise Lost;* her study concludes with a discussion of Satan's vain attempt to achieve godhead by force (pp. 264–74), which is compatible with my reading. My own view is closest to Freeman's contention that "while Milton habitually mistrusted war, the widespread belief in its efficacy prompted him to . . . evolve a subtle, learned, and progressive argument against it" (p. 61).

dence of "man" and Heaven. Milton finds the burden of singing this epic a "sad task," nevertheless his argument also enables him to sing of "Patience and Heroic Martyrdom" and other virtues that the descendants of Adam and Eve are to depend on until the joyous arrival of the promised Savior. These interiorized virtues boldly contrast with the external shows of force and emotion in classical epic, as Milton describes it: "the wrauth / Of stern *Achilles*," "the rage / Of *Turnus*" and the "ire" of Neptune or Juno. The panorama of *amor, pathos,* and *furor* that the *Metamorphoses* presents is, likewise, far from the martial heroism of Homer, but Ovid does not abandon "heroism." Rather, his depiction of mythic conflicts of human beings with the gods, with other human beings, and with themselves places "heroism" in a broad psychological context, and diffuses it among many representative figures. Many of the values that the *Metamorphoses* affirms—the piety of Baucis and Philemon, the obedience of Deucalion and Pyrrha, the fidelity of Ceyx and Alcyone, the service of Aesculapius—are precisely the values that Milton affirms as truly heroic in his Christian epic.

Though neither the *Metamorphoses* nor *Paradise Lost* would have satisfied Aristotle's expectations for "heroic" argument, both continue and develop "epic" poetry. That an epic poem may exist without a martial, heroic argument or protagonist is an important suggestion about epic offered by E. M. W. Tillyard, who derives the distinction from *The Divine Comedy*, which, he argues, is epic without being heroic.[28] As Steadman points out, the epic design of *Paradise Lost* is singular precisely because of its "startling ethical contrast" between traditional heroic values and the Christian values it advances.[29] To put the case more strongly, as John Shawcross has done, Milton mentions no hero for *Paradise Lost,* and the achievements in the poem frequently cited as "heroic" are the tragic revolt and disobedience of humanity, the corruption and uncreation of Satan, and the inimitable love and self-sacrifice of the Son.[30] These achievements fall far short of heroism on the one side, and rise far above it on the other. Without minimizing the attractiveness of the Miltonic characters, Shawcross urges that if we read the poem as

[28]E. M. W. Tillyard, *The English Epic and its Background* (London, 1954), p. 120.
[29]Steadman, *Epic and Tragic Structure,* p. v.
[30]Shawcross, pp. 92–96.

epic, the characters most fully embody ways of thinking and of exercising the will, ways among which the reader can choose. Through anthropomorphic representations of varieties of interiorized, mental heroism, therefore, Milton advances and revitalizes epic.

Taken together, Shawcross's sense of the anthropomorphic, internalized heroism of Milton's epic and Steadman's sense of the "contrast" between the values of Milton's epic and those of the tradition suggest that some sense of opposition or contrast is fundamental to the revalued genre of *Paradise Lost*. Appropriate critical terminology for this kind of poem already exists, though in a different context, in Northrop Frye's *Anatomy of Criticism*. Frye describes a certain species of epic as "the contrast-epic, where one pole is the ironic human situation and the other the origin or continuation of a divine society."[31] Frye offers two examples of contrast-epic: "The collections of myth made by Hesiod and Ovid are based on the same form: here the poet himself, a victim of injustice or exile, has a prominent place at the human pole." To make Ovid an exile before he had written the *Metamorphoses*, as Frye does, may be an attempt to make the example fit the category, which rather awkwardly conflates two poets of radically differing styles. At the same time, Frye fails to include in the category Milton, a victim of both blindness and virtual political exile, who retains a prominent place at the human pole of his epic. Like the *Metamorphoses*, *Paradise Lost* is an epic of contrast not only in its narrative structure but especially in its radical confrontation of a divine society with fallen human agents. The emphasis at one pole of con-

---

[31]Northrop Frye, *Anatomy of Criticism: Four Essays* (Princeton, N.J., 1973), p. 317. Without employing Frye's term of "contrast-epic," recent commentators on the *Metamorphoses* have drawn attention to the inventive and irreverent stance the poet takes toward classical epic. Walther Ludwig, in *Struktur und Einheit der Metamorphosen Ovids* (Berlin, 1965), pp. 75–78, discusses Ovid's conflation of historical and mythic time frames toward a more inclusive kind of epic. In "The Style of the *Metamorphoses*," in *Ovid*, ed. J. W. Binns (London, 1973), pp. 116–19, E. J. Kenney surveys a variety of suggested generic labels for the poem, including "anti-epic" (Coleman), "un-epic" (Otis), "epic of love" (Otis), "epic of rage" (Segal), and his own "epic of pathos." In *Changing Forms: Studies in the "Metamorphoses" of Ovid* (Copenhagen, 1974), pp. 120–22, Otto Steen Due approaches the generic question through a close reading of Book I and concludes that "the *Metamorphoses* have not only epic pretentions but the highest possible; they are universal, a *Weltgedicht*."

trast-epic on the "continuation" of a divine society exchanges some of the achieved order and conclusiveness of classical epic for greater processiveness. Ovid's "perpetuum carmen" stands not as the definitive epic of the founding of Rome, but as the ongoing song of Roman myth, legend, and history; and *Paradise Lost* ends not with a discrete conclusion of the Fall story but with a tentative new beginning: the first steps of Adam and Eve into an uncertain, fallen world. At the other pole of contrast-epic, the ironic human situation must be represented by narrators who, by moving their stories from their worlds' origins to open-ended conclusions, themselves absorb and reflect some of the great changes their arguments entail. What of Ovid's depiction of change was appropriate to Milton's theodicy, and how Milton adapted Ovid's narrative voice, structural techniques, and imaginative history to his Christian contrast-epic are the subjects of the next three sections.

"With mortal voice": Ovidian and Miltonic Narrators

Since Michael von Albrecht's analysis of Ovid's parenthetical remarks in the *Metamorphoses*, a number of scholars have argued that the unity of the poem inheres in the pervasive presence of the narrator.[32] In the epics of Homer and Virgil the narrator keeps the story in the foreground and only rarely interrupts the narrative to offer commentary. The narrator of the *Metamorphoses*, however, repeatedly interrupts the direct telling of a story to accomplish one of three goals: to call attention to the sources and hence the reliability of certain episodes; to comment on the action and theme; or to respond to the characters. These functions of the Ovidian narrator enable the poet to guide the reader toward his view of the material; because of the overtness of the narrator, they also enable the reader to evaluate the speaker's interpretation. That Ovid's narrative method, with its emphasis on individual interpretation of stories and myths sacred to his age, should have led many critics to attack his poem as subversive or its author as self-centered is not surprising. Nor should it be surprising that English Protestant poets such as Spenser and Milton, who prized both the skepticism toward

---

[32]See Martz, *Poet of Exile*, pp. 331, nos. 7 and 8, and Charles Segal, "Narrative Art in the *Metamorphoses*," *CJ* 66 (1971), 331–37.

received authority and the individual interpretation that Ovid's method encourages, took up and extended the technique.

For Milton, an intrusive narrator provided an ideal medium for his dialogue with Ovid, a way of imitating his work overtly and of allowing Ovid tacitly to speak through him. Beyond making the narrative more vivid because of the intrusion of personality, this form of the dialectical imitation stresses the urgency of Milton's appeal. The strategy allows Milton to guide the reader's understanding of the poem at the risk of making the poet *seem* to be the ultimate, self-styled authority. In fact, Milton humbly exposes his own poetry and his self-representation to correction from its divine source, while he distinguishes his dependent authority from poets such as Ovid and Satan who assert rhetorical self-generation. Although there are considerably fewer narrative intrusions in *Paradise Lost* (approximately 54 versus 179), Milton sustains his comments longer, on the average, than had Ovid.[33] Further, whereas Ovid's intrusions tend generally toward effervescence, Milton's tend increasingly toward lamentation, as he voices the extent of loss from the Fall to his day. Milton's additions to and limitations of Ovid's narrative voice take us far toward understanding the narrative methods of *Paradise Lost,* as well as toward seeing its significance as a fiercely individualistic poem.

Both the Ovidian and the Miltonic narrators question the sources of their material early in their works, and so begin to establish their own authority. The interpolations of Ovid's narrator are individually brief, but cumulatively they distinguish dubious stories and speakers from those having Ovid's sanction. Typical of Ovid's technique is the sequence of qualifications of the sources in the Lycaon episode. Containing the first metamorphosis of a human being in the *Metamorphoses,* this passage sets the mood for the rest of the poem. The sequence begins with an account of the impious aspirations of the giants in the Iron Age:

> Neve foret terris securior arduus aether,
> adfectasse ferunt regnum caeleste Gigantas
> altaque congestos struxisse ad sidera montes.

[33]On the intrusions of Ovid's narrator see Michael von Albrecht, *Die Parenthese in Ovids "Metamorphosen" und ihre dichterische Funktion* (Hildesheim, 1964), p. 54. See also Albrecht's Table of Parentheses, pp. 29–35.

tum pater omnipotens misso perfregit Olympum
fulmine et excussit subiectae Pelion Ossae.

(1.151–55)

High heaven was no safer than the earth, for they say that the Giants
aspired to the very throne of heaven and piled huge mountains, one
on another, clear up to the stars. Then the Almighty Father hurled
his thunderbolts and dashed Pelion down from shattered Ossa.

Readers of *Paradise Lost* may recall a remarkably similar account of
dashed aspiration early in Milton's epic:

> He trusted to have equal'd the most High,
> If he oppos'd; and with ambitious aim
> Against the Throne and Monarchy of God
> Rais'd impious War in Heav'n and Battel proud
> With vain attempt. Him the Almighty Power
> Hurld headlong flaming from th'Ethereal Skie
> With hideous ruine and combustion down
> To bottomless perdition, there to dwell
> In Adamantine Chains and penal Fire,
> Who durst defie th'Omnipotent to Arms.

(I, 40–49)

Having invoked the heavenly Muse before this description, the
Miltonic narrator reports these remote events with full confidence
in their veracity. But because the Muse's truth must be mediated to
his audience, Milton draws upon a variety of analogues from various discursive accounts, including those of Isaiah, Luke, Homer,
Aeschylus, as well as Ovid. It is precisely Milton's manner of blend-
ing these materials, of calling on the poetic resources of these texts,
that makes his account an individual interpretation of divine truth
and, simultaneously, an original poetic utterance.

A crucial difference between these passages, however, is the seed
of doubt Ovid plants in his narration through the single qualifier,
"ferunt" (they say). This might simply be taken as a concession that
the narrated event could not have been witnessed, yet Ovid repeats
the reminder and so begins to undermine the reader's trust in the
account:

obruta mole sua cum corpora dira iacerent,
perfusam multo natorum sanguine Terram
inmaduisse ferunt calidumque animasse cruorem
et, ne nulla suae stirpis monimenta manerent,
in faciem vertisse hominum. sed et illa propago
contemptrix superum saevaeque avidissima caedis
et violenta fuit: scires e sanguine natos.

(1.156–62)

When those dread bodies lay overwhelmed by their own bulk, they say that Mother Earth, drenched with their streaming blood, brought that warm gore to life again, and, lest no trace of her former offspring remain, she gave it human form. But this new stock, too, was contemptuous of the gods, rapacious for slaughter, and violent. You might know that they were sons of blood.

There is no alternate vision or witness of the event to contradict the narrator, so the story stands, if somewhat dubiously. The witty comment that rounds off the passage makes the narrator's reflexive approval of the account the main reason to accept it.

Even when Ovid accepts the source of an episode, he typically qualifies his approval by expressing doubts that a sensible reader might raise concerning the story. For example, at the critical moment in the Deucalion and Pyrrha episode, the regeneration of humanity from stones in the earth, Ovid questions the very metamorphosis he is in the midst of confirming:

saxa (quis hoc credat, nisi sit pro teste vetustas?)
ponere duritiem coepere suumque rigorem
mollirique mora mollitaque ducere formam.

(1.400–2)

And the stones (who would believe it, unless posterity vouched for it?) began at once to lose their hardness and stiffness and to grow soft slowly and, softened, to assume a form.

The best reason for trusting the myth becomes, in Ovid's subsequent summation, "the hardness of our race and our endurance for toil" (1.414). That is, human nature as Ovid sees it confirms the etiological validity of the myth, and not vice versa. As in the previous example, Ovid's question partly causes us to believe in the myth because of the way human beings behave, but partly causes us to take the myth somewhat skeptically because the narrator does. Whether humorously or judgmentally, the narrator is arguing for the principle of individual interpretation of myth. Milton relies on this principle whenever he compares pagan sources with the biblical version of his material, as in his ricocheting description of the golden fruit in Eden: "*Hesperian* Fables true, / If true, here only" (IV, 250–51). Eden verifies and subsumes, but does not destroy, the fables concerning a primitive human paradise. A critical difference here from Ovid's use of such source material is the way the Miltonic narrator, confident that his biblical fable is superior to all others, foregrounds the confluence of pagan and Christian matter and abstains from additional subjective speculation.

Ovid's method of questioning sources and converting legend to persuasive poetry informs Milton's sublime rendering of the fall of Mulciber:

> Men call'd him *Mulciber;* and how he fell
> From Heav'n, they fabl'd, thrown by angry *Jove*
> Sheer o're the Chrystal Battlements; from Morn
> To Noon he fell, from Noon to dewy Eve,
> A Summers day; and with the setting Sun
> Dropt from the Zenith like a falling Star,
> On *Lemnos* th'*Aegaean* Ile.
>
> (I, 740–46)

What Ovid had effected by "ferunt," Milton achieves by "they fabl'd," at once citing the genre of the account (a fable) and indicting its veracity (they fabled = told lies). Yet the Miltonic narrator takes a further step: he rejects the magnificent poetic account he has just given because it contradicts what for him is the supreme authority of scripture:

> thus they relate,
> Erring; for he with this rebellious rout
> Fell long before.
>
> (746–47)

The temporal primacy of the revolt in Heaven as told in Rev. 12.3–9 supports its authoritative primacy. Milton repeats this insistence on the temporal priority and hence greater veracity of Adam and Eve over Deucalion and Pyrrha in Book XI, 10–11. Ovid's narrator frequently punctuates his stories to insist on the proper temporal order of his sources, but as John Fyler points out the apparent motive of avoiding anachronism is usually disingenuous.[34] For example, the parenthetical remark on Jupiter's punishment of Lycaon—"a story still unknown because the deed was new" (1.164)—treats the legend as little told primarily to highlight his rendition, which immediately follows. Milton makes a similar use of temporal order whenever he overtly plays off the time of his narrative, or Edenic time, with his historical moment. For instance, in the epic catalog of warrior-angels, he calls the fallen angels by the names that "heathen nations" gave them centuries later (I, 364–505). Again, when Satan enters the Paradise of Fools he is, in Edenic time, alone, but the Miltonic narrator tells us that the place shall be occupied by pilgrims and Catholic monks by his time (III, 440–97). Milton thus replaces the Catholic notion of Limbo, in which the souls of infants and persons lacking the capacity for moral judgment were said to dwell, with an imaginative counterpart in which those who espoused this doctrine become the mentally deficient residents.

The prominence of both narrators in discriminating among sources suggests a congruence of narrative technique. The motives for authorial intrusiveness, however, reveal profound differences in the stances the poets take toward their poems: for Ovid, a playful tour de force sanctioned by his own creative energy; for Milton, an exacting argument, requiring his particular and extensive imagination, but sanctioned by the heavenly Muse who "brings it nightly to [his] ear." Although Ovid's voice moves away from his poetic heritage, the implicit parallels between Milton and biblical *vates,* or prophets (I, 8–10; IV, 1–5) and the explicit verses of scripture reproduced in *Paradise Lost* unite the voice of Milton with his ultimate originals and sources.

When Ovid interrupts the *Metamorphoses* to comment on the ac-

[34]Fyler, p. 4.

tion, the comments have less to do with certifying the poet's authority than with aligning the narrator's values with those of the imag-
ined reader. Put simply, these comments are essentially rhetorical,
for they attempt to persuade the reader that the narrator's evaluations of episodes are trustworthy. Such comments are particularly
prevalent in scenes involving the themes of *amor* and *pathos*, in
whose interaction some readers have seen a new kind of epic unity
in the *Metamorphoses*.[35] One example from each of these categories
must stand for many. During the unfolding of the *amor* of Pyramus
and Thisbe, the narrator interrupts the description of the "chink"
in the wall, which Shakespeare immortalized in *A Midsummer Night's
Dream,* with a brief rhetorical question:

> fissus erat tenui rima, quam duxerat olim,
> cum fieret, paries domui communis utrique;
> id vitium nulli per saecula longa notatum
> (quid non sentit amor?) primi vidistis amantes.
>
> (4.65–68)

> There was a narrow chink in the common wall of the two houses,
> which had been made when the wall was built. This chink, which no
> one had discovered for many years—but what does love not notice?—
> you lovers first saw.

Like many rhetorical questions, Ovid's is double-edged. At first,
the lovers see with such resolution and particularity that they discover the previously undetected chink, but at their appointed
meeting Pyramus's impetuous misapprehension of Thisbe's blood-
soaked cloak leads to their mutual suicides. The rhetorical question
makes only a momentary suggestion: Ovid's touch is far lighter
here than in, for example, his didactic *Ars Amatoria.* Yet it remains a
masterful and resonating phrase, both within this episode and in
other tales of love in the poem.[36]

The commentary of the Miltonic narrator on the love of Adam

<hr/>

[35]See Martz, *Poet of Exile,* p. 307, and Otis, pp. 84–85.
[36]Cf. the narrator's comment on the search of Cadmus for Europa: "For who can
comprehend the secret loves of Jove?" (3.6–7).

and Eve before the Fall also centers around a resonant rhetorical question that redirects Ovid's certainty on the ways of love:

> Our Maker bids increase, who bids abstain
> But our destroyer, foe to God and Man?
> (IV, 748–49)

Despite the similar knowing tone and sententiousness of both questions, Milton's excludes the ambiguity central to Ovid's phrase. The question approximates the form of a loose neoclassical couplet, complete with slant rhyme, which syntactically balances the favorable "increase" against "abstain," "Maker" against "destroyer." Beyond the couplet, Milton in his authorial voice gathers and extends the Ovidian remarks on love into a full discussion of married love in the Garden. The discussion is overtly rhetorical: Milton takes a clear doctrinal stand on prelapsarian sex and employs various means to lead us to share his view. The excursus begins by contrasting the cumbersome clothing of fallen man with the nakedness of Adam and Eve, continues by discrediting those "hypocrites" who deny the purity of prelapsarian sex, and culminates by celebrating love in a brief epithalamion, which relocates Ovid's imagery of Cupid's golden arrows (*Met.* 1.468–71) in the Edenic Bower (IV, 763). The whole interpretation is Ovidian, yet it is far longer than any interpolation in the *Metamorphoses*. The greater duration of Milton's comments extends the range and depth of Ovid's mercurial voice in order to represent the greater joy and sorrow in his response to the story of the Fall.

An example of Ovidian *pathos* echoed by Milton appears in the episode of Theseus and Aegeus. After rescuing his son Theseus from Medea's attempt to poison him, Aegeus joyfully plans a marvelous banquet. The Ovidian narrator, however, quickly deflates this mood of gladness with a sweeping comment on the passing of all joys:

> Nec tamen (usque adeo nulla est sincera voluptas,
> sollicitumque aliquid laetis intervenit) Aegeus
> gaudia percepit nato secura recepto.
> (7.453–55)

And yet (so true it is that there is no pleasure unmixed, and some care always comes amid our joys) Aegeus' rejoicing over his son's return was mingled with care.

Ovid's comment holds true both as an instance of narrative prolepsis within the story and as a principle of Stoic philosophy that the degeneration of human possibility in the *Metamorphoses* overall reflects. The Miltonic narrator interposes similar prolepses during his description of Paradise, most memorably in the invocation to Book IX:

> No more of talk where God or Angel Guest
> With Man, as with his Friend, familiar us'd
> To sit indulgent, and with him partake
> Rural repast, permitting him the while
> Venial discourse unblam'd: I now must change
> Those Notes to Tragic; foul distrust, and breach
> Disloyal on the part of Man, revolt,
> And disobedience.
>
> (IX, 1–8)

This transition balances the pleasant "repast" Raphael had earlier taken in the Garden with a reminder of the "Tragic," specifically politically tragic, events to come. As in the Ovidian example, a scene of gracious feasting is followed by a foreboding of disaster. As in the Ovidian example, the language of pleasure ("indulgent," "familiar," "Venial") stands close to the language of loss.

Ovid's expansion of the narrator's role in the *Metamorphoses* involves a third new function: sympathetic response to characters through direct address. Unlike Virgil, whose involvement with his epic characters, however close to their thoughts and motivations, rarely erupts in personal responses to them in his narrative voice, Ovid frequently interrupts episodes to address characters directly. Gordon Williams observes that in the *Aeneid* Virgil makes only two apostrophes to his characters: one after the deaths of Nisus and Euryalus (9.446–49), and the other before the death of Lausus (10.791–93).[37] Ovid, on the other hand, uses the apostrophe for a

---

[37]Gordon Williams, *Change and Decline: Roman Literature in the Early Empire* (Berkeley, Calif., 1978), pp. 232–33.

wide range of effects including humor and pathos. The frequent apostrophes not only add to the affective power of the poem, but also juxtapose the poet's time and place with that of his characters, and thereby induce a strange sense of incongruity between the historical setting of the speaker and the fictional world of the poem. A primary reason for Milton's imitation of Ovid's technique is the Christian poet's awareness of the many incongruities between the superior world of Eden and his own fallen condition. Like Ovid, Milton speaks to characters with whom he is closely involved, yet from whom he is forever cut off. This technique is also appropriate to the mannerist style that students of art history have seen in both Ovid's and Milton's poetry.[38] In the *Metamorphoses* Ovid uses the technique mainly for momentary effects; in *Paradise Lost* it will become an instrument enabling Milton to unite his persona with scriptural characters and events in the reader's mind. Rather than build in a mechanism to represent the process of authorial response within the action of the epic, as Dante does in the *Commedia*, Ovid and Milton choose to depict their responses to epic characters selectively and sporadically.[39] Sporadically is not randomly: The patterns of authorial response in the *Metamorphoses* and *Paradise Lost* have far-reaching implications for both poems.

Ovid directly addresses, in turn, the gods (1.2), Augustus (1.204), Python (1.438–40), Narcissus (3.432–36), Medea (7.144–46), Cyparissus and Ivy in his often imitated catalog of trees (10.99–105), Polyxena (13.483–85), and, in the prayer for the apotheosis of Augustus, the gods again (15.861). The bracketing addresses to the gods and the emperor Augustus point to the transmission of theology into history that occurs more fully within the *Metamorphoses*, especially in Book 1 and Books 12–15. Because within these brackets five of the six figures (excluding only Polyxena) reappear in *Paradise Lost*, as this and other studies have shown,[40]

---

[38]On mannerism and Ovid see Erich Burck, *Vom römischen Manierismus* (Darmstadt, 1971), pp. 20–24. On mannerism and Milton see Roy Daniells, *Milton, Mannerism and Baroque* (Toronto, 1963), and Murray Roston, *Milton and the Baroque*, pp. 13–14.

[39]Along with Dante's depiction of authorial response, his extensive addresses to the reader differentiate his narrative presence from both Ovid's and Milton's. See Erich Auerbach, "Dante's Addresses to the Reader," in *Parnassus Revisited: Modern Critical Essays on the Epic Tradition*, ed. Anthony C. Yu (Chicago, 1973), pp. 121–31.

[40] Davis Harding, in *Milton and the Renaissance Ovid*, pp. 67–84, discusses Milton's

Ovid's method of addressing them deserves close comparison with Milton's.

What provokes Ovid to speak to his characters is invariably a mixture of empathetic regard for and harsh judgment of their plights, as seen from his superior perspective. Ovid's response to Narcissus contains the most empathy, that to Medea the harshest judgment. Golding begins his translation of the Narcissus episode: "Thou fondling thou, why doest thou raught the fickle image so?" Before ominously warning Narcissus, Ovid's verses begin tenderly:

> credule, quid frustra simulacra fugacia captas?
> quod petis, est nusquam; quod amas, avertere, perdes.
> ista repercussae, quam cernis, imaginis umbra est:
> nil habet ista sui: tecum venitque manetque,
> tecum discedet, si tu discedere possis.
>
> (3.432–36)

Silly youth, why vainly seek to capture the fleeting image? What you seek is nowhere; turn, and you lose what you love. What you see is the shadow of a reflection: it has no substance of its own. With you it comes, with you it stays, with you it goes—if you can go.

The repeated negative particles pick up the negative formulation of Tiresias's prophecy, with which Ovid had begun the episode, that Narcissus would live long "si se non noverit" (if he not know himself). Both the accretion of negatives and the combination of protectiveness and prophecy in Ovid's address inform Milton's apostrophe to Adam and Eve, asleep in their Bower before the temptation:

> Sleep on
> Blest pair; and O yet happiest if ye seek
> No happier state, and know to know no more.
>
> (IV, 773–75)

---

use of Ovid's "gods" for God the Father. Martz, *Poet of Exile*, pp. 224–26, analyzes Ovid's catalog of trees as a model for Milton's geographical and angelic catalogs. The connections between Eve and both Narcissus and Medea were discussed in Chapter 2; the association of Python with Satan, in Chapter 3.

Milton's narrative voice goes beyond the Ovidian repetitions in his inventive fourfold repetition of the morpheme "nō," while his initial command gives way to a kind of lament.

Lamentation, though infrequent in the *Metamorphoses*, becomes the dominant response of the narrator to characters as *Paradise Lost* progresses. At the pivotal moment of Eve's departure from Adam on the morning of the temptation, the narrator bursts forth with a remarkably specific expression of grief:

> O much deceav'd, much failing, hapless *Eve,*
> Of thy presum'd return! event perverse!
> Thou never from that houre in Paradise
> Foundst either sweet repast, or sound repose.
>
> (IX, 404–7)

Specifically, the narrator bewails Eve's presumption that she will return to Adam unharmed; she is "deceav'd" and "hapless" in that presumption only. The "event perverse" is left unspecified. To an alert reader, however, it might recall the narrator's earlier lament that Eve was "O too like" Pandora "in sad event" (IV, 715–16). Thus, apparently scattered narrative comments may combine to heighten the audience's awareness, and to register the narrator's regret, concerning the impending Fall. After the tragic events of Book IX, the narrator continues to lament the indirect results of the Fall, most memorably in his response to the destruction of humanity by flood, which Adam glimpses in his vision of history:

> How didst thou grieve then, *Adam,* to behold
> The end of all thy Ofspring, end so sad,
> Depopulation; thee another Floud,
> Of tears and sorrow a Floud thee also drown'd,
> And sunk thee as thy Sons.
>
> (XI, 754–58)

Milton begins his lament by focusing on and sympathizing with Adam in his grief. Almost without warning, the lament ends with Adam's "Sons," who include not only men in Milton's generation but all of humanity. The more immediate connector of the generations in the passage, however, is the "Floud" linking Adam and

Noah, but even here Milton's mimetic syntax suggests that the flood of tears continues beyond the Old Testament figures.

Previously we examined Milton's use of Ovid's Medea in characterizing Eve. That analogue was used to focus the reader's response to Eve's wavering personality during the Fall, and was used implicitly. Ovid's mannered address to Medea also enters *Paradise Lost* implicitly, and again the effect is to sharpen our understanding, and ultimately our judgment, of one of Milton's characters. In this case the dialogue with Ovid takes a curious turn, for Milton aligns the commentary of the Ovidian narrator on Medea with that of Satan on Adam and Eve. Ovid's passage presents an ironic lament for Medea's plight:

> tu quoque victorem conplecti, barbara, velles;
> sed te, ne faceres, tenuit reverentia famae:
> obstitit incepto pudor. at conplexa fuisses.
>
> (7.144–46)

> You also, barbarian maid, would gladly have embraced the victor;
> your modesty stood in the way. Still you would have embraced him;
> but respect for common talk held you back.

In much the same way, Satan recoils from empathy for Adam and Eve, creatures as foreign to him, in Milton's representation, as Medea was to Jason. Satan predicts a metamorphic regression for our first parents which will simultaneously advance his falsely epic designs:

> Ah gentle pair, yee little think how nigh
> Your change approaches, when all these delights
> Will vanish and deliver ye to woe,
> More woe, the more your taste is now of joy.
>
> (IV, 366–69)

After Satan speaks, however, the Miltonic narrator immediately exposes Satan's ironic lamentation as a self-serving excuse: "So spake the Fiend, and with necessitie, / The Tyrants plea, excus'd his devilish deeds" (IV, 393–94). Throughout *Paradise Lost,* the speaker refrains from responding directly to Satan—as he does to the Spirit, light, God, the Muse, and Adam and Eve. Such reticence vitiates the reading that finds Milton "of the Devil's party without knowing it." Milton's responses to his characters are without exception deliberate, focused, and distinctive. They are, moreover, consistent in a way that Ovid's, exploiting individual opportunities for wry humor, wistfulness, or satire, are not. Milton's personal sympathies and aspirations in *Paradise Lost* emerge most clearly in the proems to Books I, III, VII, and IX, whose length and intensity are unprecedented in epic, and in the depiction of human history in Books XI and XII, which has Ovidian precedent.

Mingling Inventions: Ovidian Transitions, Multivocality, and Alternation

Critical readers of the *Metamorphoses* have repeatedly drawn attention to its innovations in narrative structure, especially its distinctive transitions and its anachronistic, imbedded narrators. Ovid's contemporary Quintilian treats the poet's use of transitions as a device brought to poetry from Roman rhetoric, and he finds Ovid's practice exceptional yet excusable: "Ovid is given to this form of affectation in his *Metamorphoses,* but there is some excuse for him owing to the fact that he is compelled to weld together [*colligentem*] subjects of the most diverse nature so as to form a continuous whole."[41] Although Quintilian does not specify how the technical innovation of "affected" or mannered transitions unites the *Metamorphoses,* a look at the operation of the first major transition in the poem supports his view. Ovid connects the Pythian games to the myth of Apollo and Daphne with a transition as light and sinuous as the ornamental wreath that captures his eye:

> hic iuvenum quicumque manu pedibusque rotave
> vicerat, aesculeae capiebat frondis honorem;
> nondum laurus erat, longoque decentia crine
> tempora cingebat de qualibet arbore Phoebus.
>
> (1.448–51)

---

[41]Quintilian, *Institutio Oratoria* 4.1.77.

At these games, every youth who had been victorious in boxing, running, or the chariot race received the honor of an oaken garland. For as yet there was no laurel, and Phoebus used to wreathe his temples, handsome with flowing locks, with a garland from any tree.

The mention of laurel suffices to introduce the tale of the timely metamorphosis of Daphne, which immediately follows. Laurel appears again as a literal garland at the end of the Daphne story, when Apollo prophesies that it shall adorn Roman victors in the days of Augustus (1.558–65). Thus an apparently extrinsic device links historical, mythic, and political subjects.

The unity of Milton's subject matter decreases the need for such ingenious transitions in *Paradise Lost*, but subtle transitions reminiscent of Ovid's nevertheless strengthen interconnections between the parts of its massive argument. The recurrent depictions of the hands of Adam and Eve, for example, at first glance merely decorative, epitomize the evolving relationship of our first "grand parents." They first appear walking through Eden "hand in hand" (IV, 321), an emblem of their unity and harmony. Eve then recounts to Adam her version of their first meeting and, by mentioning that Adam's "gentle hand" seized hers (IV, 488–89), shows how her beauty and his manly grace were joined. Adam and Eve continue "handed" even when they go to sleep (IV, 739), and Adam's first gesture to Eve next morning, "her hand first touching" (V, 17), indicates his sensitive response to the disquieting influence of the dream Satan had induced in her. "Domestic" Adam quickly dispels that disturbance, but when Eve departs from Adam on "that fateful morning," the withdrawal of her hand from Adam's (IX, 385–86) highlights her isolation and vulnerability. Thereafter, a sequence of "hand" images summarizes the degeneration of their relationship: from "her rash hand" (IX, 780) that plucks the forbidden fruit; through "his slack hand" (IX, 892) that reflects his horror at Eve's fall; to her hand that Adam, now "lascivious" rather than "gentle," seizes (IX, 1037–39). Finally, hands figure in the transition from the Fall to the start of regeneration, most significantly when "hand in hand with wandring steps and slow" a fallen but amended and reunited Adam and Eve depart from Paradise.

The frequent appearances and thematic implications of "hands" in *Paradise Lost* suggest that Milton may have developed this technique from the *Metamorphoses,* where hands (*palmas*) and arms (*bracchia*) not only appear with extraordinary frequency,[42] but also serve a special purpose. The lifting of arms to heaven is the recurrent image for supplication in the *Metamorphoses,* which typically precedes the suppliant's (or another's) transformation into a new form. All of the following lift their arms in prayer or supplication: Io (1.635–36); Callisto (2.477); Corone (2.580); Pentheus (3.723); Cadmus (4.581); Echemon (5.176); Phineus (5.215); Ilioneus (6.262); Latona (6.368); Philomela (6.533); Medea (7.188); Plexippus and Toxeus (8.432); Hercules (9.175); Alcmena (9.293); Midas (11.131); Lemnos (13.411); and Iphis (14.734). All their prayers are answered, though in a variety of ways—beneficently, ironically, literally, tragically—by ensuing metamorphoses. Milton adopts precisely this Ovidian formula in *Paradise Lost* during Adam's vision of Noah, who

> with uplifted hands, and eyes devout,
> Grateful to Heav'n, over his head beholds
> A dewie Cloud, and in the Cloud a Bow
> Conspicuous with three listed colours gay,
> Betok'ning peace from God, and Cov'nant new.
>   (XI, 863–67)

This passage extends the significance of the hand imagery from signs of the relationship between Adam and Eve to signs of the relationship between humans and God, that is, through prayer. Whereas Ovid, then, uses one basic formula, the lifting of hands to heaven, to link together similar moments in various episodes, Milton uses the same image in his epic as a transition between stages of development in the human community. Once again, Milton's imitation of Ovid transvalues an emblem of pathetic, ceaseless change into a sign of progress in repairing the Fall.

Ovid's innovative use of anachronistic narration drew the attention of Torquato Tasso in *Discourses on the Heroic Poem* (1594).

---

[42]Overall, these words appear 110 times in formulas such as "tendens bracchia caelestes" (lifting arms to heaven), according to the Deferrari, Barry, and McGuire concordance.

Tasso includes Ovid among other epic poets who practiced "min-gling the true with the false or feigned." Specifically, he discusses Ovid's device of concluding his work with a feigned didactic en-counter between a narrator imbedded in the poem and a Roman king: "Ovid took an equal liberty in his *Metamorphoses* at the end, where the Italian philosopher Pythagoras instructs the Roman King Numa, although the more reliable account has Pythagoras born centuries later."[43] Milton followed Ovid's example by con-cluding *Paradise Lost* with the instruction of Adam by the archangel Michael, a scene that Milton, having neither scriptural nor historic precedent, invented. The extensive use of imbedded, or indirect, narration in *Paradise Lost,* especially in Raphael's hexameron in Books V–VI, also has Ovidian precedent. Ovid not only uses nar-rators such as Achelous (8.549–9.97) and Nestor (12.168–13.65) who, like Raphael, tell stories in which they have an active part; he also uses those who, like Raphael, encourage their audiences to remain alert and pious (such as Lelex, narrator of the story of Baucis and Philemon, 8.618). The general effect of multiple nar-rators in both the *Metamorphoses* and *Paradise Lost* is to broaden both the scope of the subject and the range of expression over what a single epic voice could achieve.

A third innovative feature of the *Metamorphoses* generally has been either overlooked or treated as a subspecies of Ovidian transi-tions. This is Ovid's practice of narrating certain episodes in his own voice, but of drawing close to the viewpoint of various charac-ters, alternatively, as the story unfolds. Such "alternation," as the device may economically be called, is an Ovidian innovation that begins a movement toward greater flexibility and realism in the development of narration. An important precursor to alternation in epic is the suspension of human action, typically during a battle, and shift to a scene in the heavens for divine resolution of the conflict. Used extensively in the *Iliad,* this device remains a stan-dard means of representing human and superhuman views in tan-dem throughout classical and Renaissance epic. Instead of freezing one narrative level and moving to another, however, the narrator of the *Metamorphoses* moves gradually, sometimes almost impercep-

[43]Tasso, *Discourses on the Heroic Poem,* p. 59.

tibly, from the mind of one character to that of another. Alternation may prefigure both the device of *"entrelacement"* (interlacing) employed in medieval romance and the style of psychological "realism" developed by novelists George Eliot and Henry James.[44] The effect of these later devices, however, is in the one case greater formal distancing of teller from tale and in the other greater subtlety and depth of characterization than Ovid's method allows.

Alternation recurs throughout the *Metamorphoses,* notably in the episodes of Apollo's and Jupiter's *amors* (1.452–2.875), Narcissus and Echo (3.339–510), Arachne and Minerva (6.1–145), and Ceyx and Alcyone (11.410–748). The clearest and perhaps most inventive example of alternation in the *Metamorphoses,* that in the heroic narrative of Tereus, his wife Procne, and her sister Philomela (6.438–674), may also be the most illuminating for Milton's narrative technique. At first, the narrator takes the reader close to Tereus's initial response to the beautiful Philomela, a response that is apparently as natural as it is passionate:

> non secus exarsit conspecta virgine Tereus,
> quam siquis canis ignem supponat aristis
> aut frondem positasque cremet faenilibus herbas.
> digna quidem facies, sed et hunc innata libido
> exstimulat, pronumque genus regionibus illis
> in venerem est: flagrat vitio gentisque suoque.
>
> (6.455–60)

The moment he saw her Tereus was inflamed with love, quick as if one should set fire to ripe grain, or dry leaves, or hay stored in the loft. Her beauty, indeed, was worth it; but in his case his own passionate nature urged him on, and besides, the men of his region are quick to love: his own fire and his nation's burned in him.

---

[44]On "entrelacement" see Ferdinand Lot in *Etudes sur le Lancelot en Prose* (Paris, 1954), pp. 17–28. Eugene Vinaver mentions Ovid as precedent for the medieval "poetry of interlace" in *The Rise of Romance* (Oxford, 1971), pp. 71–72. On realism in fiction see Henry James's prefaces to *The Portrait of a Lady* and *The Ambassadors,* especially his remarks on the need for the character-narrator Strether to forbid the "terrible fluidity of self-revelation," in Henry James, *The Art of the Novel: Critical Prefaces* (New York, 1962), p. 321. More radical but less continuous than Jamesian or Ovidian alternation are the polyphonic narrative methods of Browning in *The Ring and the Book* and Faulkner in *Absalom, Absalom!*

The familiar pastoral imagery suggests a homely, if ardent love, little different from that of his fellow Thracians for their women. Still following the thought of Tereus, the narrator gradually reveals the horror of this situation to the reader, as if we and Tereus were realizing it simultaneously:

> iamque moras male fert cupidoque revertitur ore
> ad mandata Procnes et agit sua vota sub illa.
> facundum faciebat amor, quotiensque rogabat
> ulterius iusto, Procnen ita velle ferebat.
>
> (6.467–70)

Now, impatient of delay, he ardently repeats Procne's request and pleads his own cause under her name. Love made him eloquent, and as often as he asked more urgently than he should, he would say that Procne wished it so.

Thus far the narrator has given us the vantage of Tereus, yet Tereus is already changing, as Anderson notes, into a shrewd orator.[45] When the narrator immediately exclaims against the blindness of men and calls Tereus's designs criminal (472–73), our sympathetic involvement with the character is suddenly obliterated. Yet Ovid continues to develop the imagination of Tereus, which, as the reader can now see, is degenerating into fantasies of incest:

> spectat eam Tereus praecontrectatque videndo
> osculaque et collo circumdata bracchia cernens
> omnia pro stimulis facibusque ciboque furoris
> accipit et, quotiens amplectitur illa parentem,
> esse parens vellet: neque enim minus inpius esset.
>
> (6.478–82)

Tereus looks at her and, looking, feels her already in his arms; seeing her kisses and her arms around her father's neck all goads him, food and fuel for his passion, and whenever she embraces her father, he wishes he were her parent: indeed, if he were, he would be no less impious.

[45]Anderson, ed., *Ovid's "Metamorphoses," Books 6–10*, p. 213.

The synthetic word formation in "praecontrectatque," an Ovidian coinage, aptly depicts Tereus's imaginative anticipation of seizing the unknowing Philomela.

After briefly describing the departure of Philomela with Tereus for his kingdom, the narrator then assumes a position close to the thoughts of Philomela. By recalling and developing his previous simile of Tereus as an eagle (*"praedator"*) and Philomela as a captured hare, the Ovidian narrator characterizes the young woman as a helpless victim. He superimposes on this simile one thematically similar, but one drawn sympathetically from the victim's point of view:

> illa tremit velut agna pavens, quae saucia cani
> ore excussa lupi nondum sibi tuta videtur,
> utque columba suo madefactis sanguine plumis
> horret adhuc avidosque timet, quibus haeserat, ungues.
> mox, ubi mens rediit, passos laniata capillos,
> lugenti similis, caesis plangore lacertis,
> intendens palmas "o diris barbare factis!
> o crudelis!" ait, "nec te mandata parentis
> cum lacrimis movere piis nec cura sororis
> nec mea virginitas nec coniugialia iura."
>
> (6.527–36)

She trembled like a frightened lamb, which, torn and cast away by a gray wolf, cannot yet believe that it is safe; and like a dove which, with its own blood smeared over its plumage, still palpitates with fright, still fears those greedy claws that have pierced it. Soon, when her senses come back, she drags at the loosened hair, and like one in mourning, beating and tearing her flesh, stretching out her hands, she cries: "Oh, what a horrible thing you have done, barbarous, cruel wretch! Do you care nothing for my father's injunctions, his affectionate tears, my sister's love, my own virginity, the bonds of wedlock?"

The lifting of arms, a recurrent motif in the *Metamorphoses*, here makes an unabashed appeal to the pity of Tereus. During and beyond the mannered depiction of the rape of Philomela, including Tereus's removal of her tongue, the narrator remains close to the thoughts of the woman, as this shift from epic periphrasis to direct question shows:

> Signa deus bis sex acto lustraverat anno:
> quid faciat Philomela?
>
> (6.571–72)

Now through the twelve signs, a whole year's journey, has the sun-god passed. And what shall Philomela do?

Ovid allows the web Philomela weaves to transfer our attention from her to her sister. Procne's desperate speeches (611–19, and 631–35) recall those of Tereus at the story's beginning, as does the narrator's understated gathering of the themes of pretense, blindness, and familial piety—now given from a viewpoint closer to Procne's:

> his adhibet coniunx ignarum Terea mensis
> et patrii moris sacrum mentita, quod uni
> fas sit adire viro, comites famulosque removit.
> ipse sedens solio Tereus sublimis avito
> vescitur inque suam sua viscera congerit alvum,
> tantaque nox animi est: "Ityn huc accersite" dixit.
> dissimulare nequit crudelia gaudia Procne
> iamque suae cupiens exsistere nuntia cladis
> "intus habes, quem poscis" ait.
>
> (6.647–55)

This is the feast to which the wife invites Tereus, little knowing what it is. She pretends that it is a sacred feast according to their family custom, in which only a husband may enter, and she removes all attendants and slaves. So Tereus, sitting alone in his high ancestral banquet-chair, begins the feast and gorges himself with flesh of his own flesh. And in the total blindness of his understanding he cries: "Call my Itys here!" Procne cannot hide her cruel joy, and, eager to be the messenger of her bloody news, says: "You have within him whom you call."

I have dwelled long upon this episode, not only because of its inventiveness as epic narrative poetry, but also because of its tech-

nical similarity to one of the pivotal scenes in *Paradise Lost*: our first
view of Adam and Eve (IV, 285–355). Mario Di Cesare observes
that the narrative mediation of this scene largely controls our understanding of Adam and Eve, and he notes further that this encounter "has been prepared for by the complex structure and imagery of the preceding three books."[46] Arnold Stein, believing that
the scene represents an achievement that "can support considerable weight of meaning," analyzes Milton's delicate adjustment of
"the perspective which seems to start from Satan's view but without
transition is removed from his ken."[47] The narrator leads us into
the Garden by way of Satan's view:

> From this *Assyrian* Garden, where the Fiend
> Saw undelighted all delight, all kind
> Of living Creatures new to sight and strange.
>
> (IV, 285–87)

The lack of delight in Satan's vision differentiates his insensate
view from the active responses to Paradise by both the narrator and
its human occupants. The close correspondence between Ovid's
and Milton's descriptions of the first human beings increases the
likelihood that Ovidian narrative technique also informs the scene:

> Two of far nobler shape erect and tall,
> Godlike erect, with native Honour clad
> In naked Majestie seemd Lords of all,
> And worthie seemd, for in thir looks Divine
> The image of thir glorious Maker shon,
> Truth, wisdome, Sanctitude severe and pure,
> Severe but in true filial freedom plac't.
>
> (IV, 288–94)

> Sanctius his animal mentisque capacius altae
> deerat adhuc et quod dominari in cetera posset:
> natus homo est, sive hunc divino semine fecit

---

[46]Mario Di Cesare, "Advent'rous Song: The Texture of Milton's Epic," in *Language and Style in Milton*, ed. R. D. Emma and John T. Shawcross (New York, 1967), p. 3.
[47]Stein, *The Art of Presence*, p. 148.

ille opifex rerum, mundi melioris origo,
sive recens tellus seductaque nuper ab alto
aethere cognati retinebat semina caeli. . . .
pronaque cum spectent animalia cetera terram,
os homini sublime dedit caelumque videre
iussit et erectos ad sidera tollere vultus.

(1.76–86)

A holier creature than these, more capable of lofty thought, one who could have dominion over all the rest, was lacking yet. Then man was born: whether the god who made all else, beginning a better world, made man of his own divine substance, or whether the new earth, lately drawn away from heavenly ether, retained some seeds from its kindred sky. . . . And, though all other animals are prone and look upon the earth, he gave to man an uplifted face and bade him stand erect and lift his eyes to the heavens.

The erectness of stature, dominion over all animals, and innate regard for heaven in Ovid's account of human nature all reappear in Milton's version. Some readers have even found Ovid's theology in this passage supportive of Milton's; Sandys, in his translation of the *Metamorphoses* (1632), comments that Ovid's "god" typologically prefigures the Christian Creator. Ovid, however, wavers between god and "kindlier nature" as the source of order and creation, as we have seen (1.21). Milton is careful to particularize his "fair couple" with details drawn unmistakably from scripture. The hair-length of Adam and Eve, for instance, conforming to Paul's standards in 1 Cor. 11, reflects their hierarchical relationship under God's absolute authority. By recombining mythic and scriptural imagery, Milton transforms Ovid's humanism, which itself had transformed Virgilian piety into uncertainty concerning divine creation of mankind, into a Christianized representation of creatures who reflect the virtues of their "glorious Maker."

Milton's narrative voice then modulates from a bitter expostulation of false purity ("mere shews of seeming pure," 316), itself reminiscent of Ovid's condemnation of the false piety of Tereus (6.473–74), to a lilting celebration of Adam and Eve in motion:

So passd they naked on, nor shund the sight
Of God or Angel, for they thought no ill:

So hand in hand they passd, the lovliest pair
That ever since in loves imbraces met,
Adam the goodliest man of men since borne
His Sons, the fairest of her Daughters *Eve*.
(IV, 319–24)

With great economy of expression, Milton depicts their calm state
of mind, their posture (indicative of their closeness), and their
eventual productivity. Stein's sense that Milton's subtle narration
leaves us "seeing for ourselves" is accurate, but his feeling that the
"Serpent sly / Insinuating" is only one of the "creatures enlivening
the landscape" minimizes the daring disclosure of his "fatal guile":
so confident is Milton to mingle the reader's knowledge of the Fall
with this scene of divine creation. When Satan finally recovers
speech and responds to the sight of Adam and Eve, the reader is
aware that time has passed without significantly changing Satan's
static joylessness:

in th'ascending Scale
Of Heav'n the Starrs that usher Evening rose:
When *Satan* still in gaze, as first he stood,
Scarse thus at length faild speech recoverd sad.
O Hell! what doe mine eyes with grief behold,
Into our room of bliss thus high advanc't
Creatures of other mould, earth-born perhaps,
Not Spirits, yet to heav'nly Spirits bright
Little inferior; whom my thoughts pursue
With wonder, and could love, so lively shines
In them Divine resemblance, and such grace
The hand that formd them on thir shape hath pourd.
(IV, 354–65)

As the Ovidian narrator had alternated from seducer (Tereus) to
victim (Philomela), the Miltonic narrator alternates from Satan to
Adam and Eve. By extending the Ovidian technique and returning
to Satan's view, Milton shows Satan's persistence in his condescending, callous view of mankind despite the genial effect of seeing
innocent, graceful creatures. The narrator then presents Satan's
plan to seduce mankind, which we have heard in theory in the
Council in Hell in Book II. The plan is thus not created here but,

rather, rehearsed in private from what Satan, like Tereus, takes to be a superior view. Yet we have seen his false superiority demolished by the encompassing overview of Satan's designs, both spatially and temporally, by God in Book III. The golden scales that appear at the end of Book IV, when the detected Satan prepares to clash with Gabriel, are not simply an epic topos descending from the *Iliad* through *The Faerie Queene*. Rather, they both end the alternation of Satanic and human perspectives in this episode and figure the replacement of Fate in classical epic with a God whose ways, Milton shows, unlike those of Ovid's gods, can be clearly known and justified.

Embracing and Escaping History: Historical Conclusions of Ovid and Milton

Ever since C. S. Lewis disparaged the historical conclusion of *Paradise Lost* as "an untransmuted lump of futurity" and a "grave structural flaw," readers have risen to defend the conclusion in various ways.[48] Approaching history and epic in a different context, Joan Webber suggested that the epic hero "belongs to a community committed to history and freed from history by death, learning the way out of time by awareness of time."[49] This view of epic as educational holds not only for classical epic but for *Paradise*

---

[48]Lewis, p. 130. For a dramatistic justification of Milton's conclusion see Lawrence A. Sasek, "The Drama of *Paradise Lost*, Books XI and XII," in *Studies in English Renaissance Literature*, ed. W. F. McNeir (Baton Rouge, La., 1962), pp. 181–96; rpt. in *Milton: Modern Essays in Criticism*, ed. Arthur Barker (New York, 1965), pp. 342–56. Two excellent accounts of the typological significance of the final books are Barbara Kiefer Lewalski, "Structure and the Symbolism of Adam's Vision: Books XI and XII," *PQ* 62 (1963), 25–35, and H. R. MacCallum, "Milton and Sacred History: Books XI and XII of *Paradise Lost*," in *Essays in English Literature from the Renaissance to the Victorian Age Presented to A. S. P. Woodhouse*, ed. Millar Maclure and F. W. Watt (Toronto, 1964), pp. 149–68. Robert L. Entzminger relates the conclusion to the procedure of Puritan sermons in "Michael's Options and Milton's Poetry: *Paradise Lost* XI and XII," *ELR* 8 (1978), 197–211. Neil Hertz finds in Adam's and the narrator's responses to history a narrative structure that influenced Wordsworth's "Ruined Cottage," as he shows in "Wordsworth and the Tears of Adam," *Studies in Romanticism* 7 (1967), 15–33. See also Barker's bibliographical note in his collection, p. 356.
[49]Webber, p. 61.

Lost and the *Metamorphoses*. For if the hero of Ovid's poem is Augustus Caesar, as Brooks Otis has suggested,[50] then the historical awareness that Augustus as both reader and statesman should have gained from the *Metamorphoses* is the perfect preparation for his apotheosis. Webber's view of history and epic applies to *Paradise Lost* whether one considers Christ or Adam (or Adam and Eve) its hero, though, to be more precise, humanity is freed from history both by learning to recognize patterns of virtue and by the promise of the Redeemer in Milton's epic.

Louis Martz has discussed the structural parallels between the historical conclusions of the poems. After suggesting that the last four books of Ovid's poem may have enabled Milton to create a "subtle series of ironies" in his final two books, Martz summarizes what he sees as the major similarities and differences between the conclusions:

> The whole speech of Pythagoras evokes analogies with the instruction of Adam by the two angels: instruction by Raphael . . . and finally, Michael's story of the turning of man toward evil, the sad history of the crimes of the human race, down to Milton's own day and beyond.
>
> But Milton's poem is designed to include, transcend, and contradict teachings like those of Pythagoras, for in Milton's universe eternal flux exists only in Chaos.[51]

Martz's distinction between the cyclic flux described by Pythagoras and the replacement of flux by divine teleology is certain, but the "analogies" between Ovidian and Miltonic instruction require some clarification. The materials that the Ovidian narrator and Adam teach are similar as history, particularly the history of the founding of a people. The teaching methods of the instructors, however, differentiate the kinds and meanings of "history" in the two poems.

Ovid's historical conclusion opens with his version of the Troy story, in particular, with the two episodes of the Lapiths and Centaurs and the Judgment of the Arms. The effect of these episodes, as argued in the preceding chapter, is to counteract the martial

[50]Otis, p. 84.
[51]Martz, *Poet of Exile*, p. 242.

heroism of Homer and Virgil. Robert Coleman, aptly describing the effect of Ovid's demystifying technique, writes, "To the eye of civilized sensibility these deeds of the great heroic past, once divested of their glamorous aura, were nothing but the manifestation of brute force, a catalogue of lust, treachery, and senseless slaughter, and the vain and absurd preoccupation with honours and status. Surely an ominous preparation for the coming Aeneas-Rome sequence!"[52] To readers in Ovid's generation, steeped in the Augustan myth of a golden past, this revaluation must have been profoundly unsettling. The absurdity and senseless wrath of martial heroism are especially clear in Ovid's epic when Achilles, frustrated by his failure to pierce Cygnus with his lance, finally slays his man by choking him with his own helmet straps. There are a number of ways to slay an opponent honorably in Homeric epic; this is not one of them. In Ovid's revisionist history of the Roman empire, the rise of Rome by martial conquest is likewise subject to the bitter irony of Pythagoras's reminder of its inevitable fall, by analogy with other great cities (15.428–35). Readers of the *Metamorphoses* must reexamine, and either defend or revise, their attachment to the Augustan myth, previously reinforced by Virgil's *Aeneid.*

Milton's construction of his final books also compels a crucial revaluation, not implicitly by the reader, but explicitly by the representative reader, Adam. With the angel Michael's guidance, Adam accurately identifies death when it appears in his vision of Cain and Abel, but his precipitate discovery of hope in his vision of Cain's descendants elicits Michael's corrective reply:

> Judg not what is best
> By pleasure, though to Nature seeming meet,
> Created, as thou art, to nobler end
> Holie and pure, conformitie divine.
> (XI, 603–6)

If Milton's method is more didactic than Ovid's, it is also more reliable. The method is not lacking in the subtlety that readers have

[52]Coleman, "Structure and Intention in the *Metamorphoses*," p. 475.

found in Ovid's parodic version of the *Aeneid,* in which Aeneas becomes not a pious founder but a barbarous invader (14.574–76). Instead of allowing an uncertain reaction to historical scenes on the part of his reader, Milton represents within the poem a fully human reader who, though able to err, has a divinely appointed guide (XI, 99–116). The separate resolution of each of Adam's errant or incomplete responses by Michael offers greater control over no less scattered material than Ovid's history had surveyed.[53] The gains in both responsiveness and moderation that Adam shows during instruction, notably his tears for the destruction of humanity in the Flood and his subsequent rejoicing "For one Man found so perfet and so just, / That God voutsafes to raise another World / From him" (XI, 876–78), show that Adam is already gaining in "Patience and Heroic Martyrdom."

The historical ending of the *Metamorphoses* culminates in the long speech of Pythagoras (15.60–481). The tedious strength of the speech has led some to find it almost thoroughly ironic.[54] Certainly, as I have argued, the speech delivers a warning of the eventual fall of the Roman empire. Despite ironic moments, however, the sermon of Pythagoras argues on the whole for principles consistent with what Ovid has been at pains to depict throughout the *Metamorphoses.* The central theme of the speech is stated laconically: "omnia mutantur, nihil interit" (all things change; nothing dies). Milton's conclusion, too, teaches the mutability of all earthly things, but it goes on to promise an end to ceaseless flux at the Apocalypse in the new Heaven and Earth, "wherein the just shall dwell" (XI, 900–901). The values for which the Ovidian narrator celebrates Pythagoras—hatred of tyranny, divine thought, imagination, diligence despite public scorn, and pacifism (61–74)—exactly match those of the one good man whom Milton upholds as a hope for God's protection of the just until the Apocalypse. Even Ovid's introduction of Pythagoras, not by name, but by suggestion in high epic style (as in Virgil's introduction of Carthage by "There was an ancient city . . .") parallels Milton's introduction of Noah:

[53]Cf. Mary Ann Radzinowicz, "Man as a Probationer of Immorality," in *Approaches to "Paradise Lost,"* ed. C. A. Patrides (London, 1968), pp. 31–51.
[54]See W. R. Johnson, "The Problem of the Counter-classical Sensibility and its Critics," pp. 123–52.

So all shall turn degenerate, all deprav'd,
Justice and Temperance, Truth and Faith forgot;
One Man except, the onely Son of light
In a dark Age, against example good,
Against allurement, custom, and a World
Offended; fearless of reproach and scorn,
Or violence.

(XI, 806–11)

Owing to Christian typology, Milton has even more reason than Ovid to refrain from mentioning the "One Man's" name: Noah prefigures Moses who prefigures Jesus, the "greater Man" of the opening proem. The anonymity of the one good man, further, leads the reader to observe a pattern of virtue that followers of Christ may themselves fulfill. Milton's imaginative history itself makes these connections, and so shows the exercise of virtue by Adam's descendants as necessary preparation for the possession of a "Paradise within." Rather than present a discursive speech by his exemplary man, Milton shows us and Adam the opposition of the one good man to the confused multitude in his singular set of circumstances. Thus readers may find that the general pattern applies to their situation as well. And thus Adam gains in discrimination among fallen experience of good and evil, that is, as *Areopagitica* makes clear, of knowing good *by* evil (*CPW*, 2:514). By this dual education, the fallen Adam and the fallen reader are prepared psychologically and spiritually to descend from the height of inspiration Milton provides to the earthly level of the human future.

In describing the legacy Milton left to future epic poets in English, Stuart Curran summarizes the revised expectations readers have learned to bring to the genre: "After centuries of refinement we have come to expect definite characteristics of the epic poem: panoramic vision, encyclopedic knowledge, a heroism that defines human possibilities, a sense of the ultimate nature of the cosmos, and a justification of the cosmic order as propitious to human life."[55] By imitating and transforming previous epics in their

[55]Stuart Curran, "The Mental Pinnacle: *Paradise Regained* and the Romantic Four-Book Epic," in *Calm of Mind: Tercentenary Essays on "Paradise Regained" and "Samson Agonistes" in Honor of John S. Diekhoff,* ed. Joseph Anthony Wittreich, Jr. (Cleveland, 1971), p. 136.

poems, Ovid and Milton largely created these expectations. Their revisions in epic subject matter and narrative technique, especially, reaffirmed the viability of epic while showing that earlier epics had overemphasized, for their purposes, the heroic and martial narratives Aristotle championed in the *Poetics*. The many echoes and analogues of the *Metamorphoses* as an epic in *Paradise Lost* suggest that the narrative methods and epic design of Ovid's poem were not lost on Milton. The English poet's developments of Ovidian techniques—of a comprehensive yet coherent fable, of subtle transitions and alternation of perspective, of an epic speaker who controls the poem and guides its readers, and of history at once personal and educational—go beyond Ovid's in their scope and power. Ovid had marshaled these techniques to show that the cosmic order is antagonistic to human life; Milton transformed them to show that the actions of his God are indeed propitious and responsive to man. The many expressions of "wonder" the Miltonic narrator makes throughout *Paradise Lost*, literal translations of Ovid's pervasive exclamations ("mirum"), show that he retains the sympathy and surprise which are the most enduring contributions of the *Metamorphoses* to the epic tradition. Milton's poem is all the more wondrous for its daring use of Ovidian means to prophesy the end of all metamorphoses.

−5−

Milton's Epic Transformations:
Virgil, Ovid, and Spenser
in *Paradise Lost*

In the previous chapters we saw how Milton incorporates episodes from Ovid's *Metamorphoses* into his epic, transvaluing the
Ovidian material by a distinctive dialogue on the uses of metamorphoses. My claim that Milton's use of the *Metamorphoses* is distinctive is actually two claims: that we can distinguish the Ovidian
influence in *Paradise Lost* from the influence of other classical epic
poets, chiefly Virgil; and that we can distinguish the way Milton
uses Ovid from that of other epic poets in English, chiefly Spenser.
In the first case, the influence of Ovid versus Virgil can best be seen
by examining three pivotal passages in *Paradise Lost*—the proem to
Book I, the metamorphosis of the fallen angels into dwarfs, and
Adam's prophetic vision of history. These passages show that Virgil
provided a sublime model for majestic language and overarching
structure in Milton's epic, and Ovid enlivened this language and
structure with complex psychological insights, flexible narrative
devices, and subtle epic infrastructures. In the second case, the
distinctively Miltonic use of Ovid can best be seen by comparing
Milton's with Spenser's treatment of Ovidian scenes which appear
in both *The Faerie Queene* and *Paradise Lost;* namely, the metamorphosis of Scylla, the *locus amoenus* disturbed, and the concluding discussions of change, or mutability. Although these scenes,
transvalued in Spenser's Faeryland, support effects similar to those
in *Paradise Lost*—among them a deepening of psychological insight
and moral instruction—the allusions remain isolated, "conspic-

uous" (in a sense to be explained later), and of uncertain significance. Part of Milton's unmatched transvaluation of the *Metamorphoses* is his success in interweaving Ovidian scenes into the cohesive fabric of his epic argument, a strategy that effects a teleological completion of pagan myths in poetic spiritual history.

"Behold a Wonder!": Seeing with Virgil and Ovid

The presence of Virgil's *Aeneid* is palpable from the opening lines of *Paradise Lost* in Milton's expansive, Latinate syntax. In a headnote on "The Verse" appended to the second edition, Milton named "Homer in Greek, and Virgil in Latin" as authorities for heroic verse without rhyme. "[T]rue musical delight," Milton argues, consists not in rhyme but "onely in apt Numbers, fit quantity of Syllables, and the sense variously drawn out from one Verse into another." The harmonious composition that Milton achieves in the proem represents a brilliant fusion of Virgilian syntax and English sense. The inversion of normal word order ("Of Mans First Disobedience, . . . Sing Heav'nly Muse"), the preponderance of relative clauses ("whose mortal tast," "that on the secret top," "who first taught the chosen Seed"), and the frequent use of and-or connectives in the first sixteen lines are but three of fifteen staple features of the syntax of *Paradise Lost* that Janette Richardson finds characteristic of the *Aeneid*.[1] Richardson's statistical analysis of the two epics indicates their shared high frequency of absolute phrases, inversions and transpositions, parenthetical adjectives, ellipses, formal introductions and conclusions for speeches, relative pronouns and adjectives, appositives, participles, and coordinating connectives—all features helping to create what Alastair Fowler has called the "built order and flowing mass of the [Miltonic] verse paragraphs."[2]

More significant than reminiscences of syntax, parallels between the structures of the poems emerge when one compares the open-

[1]Janette Richardson, "Virgil and Milton Once Again," *CL* 14 (1962), 321–31.
[2]Alastair Fowler, ed., "Introduction" to John Milton's *Paradise Lost* (London, 1971), p. 13.

ing passages of the epics. Probably the most significant correspondence between Milton's proem and Virgil's is the parallel between Virgil's epic sequence of "a man . . . fugitive from Troy . . . battered by the gods . . . until he could found a city" and Milton's sequence of "Mans First Disobedience . . . loss of Eden . . . till one greater Man . . . regain the blissful Seat." The correspondences between the agency of a man, the loss of a homeland, and the delay before a restoration serve ultimately, however, to highlight the major differences between these epic arguments. Heroic man in the *Aeneid* must struggle against the will of gods to achieve his new empire; heroic man in *Paradise Lost* must seek the aid of the Redeemer, the "greater Man," to achieve not an empire but a "paradise within" the human heart. Milton's proem incorporates a number of formal elements from the *Aeneid*—the invocation of the Muse, the summary of the epic argument, the beginning *in medias res*. In every case Milton's Christian values transform these Virgilian elements. The proem to Ovid's *Metamorphoses* provided Milton with a model for transforming the inherited expectations of epic, in particular, for expanding as well as internalizing the scope of events beyond human combat to include psychological and cosmic changes.

Beyond their proems, the *Aeneid* and *Paradise Lost* continue to display remarkable correspondences of language and style. Irene Samuel has called attention to the stylistic indebtedness of the similes in *Paradise Lost,* in particular the relation among word order, repetition, and hidden allusions in them which unfolds their complex significance. "What Dante had achieved by assimilating Virgilian techniques to the Italian language in developing his own style," she concludes, "was not lost on Milton."[3] Milton's assimilation of the techniques of Ovid as well as those of Virgil and Dante may be seen clearly in Milton's version of the traditional epic council.

Toward the end of Book I of *Paradise Lost,* Milton compares Satan and the fallen angels, who are conferring in the open air of Hell before their consultation in Pandaemonium, to swarming bees. Whatever else the simile does, certainly it places Milton's

[3]Samuel, *Dante and Milton: The "Commedia" and "Paradise Lost,"* pp. 272–73.

scene in an epic context, for early in both the *Iliad* (2.87–90) and the *Aeneid* (1.430–36) bee similes had described complex political groups in the heroic mode. Immediately after Milton establishes the connection between bees and the demonic council, however, the pace of action and allusion in his verse accelerates in a way unlike anything in Homeric or Virgilian narration, but in a way reminiscent of the *Metamorphoses*:

> So thick the aerie crowd
> Swarm'd and were straitn'd; till the Signal giv'n,
> Behold a wonder! they but now who seemd
> In bigness to surpass Earths Giant Sons
> Now less then smallest Dwarfs, in narrow room
> Throng numberless, like that Pigmean Race
> Beyond the *Indian* Mount, or Faerie Elves,
> Whose midnight Revels, by a Forrest side
> Or Fountain some belated Peasant sees,
> Or dreams he sees, while over-head the Moon
> Sits Arbitress, and neerer to the Earth
> Wheels her pale course, they on thir mirth and dance
> Intent, with jocond Music charm his ear;
> At once with joy and fear his heart rebounds.
>
> (I, 775–88)

Before attempting to isolate the Ovidian components of this passage, we do well to see how playful, how evocative, and how open to critical speculation it is. More than the "jocond" music and dance of the midnight revelers make it playful: Unusually lush consonance (*s* in lines 775–76; *w* in 777; *n* in 779–81), a cascading syntax ("So . . . till . . . like . . . or . . . whose . . . by . . . or . . . while . . . and . . . at once . . . rebounds"), and the swift unfolding of marvelous action all contribute. The evocative quality derives both from the passage's literary allusiveness and its radical ambiguity. Central to the scene is the "belated Peasant" who "sees, / Or dreams he sees" the antics of elves by clear moonlight. Dreaming in *Paradise Lost* is usually a sign of imaginative fancy, as in Eve's dream of flying, and is in every case a Miltonic invention. Yet this phrase also alludes to *Aeneid* 6.453–54, in which Aeneas encounters Dido for the last time in the Underworld. What is immediately striking about the peasant is his confused response to the sight or vision, his mixed feelings, capturing both his joy in the scene and his fear of its strangeness. If the peasant is passively dreaming, his delusion nevertheless entails a strong physiological reaction: "His heart rebounds." If he is imagining all he sees, then the fanciful parade of images—pygmies and elves, moon and earth, music and dance— nevertheless retains its own vitality. In a fundamental way, the peasant is an unpretentious example of humanity, needed to stand between and so indicate the huge shift from angelic to fairy dimensions. In addition to indicating human scale, the peasant embodies a representative human response to the devils' change. The peasant's reaction to the scene suggests how it might affect the reader as well; the peasant, in other words, becomes a surrogate for the audience. This type of surrogate audience is a device common to both epic (the woodsmen and hunters in Homeric similes) and drama (choral figures). The dramatic aspect of Milton's scene is reinforced by its similarity to both Puck's playful confusion in *A Midsummer Night's Dream* and to Mercutio's Queen Mab speech in *Romeo and Juliet* (I. iv.53–103).[4]

But why a belated peasant? The *OED* cites this usage as an instance of belated as "benighted" or darkened, surely a sense appropriate to the "darkness visible" of Hell. But two other current senses of belated, "delayed in time" and "out of date," may also operate in Milton's essentially retrospective and frequently anachronistic poem. Because Milton's readers necessarily take a darkened, retrospective, and anachronistic view of the demonelves, we share in the peasant's belatedness.

Underlying the narrative and dramatic effects of this passage, its lexical complexities—resonant puns, emotional ambiguity, rapid shifts in action and perspective—may strike some readers as features associated more with metaphysical wit than with the "grand" Miltonic style, though these readers would have no trouble differ-

---

[4]In *A Map of Misreading* (New York, 1975), p. 141, Harold Bloom notes the allusion to *A Midsummer Night's Dream*, 2.1.28–57. More significantly, Bloom (p. 129) upholds the argument of Angus Fletcher that "from Shakespeare Milton learned to contain the Spenserian elegiacism or 'prophetic strain' within what Fletcher calls 'transcendental forms.'" See Fletcher, *The Prophetic Moment: An Essay on Spenser* (Chicago, 1971), p. 301.

entiating this passage from one in Donne's *Songs and Sonnets*. Having a too fixed or predetermined notion of Miltonic style in mind, one might easily underestimate the flexibility and humor of Milton's verse which both sustain the reader's interest and increase, in Barthes's phrase, the pleasure of the text. Because these features show strong similarities with those in the *Metamorphoses*, we do well to consider how Milton adapts Ovid's humor and narrative effects. Ovid's influence on this passage is reflected in three areas: the actual metamorphosis, the emphasis on the "wonder" of this change, and the exuberant wordplay. We have already examined the counterheroic effect of this metamorphosis on the characterization of Satan in Chapter 3—it remains to be seen how closely and how extensively Milton's depiction of this change follows Ovidian precedent.

The pressure for the diminution of the devils, "So thick the aerie crowd / Swarm'd and were straitn'd," recalls the pressure leading to the expansion of the dwelling of Baucis and Philemon in Book 8 of the *Metamorphoses*. Ovid's fable turns, in fact, on a question of proper dimensions or scale. Essentially, the fable asks, what relation does godhead bear to grandeur or size? In Ovid's account (8.611–724), Jupiter and Mercury take on human form in order to wander undetected among the Phrygians. Seeking rest, they go to a thousand homes, all of which reject them. Finally the gods arrive at the small cottage of Baucis and Philemon, where they receive an unexpectedly warm welcome:

> tamen una recepit,
> parva quidem stipulis et canna tecta palustri,
> sed pia Baucis anus parilique aetate Philemon
> illa sunt annis iuncti iuvenalibus, illa
> consenuere casa paupertatemque fatendo
> effecere levem nec iniqua mente ferendo.
> nec refert, dominos illic famulosne requiras:
> tota domos duo sunt, idem parentque iubentque.
> ergo ubi caelicolae parvos tetigere penates
> submissoque humiles intrarunt vertice postes,
> membra senex posito iussit relevare sedili.
>
> (8.629–39)

Yet one house did receive them, a tiny house indeed, thatched with straw and marshy reeds. Pious old Baucis and Philemon, equal in years, were wedded in that cottage in their youth, in that cottage they had grown old together, and by acknowledging their poverty, and by bearing it in a contented spirit, they had made it light. It was meaningless to ask for masters or servants in that house: these two are the whole household; they served and ruled alike. And so when the high gods had touched the little household gods and, stooping, came in by the low door, the old man, setting out a bench, bade them rest their legs.

The relationship between deity and magnitude enters this scene comically, both when the gods must bow their heads to enter the cottage and when they respectfully observe the household gods, the *penates*. When the old people try unsuccessfully to catch their one goose to make a dinner for their guests, Mercury and Jupiter casually mention, in one of Ovid's wittiest moments: "'di' que 'sumus'" ("By the way, we're gods"). As gods, of course, they possess great power, some of which they confer upon the pious and hospitable couple. The gods destroy the homes of the other Phrygians, but they reward Baucis and Philemon with a beneficent metamorphosis:

> dum deflent fata suorum,
> illa vetus, dominis etiam casa parva duobus
> vertitur in templum: furcas subiere columnae,
> stramina flavescunt, adopertaque marmore tellus
> caelataeque fores aurataque tecta videntur.
>
> (8.698–702; Loeb)

While they wept for the fate of their neighbors, that old house, which had been small even for the two of them, was changed into a temple. Marble columns replaced the wooden beams; the straw brightened and became a golden roof; richly carved gates appeared, and marble pavement covered the ground.

The metamorphosed cottage bears some resemblance to Pandaemonium in *Paradise Lost:* "Built like a Temple, where *Pilasters* round / Were set, and Doric pillars overlaid / With Golden Architrave; nor did there want / Cornice or Freeze, with bossy Sculptures grav'n, / The Roof was fretted Gold" (I, 713–17). Despite this resemblance of surfaces, the demonic temple falls short of the temple of Baucis and Philemon in two important respects. Even the pagan temple could boast its origin in pious service to the gods; Pandaemonium is a temple for the devils' self-worship. Second, the gods' condescension in Ovid draws the divine and human beings into proximity. As the narrator argues in concluding the tale: "cura deum di sint, et, qui coluere, colantur" (724), (Let those beloved of the gods be gods, and let those who have worshiped, be worshiped). The dwarfing of the fallen angels, beyond enabling those of lower rank to enter the hall of Pandaemonium, serves no such purpose. Rather, as Ricks observes, the shift in scale effectively belittles the inferior angels.[5] At the same time, the "great Seraphic Lords" assume the posture of pretenders to godhead: "[i]n close recess and secret conclave sat / A thousand Demy-Gods on golden seat's" (I, 795–96). The conjunction of these ornate ecclesiastical furnishings and these cacophonous sounds, especially the clicking *c*'s and sibilant *s*'s, undermines the apparent divinity of these creatures. Whereas in Ovid the metamorphosis ends the fable with epigrammatic finality and economy, in Milton the metamorphosis ends this episode with a promise of ongoing duplicity on the devils' part.

Virgil's contribution to Milton's passage is less narrative and ideological than tonal, or atmospheric. As part of the narrative, Milton's peasant requires little explanation; rather, he aids explanation by figuring a representative human response to the devils' change in size. As part of a resonant allusion to the *Aeneid*, however, the response of the peasant superimposes one moment of doubt on a thematically quite different one:

> inter quas Phoenissa recens a vulnere Dido
> errabat silva in magna; quam Troius heros
> ut primum iuxta stetit agnovitque per umbras
> obscuram, qualem primo qui surgere mense
> aut videt aut vidisse putat per nubila lunam,

[5]Ricks, *Milton's Grand Style*, p. 15.

demisit lacrimas dulcique adfatus amore est:
"infelix Dido, verus mihi nuntius ergo
venerat exstinctam ferroque extrema secutam?"

(6.450–57)

Among them, wandering in that great forest, and with her wound still fresh: Phoenician Dido. And when the Trojan hero recognized her dim shape among the shadows (just as one who either sees or thinks he sees among the cloud banks, when the month is young, the moon rising), he wept and said with tender love: "Unhappy Dido, then the word I had was true? That you were dead? That you pursued your final moment with the sword?"[6]

This final encounter between Aeneas and Dido in the Underworld is charged with the pathos of tragic human love, love that Aeneas has abandoned in deciding to heed the divine command to found a new empire in Latium. The theme of lost romantic love is absent from Milton's epic simile, yet the tone of "haunting uncertainty," which Bowra found characteristic of Virgil's epic,[7] seems equally present in Milton's scene. Because it recalls the sense of loss inherent in the mission of Aeneas, the Virgilian echo emphasizes the "fear" and diminishes the "joy" the reader may share with the peasant. Milton's slight alteration of the line from Virgil indicates the limits of the allusion. Whereas Virgil's hunter sees a pale moon, a romantic emblem of Dido, the moon in Milton's simile "[s]its arbitress" over the changing devils. Virgil's emblem of romantic love has become in Milton's poem an emblem of ethical judgment on the self-debasing antics of the fallen angels. However dreamlike the scene or uncertain the viewer, the moon coolly exposes the scheming devils.

Viktor Pöschl has observed that the entire *Aeneid* "may be viewed as a sequence of moods, a series of changing sensations."[8] It is the integrity of the narrative, however, which makes the sequence of moods engaging, and the integrity of the poem which provided

---

[6]*The "Aeneid" of Virgil*, ed. with intro. and notes R. D. Williams (London, 1975). The English version is Allen Mandelbaum's, *The "Aeneid" of Virgil: A Verse Translation*.

[7]Bowra, *From Virgil to Milton*, p. 83.

[8]Viktor Pöschl, *The Art of Virgil: Image and Symbol in the "Aeneid,"* trans. Gerda Seligson (Ann Arbor, Mich., 1962), p. 140.

Milton with the best model for the overall structure of his "diffuse" epic. The twelve-book division of *Paradise Lost* is only the largest and most obvious parallel to the structure of the *Aeneid*.[9] The beginning of *Paradise Lost in medias res,* the catalog of Satan's warrior-followers, the account of the games in Hell, ekphrastic descriptions such as that of Satan's shield (I, 284–91), and formal indications of structure such as the proem to Book VII ("Half yet remaines unsung"; cf. *Aen.* 7.37–45) all show Milton's ample use of Virgilian structural devices.

One crucial element of epic structure—the adjustment of narrative sequence by retrospect and prophecy—reveals both Milton's reliance on Virgil for structural components and his reliance on Ovid for dynamic transvaluation of these structures. By isolating and foregrounding the implicit use of prophecy and retrospect from the Homeric poems, Virgil had established in the *Aeneid* the utility and place of these techniques in all succeeding literary epics. The major instance of history as prophecy in the *Aeneid* occurs in Book 6, in which Anchises shows Aeneas the "future" generations of illustrious Romans. Like the archangel Michael in Book XI of *Paradise Lost,* Anchises is a reliable guide to the future because he dwells for eternity among the blessed. Michael speaks as a servant and interpreter of God; Anchises studies the fates and speaks of them to his son:

> Nunc age, Dardaniam prolem quae deinde sequatur
> gloria, qui meneant Itala de gente nepotes,
> inlustris animas nostrumque in nomen ituras,
> expediam dictis, et te tua fata docebo.
>
> (6.756–59)

> Listen to me: my tongue will now reveal the fame that is to come from Dardan sons and what Italian children wait for you—bright souls that are about to take your name; in them I shall unfold your fates.
> (Mandelbaum)

---

[9]Martz, *Poet of Exile,* p. 203, suggests that the twelve-book division of *Paradise Lost* has "led us somewhat to over-estimate the example of Virgil." He finds the "panel" construction of the *Metamorphoses* a closer model to Milton's epic structure. The Ovidian panels Martz adduces, though, contain only arrangements of scenes within individual books. For a recent restatement of the strong role of the *Aeneid* in Milton's overarching design, see G. K. Hunter, *"Paradise Lost,"* pp. 37–40.

As Anchises goes on to show, the descendants of Aeneas include Romulus, Augustus, Brutus, and the ill-fated Marcellus. By thus tracing the descendants of Aeneas from the "Alban fathers" to Augustan princes, Virgil achieves two main goals. In terms of the characterization of Aeneas, the pageant of Roman heroes confirms him in his mission to found his new city, so that these heroes and the glorious events to come should actually take place. In terms of the expectations of the Roman reader, the pageant presents models of patriotic, martial heroism to be emulated.

The similarities in structure between Aeneas's dialogue with Anchises and Adam's dialogue with Michael are clear. From the *Aeneid* Milton takes the dialectical structure of viewer and interpreter, as well as the visionary pageant of heroes exemplary either for vice or virtue. In explaining to Adam the method of his presentation, Michael almost literally repeats the words of Anchises in *Aeneid* 6.780: "Things by thir names I call though yet unnam'd" (XII, 140). As in the *Aeneid*, Milton's presentation of history as prophecy prepares its immediate audience for his earthly mission and presents the reader with models of ideal or lamentable lives.

The preceding chapter examined the many parallels between the historical and prophetic conclusions of the *Metamorphoses* and *Paradise Lost*. Both are concerned with the problem of natural flux, with the persistence of evil in various forms, with the need for individual virtue. Ovid's conclusion offered Milton both a radical revaluation of martial heroism (in the parody of the battle between the Lapiths and the Centaurs) and a view of human history (in the speech of Pythagoras) which places asceticism and temperance above conquest or self-indulgence. We saw that Ovid's transvaluation of martial heroism was, for Milton, significant but incomplete. In *Paradise Lost* the Stoic temperance and vegetarianism of Pythagoras, along with the martial prowess of Hector and Aeneas, yield to the "better fortitude / Of Patience and Heroic Martyrdom" (IX, 31–32), along with faith and love. These Christian virtues are vital aspects of the heroism of interiorized virtue that Adam sees exemplified in Noah, Abraham, and Christ.

We saw further that Ovid's method of presenting history as prophecy, in particular, his use of the long didactic monologue by Pythagoras, was unreliable for Milton's purposes. The dialogic method preferred by Virgil is both much closer to Milton's structure and far more applicable to his concern with delighting while educating the reader. The actual dialogue between Michael and Adam, in which Adam learns both from his errant questions and responses and from the angel's explanations, transforms Aeneas's passive absorption of history to suit the twin demands of dramatic action and Christian education. Moreover, Milton's conclusion transforms the doctrine of unending flux preached by Pythagoras into the promise of the Redeemer. In short, the conclusion of *Paradise Lost* represents a remarkable amalgam of Virgilian structure and Ovidian philosophy, while it transvalues both toward Milton's theodicy.

"So many pathes": Wandering with Ovid and Spenser

If Virgil represents the chief rival to Ovid among classical influences on Milton, the chief rival to Milton for the distinction of being the English poet most influenced by Ovid must be Edmund Spenser. Bush and Lotspeich have shown how thoroughly Spenser relies on Ovid for mythological figures, and a number of scholars have examined how Spenser modeled certain episodes in *The Faerie Queene* on Ovidian patterns.[10] Of these scholars, William Nelson perhaps best characterizes Spenser's use of Ovid as "free adaptation." Accordingly, Nelson points out that in the Mutabilitie Cantos Spenser "derived from the *Metamorphoses* not only his resolving symbol, the goddess Natura, but also the inspiration for each of the three sections that make up the cantos, Mutabilitie's challenge to the gods, the episode of Faunus and Diana, and the pageant of the

---

[10]See, inter alia, William P. Cumming, "The Influence of Ovid's *Metamorphoses* on Spenser's 'Mutabilitie Cantos,'" *SP* 28 (1931), 241–56; Anthony E. Friedmann, "The Diana–Acteon Episode in Ovid's *Metamorphoses* and the *Faerie Queene*," *CL* 18 (1966), 289–99; Helen C. Gilde, "Spenser's Hellenore and some Ovidian Associations," *CL* 23 (1971), 233–39; M. N. Holahan, "'Iamque opus exegi': Ovid's Changes and Spenser's Brief Epic of Mutability," *ELR* 6 (1976), 244–70; Richard N. Ringler, "The Faunus Episode," *MP* 63 (1965), 12–19; rpt. in *Essential Articles for the Study of Edmund Spenser*, ed. A. C. Hamilton, pp. 289–98. (Hamden, Conn.: Archon Books, 1972). Still useful are Bush, *Mythology and the Renaissance Tradition in English Poetry*, and Henry G. Lotspeich, *Classical Mythology in the Poetry of Edmund Spenser* (Princeton, N.J., 1932).

changeful world."[11] But whereas Ovid qualifies the prospect of endless change with a proclamation of immortality for Augustus Ceasar and for his own poem, Nelson argues that Spenser's Christian solution must apply both to the "perdurable" world of Mutabilitie and to the "eternal" realm of "that great Sabbaoth God": hence the double conclusion of the Cantos.[12] Spenser's distinction between the realms of Mutabilitie and Eternity improves on the conclusion of the *Metamorphoses* from the viewpoint of Christian doctrine. For Milton, it seems likely that Spenser's imitation of Ovid in the Cantos would have provided a poetic model for his epic's conclusion.

In *Areopagitica*, Milton expressed his high regard for Spenser by calling him "our sage and serious Poet . . . whom I dare be known to think a better teacher then *Scotus* or *Aquinas*" (*CPW*, 2:516). The contrast with the schoolmen not only distinguishes Spenser's superior method of instruction through poetry, but reminds us that Spenser and Milton share a common cultural, religious, and ethical heritage. Not surprisingly, then, the allusions to the *Metamorphoses* by Spenser and Milton serve similar ends: In both, the pagan myths of Ovid illuminate scenes of psychological or moral conflict; in both, the Ovidian allusions signal the superiority of the inclusive Christian mythos. The differences between the Ovidian figurations in *The Faerie Queene* and *Paradise Lost* lie in the divergent manner of their application to epic structure and characterization. In *The Faerie Queene* the Ovidian material remains both tantalizingly engaging and "conspicuously irrelevant," as Berger has observed of Spenser's allusions in general.[13] In *Paradise Lost* the same material, subsumed in Milton's epic argument, more directly illustrates the unfolding action. These points emerge more clearly when we examine two more Ovidian scenes used by both poets: the metamorphosis of Scylla, and the Ovidian *locus amoenus*.

Although Ovid mentions the final transformation of Scylla into the rock that endangered the ships of Ulysses and Aeneas, the account of Scylla in the *Metamorphoses* concentrates on another

---

[11]William Nelson, *The Poetry of Edmund Spenser: A Study* (New York, 1963), p. 297.
[12]Ibid., pp. 308–9. All quotations from Spenser are from *Edmund Spenser: "The Faerie Queene,"* ed. A. C. Hamilton (London, 1977).
[13]Harry Berger, Jr., *The Allegorical Temper: Vision and Reality in Book II of Spenser's "Faerie Queene"* (Hamden, Conn., 1967), pp. 122–25.

change. According to Ovid, the goddess Circe, enraged that Glaucus loves Scylla rather than herself, poisons the pool in which the nymph habitually bathes (14.51–58). Graphically yet in a completely detached manner, Ovid describes the ill effects on the body and psyche of Scylla: namely, the transformation of her body below the waist into a pack of wild dogs that ceaselessly consume and terrify her (14.59–67). As noted briefly in Chapter 1, Ovid's figure of an alluring female disfigured by monstrous forms below the waist reappears in the allegorical and moralized figures of Spenser's Error and Milton's Sin. What we have yet to see is the place of Ovid's Scylla, considered as a narrative episode, within the structure of the *Metamorphoses*, *The Faerie Queene*, and *Paradise Lost*.

Scylla and her descendants serve a common narrative purpose. They stand as obstacles a heroic figure must elude in order to continue on his journey. A trace of Scylla as the personification of an actual rock, which the primary epics of Homer and the secondary epic of Virgil had emphasized, still lingers in the Scylla-based episodes of the "tertiary epics," as Alastair Fowler has distinguished the literarily self-conscious and inward-tending epics of Spenser and Milton.[14] The continuity among these episodes shows that Ovid, Spenser, and Milton are readapting a still significant narrative element from the epic tradition.

With the turn in tertiary epic toward interiorizing formerly external heroic behavior, however, comes a turn toward internalizing, within the hero's mind, the obstacles to heroic progress. Error in Spenser's text is less a dragon external to Redcross than a manifestation of his own tendency to err in the ways of Holiness. Sin in Milton's text is likewise not a foreign, external opponent to Satan, but the first offspring of his brain when he conceives of revolting from God's empire. In both cases, moreover, these confrontations have shifted from the main line of narrative to a digression. Redcross must go on to conquer a more potent dragon to complete his quest: the encounter with Error is, in terms of that quest, at best a

[14]Fowler, "The Life and Death of Literary Forms," p. 89. In *The Faerie Queene*, 2.12, for example, the Gulf of Greediness and the Rock of Reproach, counterparts to the classical Charybdis and Scylla, retain the threat of physically sinking the bark of Guyon and the Palmer. As their names suggest, however, they are fundamentally psychological threats, fatal to those persons who "hauing all their substance spent / In wanton joyes, and lustes intemperate, / Did afterwards make shipwracks violent" (12.7).

prologue and at worst a departure from the way. And although Satan's journey seems at first to be the main heroic narrative in *Paradise Lost,* we soon learn that his journey is a counterheroic one, and this encounter with Sin an awkward reunion with his own forgotten offspring.

The role of the Scylla episode in the *Metamorphoses* points the way for these shifts in both significance and narrative structure. Ostensibly, the Scylla episode (13.738–897) is a digression from Ovid's version of the *Aeneid,* which occupies parts of the last three books of the *Metamorphoses* (13.623–15.806). Before this digression we hear how Aeneas bears away his father, his son, and his vestal gods from Troy; after it we hear how Aeneas meets Dido in Libya. The experience of reading this complete "Aeneid," however, suggests exactly the opposite: that Ovid's story of Aeneas is a frame for, if not a digression from, his primary concerns, namely the pursuit of Scylla, the Song of Cyclops, and the *amor* of Vertumnus and Pomona.

Whether Ovid's "Aeneid" reinforces or undermines the view of Aeneas in Virgil's epic, certainly Ovid succeeds in retelling the story in a radically new way. Galinsky captures this quintessentially Ovidian principle in a phrase from the *Ars Amatoria:* "referre aliter idem" (to recount the same thing differently).[15] The paradox inherent in this Ovidian maxim hints at the unsettling effect of Ovid's method of narration. His penchant for retelling a story rendered earlier, whether by another poet or himself, has the immediate effect of causing readers to expect a certain mode of treatment and certain details from the familiar story. The technique has the corollary effect of introducing startling variations on the expected pattern. Thus, readers familiar with Virgil's *Aeneid* may be either shocked, or delighted, or both, when they confront Ovid's amplified, sympathetic treatment of Scylla in his "Aeneid."

This method of varying previously used material has immediate applications for such highly allusive poems as *The Faerie Queene* and *Paradise Lost.* In alluding to classical precedents generally, Milton establishes appropriate connections between them and his epic while he measures the historical distance that separates them: "thus

---

[15]Galinsky, *Ovid's "Metamorphoses,"* p. 4.

they relate / Erring; for he with this rebellious rout / Fell long before" (I, 746–48).[16] In imitating Ovid specifically, Milton creates a dialogue in which Ovid's mythic figures are clearly "less ancient yet than these" (XI, 11) but still useful in illuminating the more distant mythic figures in Eden. The subtle appropriateness of Milton's allusions to his narrative sets them apart from the shocking variations of Ovid and the "conspicuously irrelevant" allusions of Spenser. In *Paradise Lost,* as we have seen, Ovid's Scylla illuminates both the deformed figure of Sin and the counterheroic narrative of Satan, but Milton suggests these points of relevance without leading us to dwell on Ovid's (or Spenser's) poem as their source. In adapting Scylla to Error, Spenser, in contrast, overtly draws our attention to her source in Ovid in a number of ways: by leading us to Error's den through a patently Ovidian catalog of trees; by dwelling on her disfigured anatomy and horrible offspring; and by following Ovid's account of spontaneous generation (*Met.* 1.416–37) to describe the prodigious vitality of Error's vomit. Fletcher characterizes this method of conspicuously adapting source material as "collage," which he defines as "parody drawing attention to the *materials* of art and life." The effect of this method on Spenser's reader, Fletcher astutely argues, is that we "remain aware of *source,* that is, of the secondariness of his epic, as a quality in itself."[17] The method does more than contribute to the anachronistic and elegiac qualities of Spenser's verse. Most of all, it maintains the fruitful distinction between the world Spenser's characters inhabit and the world we see, a distinction that enables us to "read" their stories with a maximum of knowledge and understanding.[18] While accruing these gains, Spenser's method of allusion risks losing both the straightforward progression and the undivided interest of more monolithic narratives such as *Paradise Lost.*

Along with its figural and narrative influence, the Scylla episode in the *Metamorphoses* bears on *The Faerie Queene* and *Paradise Lost* in yet another way. It contributes to the imagery and iconography of the *locus amoenus,* the pleasant place, usually a garden. For his

[16]Greene, *The Light in Troy,* p. 40.
[17]Angus Fletcher, *The Prophetic Moment,* pp. 102, 294.
[18]For this valuable insight I am indebted to Isabel MacCaffrey, *Spenser's Allegory: The Anatomy of Imagination* (Princeton, N.J., 1976), pp. 159–63.

depiction of Eden, Milton was of course free to draw upon a large number of *loci amoeni*.[19] Among these varied places, Ovid's *loci* are remarkable for two features: metamorphosis and violence within the delightful spot. That Milton in *Paradise Lost* welcomed the suggestion of these Ovidian possibilities is certain from his close imitation of Ovid's account of the rape of Proserpina in his celebrated Enna simile, which, as noted in Chapter 2, proleptically laments both Eve's fall and the pain of Christ in redeeming humankind.

The Scylla episode presents two complementary versions of the Ovidian *locus amoenus*. In attempting to seduce Scylla, the sea-god Glaucus describes the first, the unspoiled meadow where he was transformed from man to fish:

> sunt viridi prato confinia litora, quorum
> altera pars undis, pars altera cingitur herbis,
> quas neque cornigerae morsu laesere iuvencae,
> nec placidae carpsistis oves hirtaeve capellae;
> non apis inde tulit collecto semine flores,
> non data sunt capiti genialia serta, neque umquam
> falciferae secuere manus. ego primus in illo
> caespite consedi, dum lina madentia sicco,
> utque recenserem captivos ordine pisces,
> insuper exposui, quos aut in retia casus
> aut sua credulitas in aduncos egerat hamos.
> res similis fictae: sed quid mihi fingere prodest?
>
> (13.924–35)

There is a shore, bound by a verdant meadow, of which one part is encircled with waves and the other part with grasses, which neither horned cattle nor quiet she-goats nor fleecy sheep have disturbed by grazing. No bee having gathered seeds ever bore off flowers from there; no festal wreaths for the head were ever given from there, no

---

[19]First of all, Milton was careful to contradict nothing written in Genesis 1–2 about Eden. Other gardens of which the poet almost certainly was aware include Homer's garden of Alcinous in *Odyssey* 7.112–19; Dante's Earthly Paradise in *Purgatorio* 28.28–30; 33.109–11 and its celestial counterpart in *Paradiso* 30.61–63; the Garden of Deduit (1375–1438) and the Park of Genius (19907–20667) in the *Roman de la Rose;* Ariosto's paradise in *Orlando Furioso* 34.19; and Tasso's Garden of Arminda in *Gerusaleme Liberata* 16.10. Beyond the Ovidian *loci* examined here, Diana's grotto (*Met.* 3.138–252) and the stream Arethusa (5.577–641) may also have influenced Milton's Eden. See further Joseph E. Duncan's, *Milton's Earthly Paradise* (Minneapolis, 1972) and Giamatti, *The Earthly Paradise and the Renaissance Epic.*

hands with sickles ever mowed there. It was I who first sat on that turf while I was drying my matted lines, so that I could count in order my netted fish, which either chance had sent to my nets or their own guilelessness had sent to my hooks. The thing sounds like fiction, but what would I gain by deceiving you?

The inviolate privacy, the potential for metamorphosis, the spatial design of arcs within arcs, and the narrator's anticipation of disbelief in this place will figure largely in both Spenser's Garden of Adonis and Milton's Garden of Eden. In particular, Glaucus's protestation that his story sounds like fiction yet intends no deception approximates Milton's strategy of coalescing fiction and fact in his description of Eden: "*Hesperian* fables true, if true, here only." In Spenser's self-consciously literary boast that "this same [Garden of Adonis] / All other pleasant places doth excell" (3.6.29), Milton's great teacher may have provided him with the tone of superiority that he claims for his paradise above all others.

The second *locus amoenus* in Ovid's Scylla episode has less bearing on poetic landscape than on the psychology of Spenserian and Miltonic characters. At noon, according to her habit, Scylla returns to an isolated and shadowed pool to rest:

> Parvus erat gurges curvos sinuatus in arcus,
> grata quies Scyllae; quo se referebat ab aestu
> et maris et caeli, medio cum plurimus orbe
> sol erat et minimas a vertice fecerat umbras.
>
> (14.51–54)

There was a little whirlpool, bent inwards into curved bows, a restful place pleasing to Scylla. There she used to retire from the heat of both sea and sky, when the sun in mid-circuit was greatest and, from his apex, had made the shadows smallest.

Since Circe has poisoned the pool, the *locus amoenus* turns out to be a setting for violent destruction by an interloper and degenerative change in the victim, as happens so often in the *Metamorphoses*.[20] The pool in which Salmacis sexually molests Hermaphroditus

[20]See Charles Segal, *Landscape in Ovid's "Metamorphoses": A Study of the Transformation of a Literary Symbol* (Wiesbaden, 1969). On the general aspects of the *locus amoenus* see Curtius, *European Literature and the Latin Middle Ages*, pp. 182–202.

(4.285–386) and that in which Narcissus becomes infatuated with his shadowy reflection (3.402–510) are two closely related Ovidian places that foster such changes. The possibilities of monstrous reproduction, sexual incontinence and enervation, and self-enclosure which Scylla, Salmacis, and Narcissus depict seem to inhere not in the *locus amoenus* per se but in its occupant's mental state, typically one of "wavering identity," as Fraenkel has put it. As we have seen in Chapter 2, moments of these perilous mental states arise for Eve in her willingness to bring death into being for herself and her descendants, in her carnal desire for Adam after consuming the forbidden fruit, and in her fascination with her image in the pool when she first awakens to creation. Milton has arranged the Ovidian aspects of Eve's behavior to show her development through a series of metamorphic phases. Eve's individual development, we recall, increased her vulnerability before Satan, in that the temper was able to conflate her eventual improvement with the immediate means of perfecting her self, of gaining "God-head."

If we compare Spenser's developments of the Ovidian *locus amoenus* with Milton's, their similar psychological and moral significance as well as their divergent implications for characterization and structure come into sharp focus. A look first at Spenser's pleasant places in the Legend of Holiness, and then at his Garden of Adonis, in comparison with Milton's Eden, will specify and elucidate these claims.

The opening adventure of *The Faerie Queene* finds Redcross and Una entering a "shadie groue" to avoid a sudden rainstorm (1.1.7). Even before they become lost in the grove, they might have suspected these trees "that heauens light did hide," and that comprise a seductive Ovidian catalog, but "in they entred arre":

> And foorth they passe, with pleasure forward led,
>> Ioying to heare the birdes sweete harmony,
>> Which therein shrouded from the tempest dred,
>> Seemd in their song to scorne the cruell sky.
>> Much can they prayse the trees so straight and hy,
>> The sayling Pine, the Cedar proud and tall,
>> The vine-prop Elme, the Poplar neuer dry,
>> The builder Oake, sole king of forrests all,
> The Aspine good for staues, the Cypresse funerall.

> The Laurell, meed of mightie Conquerours
>> And Poets sage, the Firre that weepeth still,
>> The Willow worne of forlorne Paramours,
>> The Eugh obedient to the benders will,
>> The Birch for shaftes, the Sallow for the mill,
>> The Mirrhe sweete bleeding in the bitter wound,
>> The warlike Beech, the Ash for nothing ill,
>> The fruitfull Oliue, and the Platane round,
> The caruer Holme, the Maple seeldom inward sound.
>> (1.1.8–9)

Virtually the same trees appear together in Books 10 and 11 of the *Metamorphoses*, where they sympathetically gather to provide shade on a grassy hilltop for the bard Orpheus. In fact, Spenser's catalog of trees so closely follows Ovid's that the scene appears to have been dislocated from the *Metamorphoses* and relocated intact in *The Faerie Queene*. The allusion boldly adapts the mythic natural scenery of Ovid, though, to the mental terrain, the Coleridgean "mental space" of Faeryland. In the *Metamorphoses*, the trees could provide Orpheus with no protection against the Bacchantes, who stone him to death. Spenser uses the catalog of trees to represent a like vulnerability in the presence of apparent safety and sensuous charm (the birdsong). Spenser centers this vulnerability in the consciousness of the knight and the lady, who have wandered away from their quest while praising and exploring the trees. Both in its involved syntax and in the new principle of movement that opens the stanza, the next stanza brilliantly reflects the wanderers' plight.

> Led with delight, they thus beguile the way,
>> Vntill the blustring storme is ouerblowne;
>> When weening to returne, whence they did stray,
>> They cannot finde that path, which first was showne,
>> But wander too and fro in wayes vnknowne,
>> Furthest from end then, when they neerest weene,
>> That makes them doubt, their wits be not their owne:
>> So many pathes, so many turnings seene,
> That which of them to take, in diuerse doubt they been.

Spenser's syntax makes Redcross and Una simultaneously doubt which path to take (1.9) and whether they are in possession of their wits (1.7). Their "wits" are, to a large extent, the reader's as well, as we have delighted in the "turnings" of the verse through the catalog of trees, praising them as we went, as much as Redcross and Una. Unlike the characters, however, we can see where we have erred, and so learn to anticipate and detect future dangers.

Before proceeding to any further Ovidian *loci* in *The Faerie Queene*, we might pause to observe that Milton adapted the same catalog of trees to the characterization of Eve in *Paradise Lost*. Martz has shown that the rhetorical patterning of Ovid's tree catalog matches that of Eve's intricate, splendid declaration of love for Adam (IV, 641–56).[21] In contrast with Spenser's use of the catalog, Milton's adaptation leaves out the original content (trees) and adapts the catalog to a thoroughly positive moral and psychological scene. Because few readers of *Paradise Lost* could be expected to hear and respond to this imbedded use of Ovid, no comparing of Eve's situation with that of Orpheus is needed. The reader can respond more directly to Eve's speech as an expression of her unfallen joy and love, that is, as an expression of her character and of her surroundings. The reader may, in this case, follow the mental operations of Milton's characters, but their ways in Eden remain distinct from our usual wanderings.

Redcross's further encounters in Ovidian *loci* subtly develop his character while delightfully instructing the reader. Along the way, a second major difference between Spenserian and Miltonic characterization emerges. The sequence of episodes in the Legend of Holiness is not merely important; it is crucial to the knight's growth and progress. When Redcross lies down and toys with Fidessa in a "ioyous shade" (1.7.4), therein to take some relief from the "boyling heat," he has already talked at length with Fradubio, a man-turned-tree, in a similar cool shade (1.2.24–44). From that meeting, Redcross might conceivably have gone on prepared to decode "Fidessa's" intentions in dallying with him and leading him to drink in a stream that immediately saps his strength (1.7.6), for the false Duessa has done much the same to Fradubio. The place in which "Fidessa" tempts Redcross is recognizable to a reader schooled in Ovid, as it artfully conflates details from the myths of Actaeon

---

[21]Martz, *Poet of Exile*, pp. 214–15.

(Diana's dissatisfaction with her nymph), Salmacis (the enervating water), and Scylla (the shadowed retreat). Yet Spenser's rhetorical question opening the Canto strenuously reminds the reader that no one is able to detect hypocrisy, a view Milton adopts in excusing Uriel for allowing Satan to enter Eden (III, 681–85). Accordingly, Redcross fails to comprehend Duessa's intentions, and arises feebly from the grass without his armor (glossed in Spenser's Letter to Raleigh as "the armour of a Christian man specified by Saint Paul v. Ephes."), whereupon he hears the dreadful approach of Orgoglio, a sign of his own swollen pride.

Spenser's poetry, like Milton's, would seem to provide its characters with a maximum of both dangers and excuses at once. On close examination, however, the "danger" varies widely between the poems. Redcross inhabits a fallen world whose dangers are legion. Because of Spenser's allegorical method, Redcross's many slips into these dangers give the reader ample opportunity to understand and, when possible, to avert them. In their sensuous and distracting appeal, the Ovidian allusions in *The Faerie Queene* themselves often number among the dangers. The Ovidian allusions in *Paradise Lost,* for the most part, foreshadow a host of prospective dangers, but all of them remain merely prospective until Adam and Eve face the single, pivotal danger of the temptation. The beauty, diversity, and danger depicted in the *Metamorphoses* reappear in *Paradise Lost* to support and magnify the biblical account of the Fall and its consequences. Milton's allusions in his epic function much like the ornamented braces on the vault of a Baroque cathedral: not central to the body of the main structure, but indicative of its expansive design and conflicting forces.

Among Spenser's many vividly rendered gardens and pleasant retreats, the Garden of Adonis best merits comparison with Milton's Eden. Spenser's Bower of Bliss represents, in C. S. Lewis's words, "artifice, sterility, death," but the Garden of Adonis is "nature, fecundity, life."[22] Both the Garden of Adonis and Eden represent, of course, safe, joyous, and beneficent paradises. Although they would seem to have little in common with the Ovidian *loci amoeni* described earlier, they nevertheless recombine and ide-

---

[22]C. S. Lewis, *The Allegory of Love* (New York, 1958), p. 326.

alize certain Ovidian details. Both expand upon Ovid's description of the earth in the Golden Age:

> Ver erat aeternum, placidique tepentibus auris
> mulcebant Zephyri natos sine semine flores;
> mox etiam fruges tellus inarata ferebat,
> nec renovatus ager gravidis canebat aristis:
> flumina iam lactis, iam flumina nectaris ibant,
> flavaque de viridi stillabant ilice mella.
>
> (1.107–12)

Then spring was eternal, and gentle zephyrs with mild breath stroked flowers born from no seed. Then the earth, yet untilled, brought forth its fruits, and the field, without having been plowed, grew white with full harvests. Streams of milk and streams of nectar flowed, and yellow honey dripped from the fresh oak.

In describing the Garden of Adonis, Spenser adopts Ovid's *ver erat aeturnum,* depicts nature as a harmony of sights, sounds, and sensations there, and emphasizes its natural fecundity:

> There is continuall spring, and haruest there
> > Continuall, both meeting at one time:
> > For both the boughes doe laughing blossoms beare,
> > And with fresh colours decke the wanton Prime,
> > And eke attonce the heauy trees they clime,
> > Which seeme to labour vnder their fruits lode.
> >
> > (3.6.42.1–6)

Milton's summary description of Eden stresses, in turn, its variety, luxuriance, and harmony (IV, 246–87), and concludes with two Ovidian details, "th'Eternal Spring" and the myth of Proserpina. The whole passage shifts subtly from a description of nature, such as the poet could have seen at Vallombrosa or Penshurst ("happy rural seat"), to an amalgam of myths, such as he read in Ovid and Spenser. In addition to these correspondences, both the Garden of Adonis and Milton's Eden feature a mount in the center, with an arbor in the center of that. Most important for their occupants, both gardens contain the source of death as well as life: Time with his scythe in Adonis, and the Tree of Knowledge in Eden. Spenser's garden is closer to the Ovidian *loci* in one important respect: its colors and forms change, while their substance remains. This procedure follows the rule of Ovid's Pythagoras: "nec perit in toto . . . mundo, / sed variat faciemque novat" (nothing dies in the universe; it varies and renews its aspect), (15.254–55). Nature in the Mutabilitie Cantos reaches the same conclusion, but adds the apocalyptic prophecy of a time when "all shall changed bee" (7.7.59).

Where these two gardens ultimately differ is in the range of their significance within their poetic contexts. The Garden of Adonis is significant locally and synchronically; Eden, universally and diachronically. Despite its suggestions of universal fecundity, the Garden of Adonis appears in the Legend of Chastity for a specific reason: to account for Amoret's growth and training in "true feminitee" (3.6.51), or perfect womanhood. By describing the garden as Amoret's nursery both before and after giving his detailed account of it (3.6.29; 3.6.51), Spenser effectively restricts the garden's significance within the narrative to the education of Amoret. Once Amoret leaves her nursery, the Garden of Adonis may continue to bear new flora, and may remain an intriguing poetic construct, but it holds little or no further significance for either Amoret or the narrative. The Garden of Adonis is extremely significant for *The Faerie Queene* nevertheless, because it depicts the cooperation of chastity and fecundity, a theme crucial to Books 3 and 4 as well as to the Mutabilitie Cantos.

Milton's Eden, on the other hand, though at first the localized mythological home of our first parents, eventually becomes in *Paradise Lost* a reflection of their unfolding relationship and an image for their ultimate consolation (after the Fall). In contrast to the vegetative labor in Ovidian and Spenserian gardens, Adam and Eve work actively in Eden. Their trimming of overluxuriant growth and their wedding of the vine and elm reflect their own temperance and mutual love. After their Fall, Michael informs Adam and Eve not only that they must leave Eden, but that Eden shall be moved out of its present location and into the sea. Michael points out that this move is meant to be spiritually enlightening: "To teach thee that God attributes to place / No sanctitie" (XI,

836–37). The spiritual concept of Paradise, however, does remain. Building on his previous lesson, Michael exhorts Adam finally to join the practice of Christian virtues to his sadly gained knowledge, so that he "shalt possess / A paradise within" (XII, 586–87).

Milton's paradise enjoys a metamorphic afterlife unseen in the paradises of Ovid and Spenser largely because of the cohesive narrative structure of *Paradise Lost*. Despite Milton's development of two major Ovidian structural devices, the pervasive narrator who comments freely on his story and the alternation of point of view among various characters, it is Spenser whose epic best approximates the structure of the *Metamorphoses*. At the same time, what Spenser developed from Ovidian precedents in *The Faerie Queene*— complex moments of psychological insight such as Redcross's wandering into error; lush, dangerous *loci amoeni* such as the Garden of Adonis and the "ioyous shade"; and an epic structure moving through Ovidian changes toward a poetic debate on change itself— became for Milton valuable lessons from that "better teacher." Ovid provided sensuous scenes leading to thrilling action; the Christian poets saw in them opportunities for exercising reason, for choice.

Epilogue

One of the lessons Milton found expressed in Spenser was the notion of purification through trial. That lesson was the reason, in Milton's view, for Spenser to bring Guyon through the Cave of Mammon and the Bower of Earthly Bliss: "that he might see and know, and yet abstain." Because Milton cites this example in his campaign for unlicensed printing in *Areopagitica*, the argument for informed choice applies to reading as well. In reading books generally and in reading his books specifically, Milton's reader is urged with Guyon to see and know, and yet abstain from the allure and seeming pleasures of vice, and to prefer that which is truly better. The contrary errant choices do not cease to be attractive options— they become rather opportunities for exercising virtue, for purification.

This lesson extends to Milton's use of Ovid as traced throughout this study. In his dialogue with Ovid in *Paradise Lost*, Milton brings the reader through a series of opportunities to see and know apparent pleasures and yet prefer a better way. Thus Eve's fascination with her reflection, based on Ovid's account of Narcissus, becomes a "seeming pleasure" when one compares it with her more productive Ovidian stances as Pomona and Pyrrha. Satan's initially attractive heroism, conveyed through Ovidian analogues, is gradually exposed as a vain approach to godhead; his version of heroism, too, once well seen and known, can be replaced by the "better fortitude / Of Patience and Heroic Martyrdom." Even the Miltonic narrator confronts attractive, specious choices presented by Ovid: to sanction his poem on the authority of his own rhetorical self, to accept the apparently ceaseless flux of change, to make verbal curiosities the end of his poesis. Rather than slink away from these possibilities, Milton confronts them in a free and open encounter by including palpably Ovidian figures, rhetoric, and structures within his Christian epic. The presence of these Ovidian elements suggests that, like the *Metamorphoses, Paradise Lost* is an epic of change. It is more flexible in its style and rhetoric, more varied in its suggestiveness because of Milton's encounter with Ovid. For the fit audience of *Paradise Lost,* however, the partial illumination of Ovid's *Metamorphoses* provides at best a way out of eternal, restless change toward Milton's vision of eternal Providence. "[T]hat fair field / Of *Enna*" which Ovid so movingly described must ultimately fail to describe Eden. But even as it fails, Milton's allusion works to suggest the greater beauty, danger, woe, and salvation of his Christian mythos.

Milton's imitation of Ovid epitomizes the heroic, at times perilous struggle between poetic fiction and Christian truth which characterizes *Paradise Lost.* For Andrew Marvell, among the first and best critics of the poem, that struggle was the fundamental problem Milton posed. In Marvell's view, Milton threatened to "ruin (for I saw him strong) / The sacred Truths to Fable and old Song." Marvell's concern might alert later critics to recover a sense of the fundamental danger that Milton's struggle with the pagan classics involves. Alerted to this danger, we might return to *Paradise Lost* with greater awareness of its "vast Design" and openness to its power to purify.

After *Paradise Lost,* the dialectical imitation of Ovid comes to an end. In *Paradise Regained* and *Samson Agonistes,* Milton would withdraw from the extensive use of Ovid (and of pagan fables generally) that we have seen in *Paradise Lost.* It may be that the rational skepticism in Milton's view of pagan literature eventually triumphed, or that Milton himself adopted the severe view on the pagan poets that the Savior maintains in *Paradise Regained:* "But these are false, or little else but dreams, / Conjectures, fancies, built on nothing firm" (IV, 291–92). If there is a greater consistency in this stance, there is also a corresponding loss of that creative struggle with the pagan classics which we have seen in *Paradise Lost.* In English literary history, too, *Paradise Lost* is the high-water mark of Ovidian imitation. Poets such as Dryden, Pope, and Keats would inevitably read the Latin poet through Milton's epic, and never again would a student and critic of Ovid so thoroughly imitate his metamorphic verse. Yet with each new reading of *Paradise Lost* Ovid may come to life again, revived uneasily in an argument of sublime wonder, danger, woe, and promised redemption.

Appendix: Verbal Echoes of Ovid's
Metamorphoses in *Paradise Lost*

Paradise Lost	Metamorphoses	Paradise Lost	Metamorphoses
I, 1–26	1.1–4	968	12.43–47
9–10	1.5–7; 1.21–23	1020	13.730
33–36	1.128–31		
36–49	1.151–56;	III, 56–61	1.177–81
	2.304–20	359	2.364–66
48	7.412	364	2.113–14
69	15.350–52	380	2.181
87–91	1.351–53	381–82	2.21–23
196–200	1.156; 1.438–40	455–59	1.7–9
230–38	15.296–355	501–9	2.1–7
476–82	5.319–31	579–84	2.25–30
591–92	1.1	591–608	2.1–4
619–20	11.419	636–39	2.733–34
670–74	5.352–58	708–21	1.5–31
685–90	1.138–42	718–21	1.69–71
723–26	4.762–63	730–31	15.196–98
710–17	2.1–7		
		IV, 218–20	4.637–38;
II, 1–6	1.176–80		10.647–50
28	1.154; 1.70;	223–35	5.501–5
	1.197	236–40	1.111
306–7	4.657–62	248–51	4.637–38;
397–98	1.45–51		10.647–50;
530	1.445–49		11.113–14
539–41	5.349–58	261–63	9.334–35
542–46	9.134–231	264–68	1.107–12
552–55	10.40–48	268–72	5.385–96;
650–61	14.59–67		5.438–41
890–906	1.5–20	277	5.327–28
922	5.155–56	288–92	1.76–86

Paradise Lost	Metamorphoses	Paradise Lost	Metamorphoses
396–98	5.327–31	453–55	1.416–21;
453–69	3.407–36		1.434–37
641–56	10.90–105	506–16	1.76–88
705–8	3.155–62	574–81	1.168–71
763–65	1.468–70	624	1.30–31
802–9	11.613–15		
976	1.168–71	VIII, 54–57	10.558–59
987–88	4.657–62	610–11	7.20–21
V, 137	12.212	IX, 390–96	14.623–31
166	2.114–15	494–507	3.31–45; 4.571–
171	4.228		603
193–94	1.566–67	782–84	1.202–3
215–19	14.661–68		
377–79	14.623–27;	X, 282–88	1.5–20
	14.635–36	295–96	15.336–37
699–701	9.588–89	311	11.491
753–59	2.1–7	355	13.140–41
		504–21	4.571–80
VI, 2–4	2.112–14	526–28	4.617–20
82–83	8.285	529–31	1.434–40
478–83	15.346–55	540–45	4.581–603
521–22	13.15	651–56	1.116–20
643–46	12.507–9;	664–67	1.55–66
	13.882–84	678–79	1.107–8
673	2.300		
		XI, 8–14	1.318–23
VII, 4	4.785–86	57–60	1.661–63
32–38	11.1–43	129–33	1.625–716
89–90	1.12	323–24	15.573–74
98–99	2.63–67	586–91	4.758–64
239–42	1.12–31	738–45	1.264–69
278–81	1.416–21	747–50	1.288–92
285–89	1.43–44	777–79	1.311–12
290–94	1.38–42	841–43	1.328
387–89	1.72–75		
416	3.686	XII, 13–19	1.123–27
417	2.269	24–32	1.127–50

Bibliography

Albrecht, Michael von. *Die Parenthese in Ovids "Metamorphosen" und ihre dichterische Funktion*. Hildesheim: Georg Olms, 1964.

Allen, Don Cameron. *The Harmonious Vision: Studies in Milton's Poetry*. Baltimore: Johns Hopkins University Press, 1970.

———. *Mysteriously Meant: The Rediscovery of Pagan Symbolism and Allegorical Interpretation in the Renaissance*. Baltimore: Johns Hopkins University Press, 1970.

Alpers, Paul. "Narration in *The Faerie Queene*." *ELH* 44 (1977), 19–39.

Anderson, W. S. "The Orpheus of Virgil and Ovid: *flebile nescio quid*." In *Orpheus: The Metamorphosis of a Myth,* ed. John Warden. Toronto: University of Toronto Press, 1982.

Aristotle. *On The Art of Poetry*. Trans. Ingram Bywater. Preface by Gilbert Murray. Oxford: Clarendon Press, 1920; rpt. 1962.

Auerbach, Erich. "Dante's Addresses to the Reader." In *Parnassus Revisited: Modern Critical Essays on the Epic Tradition,* ed. Anthony C. Yu, pp. 121–31. Chicago: American Library Association, 1973.

———. *Mimesis: The Representation of Reality in Western Literature*. Trans. Willard R. Trask. Princeton: Princeton University Press, 1953.

Avery, Mary Myrtle. "The Use of Direct Speech in Ovid's *Metamorphoses*." Diss. University of Chicago, 1937.

Baldwin, T. W. *William Shakespeare's Small Latine & Lesse Greeke*. 2 vols. Urbana: University of Illinois Press, 1944.

Berchorius [Bersuire], Petrus. *Metamorphosis Ovidiana moraliter*. Paris, 1509.

Berger, Harry, Jr. *The Allegorical Temper: Vision and Reality in Book II of Spenser's "Faerie Queene."* New Haven: Yale University Press, 1957; rpt. Hamden, Conn.: Archon Books, 1967.

Binns, J. W., ed. *Ovid*. London: Routledge & Kegan Paul, 1973.

Blessington, Francis C. *"Paradise Lost" and the Classical Epic*. Boston: Routledge & Kegan Paul, 1979.

Bloom, Harold. *The Anxiety of Influence: A Theory of Poetry*. New York: Oxford University Press, 1973.

Bibliography

———. *A Map of Misreading*. New York: Oxford University Press, 1975.

Bono, Barbara J. *Literary Transvaluation from Vergilian Epic to Shakespeare.* Berkeley: University of California Press, 1984.

Boswell, Jackson Campbell. *Milton's Library: A Catalogue of the Remains of John Milton's Library and an Annotated Reconstruction of Milton's Library and Ancillary Readings.* New York: Garland, 1975.

Bouchard, Donald F. *Milton: A Structural Reading.* Montreal: McGill-Queen's University Press, 1974.

Bowra, C. M. *From Virgil to Milton.* London: Macmillan, 1945.

Boyette, Purvis E. "Milton and the Sacred Fire: Sex Symbolism in *Paradise Lost.*" *Literary Monographs* 5 (1973), 63–138.

Brenkman, John. "Narcissus in the Text." *Georgia Review* 30 (1976), 293–327.

Brill, Mary Campbell. "Milton and Ovid." Diss. Cornell University, 1935.

Brinsley, John. *Ludus Literarius.* London, 1612.

Broadbent, J. B. "Milton's Rhetoric." *MP* 56 (1959), 224–42.

Brownlee, Kevin. "Dante and Narcissus." *Dante Studies* 96 (1978), 201–6.

Burck, Erich. *Vom römischen Manierismus.* Darmstadt: Wissenschaftliche Buchgesellschaft, 1971.

Burden, Dennis H. *The Logical Epic: A Study of the Argument of "Paradise Lost."* Cambridge, Mass.: Harvard University Press, 1967.

Bush, Douglas. *English Literature in the Earlier Seventeenth Century: 1600–1660.* 2d rev. ed. The Oxford History of English Literature, ed. John Buxton and Norman Davis. Oxford: Clarendon Press, 1962; rpt. 1976.

———. "Ironic and Ambiguous Allusions in *Paradise Lost.*" *JEGP* 60 (1961), 638–39.

———. *Mythology and the Renaissance Tradition in English Poetry.* Minneapolis: University of Minnesota Press, 1932; new rev. ed. New York: Norton, 1963.

Cartari, Vincent. *Images des dieux.* Lyons: Paul Frellon, 1610.

Clark, Donald L. *John Milton at St. Paul's School.* New York: Columbia University Press, 1948.

Clarke, Martin L. *Classical Education in Britian: 1500–1900.* Cambridge: Cambridge University Press, 1959.

Cohen, Ralph, ed. *New Directions in Literary History.* London: Routledge & Kegan Paul, 1974.

Coleman, R. "Structure and Intention in the *Metamorphoses.*" *CQ* 65 (1971), 461–76.

Colie, Rosalie L. *The Resources of Kind: Genre-theory in the Renaissance.* Ed. Barbara K. Lewalski. Berkeley: University of California Press, 1973.

Comes, Natalis. *Mythologiae sive Explicationis Fabularum.* Rpt. in The Philosophy of Images, ed. Stephen Orgel. New York: Garland, 1979.

Cumming, William P. "The Influence of Ovid's *Metamorphoses* on Spenser's 'Mutabilitie Cantos.'" *SP* 28 (1931), 241–56.

Curran, Stuart. "The Mental Pinnacle: *Paradise Regained* and the Romantic

Four-Book Epic." In *Calm of Mind: Tercentenary Essays on "Paradise Regained" and "Samson Agonistes" in Honor of John S. Diekhoff*, ed. Joseph A. Wittreich, Jr., pp. 133–62. Cleveland: Case Western Reserve Press, 1971.

Curtius, Ernst Robert. *European Literature and the Latin Middle Ages.* Trans. Willard R. Trask. Princeton: Princeton University Press, 1953.

Daniells, Roy. *Milton, Mannerism and Baroque.* Toronto: University of Toronto Press, 1963.

Dees, Jerome S. "The Narrator of *The Faerie Queene:* Patterns of Response." *TSLL* 12 (1971), 537–68.

Deferrari, Roy J., Sister M. Inviolata Barry, and Martin R. P. McGuire, eds. *A Concordance of Ovid.* Washington, D.C.: Catholic University of America Press, 1939.

De Quincey, Thomas. *The Collected Writings of Thomas De Quincey.* Ed. David Masson. 14 vols. Edinburgh: Adam and Charles Black, 1889–90; rpt. New York: AMS Press, 1968.

Di Cesare, Mario. "Advent'rous Song: The Texture of Milton's Epic." In *Language and Style in Milton*, ed. R. D. Emma and John T. Shawcross, pp. 1–29. New York: Frederick Ungar, 1967.

_____. "*Paradise Lost* and Epic Tradition." *MS* 1 (1969), 31–50.

Dixon, Peter. *Rhetoric.* London: Methuen, 1971.

Dryden, John. *Essays of John Dryden.* Ed. W. P. Ker. 2 vols. Oxford: Clarendon Press, 1900.

Due, Otto Steen. *Changing Forms: Studies in the "Metamorphoses" of Ovid.* Copenhagen: Gyldendal, 1974.

Duncan, Joseph E. *Milton's Earthly Paradise.* Minneapolis: University of Minnesota Press, 1972.

Durling, Robert M. *The Figure of the Poet in Renaissance Epic.* Cambridge, Mass.: Harvard University Press, 1965.

Ellwood, Thomas. *The History of Thomas Ellwood, Written by Himself.* London: George Routledge and Sons, 1885; rpt. Methuen, 1900.

Else, Gerald F. *Aristotle's "Poetics": The Argument.* Cambridge, Mass.: Harvard University Press, 1957.

Emma, R. D., and John T. Shawcross, eds. *Language and Style in Milton.* New York: Frederick Ungar, 1967.

Entzminger, Robert L. "Michael's Options and Milton's Poetry: *Paradise Lost* XI and XII." *ELR* 8 (1978), 197–211.

Ferry, Anne Davidson. *Milton's Epic Voice: The Narrator in "Paradise Lost."* Cambridge, Mass.: Harvard University Press, 1963.

Fish, Stanley. *Surprised by Sin: The Reader in "Paradise Lost."* London: Macmillan, 1967.

Fletcher, Angus. *Allegory: The Theory of a Symbolic Mode.* Ithaca, N.Y.: Cornell University Press, 1964.

_____. *The Prophetic Moment: An Essay on Spenser.* Chicago: University of Chicago Press, 1971.

Fletcher, Harris Francis. *The Intellectual Development of John Milton*. 2 vols. Urbana: University of Illinois Press, 1956.

Fowler, Alastair. *Kinds of Literature: An Introduction to the Theory of Genres and Modes*. Cambridge, Mass.: Harvard University Press, 1982.

――. "The Life and Death of Literary Forms." In *New Directions in Literary History*, ed. Ralph Cohen, pp. 77–94. Baltimore: Johns Hopkins University Press, 1974.

Fraenkel, Hermann. *Ovid: A Poet between Two Worlds*. Berkeley: University of California Press, 1945.

Freeman, James A. *Milton and the Martial Muse*. Princeton: Princeton University Press, 1980.

French, J. Milton, ed. *The Life Records of John Milton*. 5 vols. New Brunswick, N.J.: Rutgers University Press, 1949–58.

Friedmann, Anthony E. "The Diana–Acteon Episode in Ovid's *Metamorphoses* and the *Faerie Queene*." *CL* 18 (1966), 289–99.

Frye, Northrop. *Anatomy of Criticism: Four Essays*. Princeton: Princeton University Press, 1957; rpt. 1973.

Fyler, John. *Chaucer and Ovid*. New Haven: Yale University Press, 1979.

Galinsky, G. Karl. *Ovid's "Metamorphoses": An Introduction to the Basic Aspects*. Berkeley: University of California Press, 1975.

Gardner, Helen. "Milton's 'Satan' and the Theme of Damnation in Elizabethan Tragedy." *English Studies* 1 (1948), 46–66; rpt. in *Milton: Modern Essays in Criticism*, ed. Arthur Barker, pp. 205–17. New York: Oxford University Press, 1965.

Giamatti, A. Bartlett. *The Earthly Paradise and the Renaissance Epic*. Princeton: Princeton University Press, 1966.

Gilde, Helen C. "Spenser's Hellenore and some Ovidian Associations." *CL* 23 (1971), 233–39.

Giraldi Cinthio. *On Romances*. Trans. with intro. and notes by Henry L. Snuggs. Lexington: University of Kentucky Press, 1968.

Gmelin, Hermann. "Das Prinzip der Imitatio in den romanischen Literaturen der Renaissance." *Romanische Forschungen* 46 (1932), 82–360.

Grandsen, K. W. "*Paradise Lost* and the *Aeneid*." *Essays in Criticism* 17 (1967), 281–303.

Greenblatt, Stephen, ed. *The Forms of Power and the Power of Forms in the Renaissance*. Special Topics Issue # 7, *Genre* 15 (1982).

Greene, Thomas M. *The Light in Troy: Imitation and Discovery in Renaissance Poetry*. New Haven: Yale University Press, 1982.

Grose, Christopher. *Milton's Epic Process*. New Haven: Yale University Press, 1973.

Guillory, John. *Poetic Authority: Spenser, Milton, and Literary History*. New York: Columbia University Press, 1983.

Hagin, Peter F. *The Epic Hero and the Decline of Heroic Poetry: A Study of the Neoclassical English Epic with Special Reference to Milton's "Paradise Lost."* Solothurn, Switzerland: Gassman, 1964.

Bibliography

Hanford, James Holly. *The Youth of Milton: Studies in Shakespeare, Milton, and Donne.* New York: Haskell House, 1964.

———, and James G. Taaffe. *A Milton Handbook.* 5th ed. New York: Appleton-Century-Crofts, 1970.

Harding, Davis P. *Milton and the Renaissance Ovid.* Urbana: University of Illinois Press, 1946.

Hartman, Geoffrey. "Adam on the Grass with Balsamum." *ELH* 36 (1969), 168–92.

———. "Milton's Counterplot." *ELH* 25 (1958), 1–12.

Herbst, Edward L. "Classical Mythology in *Paradise Lost.*" *CP* 29 (1934), 147–48.

Herford, C. H. "Dante and Milton." *Bulletin of the John Rylands Library* 8 (1924), 191–235.

Hertz, Neil. "Wordsworth and the Tears of Adam." *Studies in Romanticism* 7 (1967), 15–33; rpt. in *Wordsworth: A Collection of Critical Essays,* ed. M. H. Abrams, pp. 107–22. Englewood Cliffs, N.J.: Prentice-Hall, 1972.

Hieatt, A. Kent. *Chaucer, Spenser, Milton: Mythopoeic Continuities and Transformations.* Montreal: McGill-Queens University Press, 1975.

Hill, Christopher. *Milton and the English Revolution.* New York: Viking, 1978.

Hinton, Stan. "The Poet and His Narrator: Spenser's Epic Voice." *ELH* 41 (1974), 165–81.

Hirsch, E. D., Jr. *Validity in Interpretation.* New Haven: Yale University Press, 1967.

Holahan, M. N. "'Iamque opus exegi': Ovid's Changes and Spenser's Brief Epic of Mutability." *ELR* 6 (1976), 244–70.

Hollander, John. *The Figure of Echo: A Mode of Allusion in Milton and After.* Berkeley: University of California Press, 1981.

Homer. *The Odyssey of Homer.* Trans. with intro. by Richmond Lattimore. New York: Harper & Row, 1965; rpt. 1975.

Hoole, Charles. *A New Discovery of the Old Art of Teaching Schoole.* London, 1660.

Hübener, Gustav. *Die Stilistische Spannung in Milton's "Paradise Lost."* Göttingen: Halle, 1913.

Hulse, Clark. *Metamorphic Verse: The Elizabethan Minor Epic.* Princeton: Princeton University Press, 1981.

Hume, Patrick. *Annotations on Milton's "Paradise Lost."* London: J. Tonson, 1695.

Hunter, G. K. *"Paradise Lost."* Unwin Critical Library, gen. ed. Claude Rawson. London: George Allen and Unwin, 1980.

Ingram, W., and Kathleen M. Swaim, eds. *A Concordance to Milton's English Poetry.* Oxford: Clarendon Press, 1972.

James, Henry. *The Art of the Novel: Critical Prefaces by Henry James.* Intro. by R. P. Blackmur. New York: Scribner's, 1934; rpt. 1962.

Johnson, W. R. "The Problem of the Counter–classical Sensibility and Its Critics." *California Studies in Classical Antiquity* 3 (1970), 123–52.

Jonson, Ben. *Works.* 11 vols. Ed. C. H. Herford, Percy Simpson, and Evelyn Simpson. Oxford: Clarendon Press, 1925–52.

Kates, Judith A. "The Revaluation of the Classical Heroic in Tasso and Milton." *CL* 26 (1974), 299–317.

Kennedy, George A. *The Art of Rhetoric in the Roman World.* Princeton: Princeton University Press, 1972.

Kennedy, William J. *Rhetorical Norms in Renaissance Literature.* New Haven: Yale University Press, 1978.

Kent, Thomas L. "The Classification of Genres." *Genre* 16 (1983), 1–20.

Kermode, J. F. *The Classic: Literary Images of Permanence and Change.* New York: Viking, 1975.

Kranidas, Thomas. *The Fierce Equation: A Study of Milton's Decorum.* London: Mouton, 1965.

Lanham, Richard A. *The Motives of Eloquence.* New Haven: Yale University Press, 1976.

Le Comte, Edward. *Milton and Sex.* New York: Columbia University Press, 1975.

Lewalski, Barbara Kiefer. "The Genres of *Paradise Lost:* Literary Genre as a Means of Accommodation." In *Composite Orders: The Genres of Milton's Last Poems,* ed. Richard S. Ide and Joseph Wittreich, Jr. *MS* 17 (1983), 75–103.

——. "Innocence and Experience in Eden." In *New Essays on "Paradise Lost,"* ed. Thomas Kranidas, pp. 86–117. Berkeley: University of California Press, 1969.

——. "Structure and the Symbolism of Adam's Vision: Books XI and XII." *PQ* 62 (1963), 25–35.

Lewis, Charlton T., and Charles Short, eds. *A Latin Dictionary.* Oxford: Clarendon Press, 1969; rpt. 1980.

Lewis, C. S. *The Allegory of Love.* Oxford: Clarendon Press, 1936; rpt. New York: Macmillan, 1958.

——. *A Preface to "Paradise Lost."* New York: Oxford University Press, 1942; rpt. 1961.

Lieb, Michael. *Poetics of the Holy: A Reading of "Paradise Lost."* Chapel Hill: University of North Carolina Press, 1981.

Longinus. *On the Sublime.* Trans. W. Rhys Roberts. Cambridge: Cambridge University Press, 1907.

Lot, Ferdinand. *Etudes sur le Lancelot en prose.* Paris: E. Champion, 1918; rev. ed. 1954.

Lotspeich, Henry G. *Classical Mythology in the Poetry of Edmund Spenser.* Princeton: Princeton University Press, 1932.

Ludwig, Walther. *Struktur und Einheit der Metamorphosen Ovids.* Berlin: De Gruyter, 1965.

MacCaffrey, Isabel G. *"Paradise Lost" as "Myth."* Cambridge, Mass.: Harvard University Press, 1959.

———. *Spenser's Allegory: The Anatomy of Imagination*. Princeton: Princeton University Press, 1976.

MacCallum, H. R. "Milton and Sacred History: Books XI and XII of *Paradise Lost*." In *Essays in English Literature from the Renaissance to the Victorian Age Presented to A. S. P. Woodhouse*, ed. Millar Maclure and F. W. Watt, pp. 149–68. Toronto: University of Toronto Press, 1964.

McColley, Diane Kelsey. *Milton's Eve*. Urbana: University of Illinois Press, 1983.

Martz, Louis L. *Poet of Exile: A Study of Milton's Poetry*. New Haven: Yale University Press, 1980.

———. "The Rising Poet." In *The Lyric and Dramatic Milton*, ed. Joseph H. Summers, pp. 3–33. New York: Columbia University Press, 1965.

Milton, John. *The Columbia Edition of the Works of John Milton*. 23 vols. Ed. Frank Allan Patterson et al. New York: Columbia University Press, 1931–40.

———. *The Complete Poems and Major Prose of John Milton*. Ed. Merritt Y. Hughes. Indianapolis: Odyssey Press, 1957.

———. *The Complete Prose Works of John Milton*. 8 vols. Ed. Don M. Wolfe et al. New Haven: Yale University Press, 1953–82.

———. *John Milton: The Complete Shorter Poems*. Ed. John Carey. London: Longman, 1968; rpt. 1978.

———. *John Milton's Complete Poetical Works*. Reproduced in Photographic Facsimile. 4 vols. Ed. Harris F. Fletcher. Urbana: University of Illinois Press, 1948.

———. *Milton's "Paradise Lost": A New Edition*. Ed. Richard Bentley. London: J. Tonson, 1732.

———. *Paradise Lost*. Ed. Scott Elledge. New York: Norton, 1975.

———. *Paradise Lost*. Ed. Alastair Fowler. London: Longman, 1971.

———. *A Variorum Commentary on the Poems of John Milton*. 3 vols. Ed. Merritt Y. Hughes et al. New York: Columbia University Press, 1970–.

Miner, Earl. *The Metaphysical Mode from Donne to Cowley*. Princeton: Princeton University Press, 1969.

Murray, Gilbert. *The Rise of the Greek Epic*. New York: Oxford University Press, 1924.

Naumann, Heinrich. "Ovid und die Rhetorik." *Altsprachliche Unterricht* 11 (1968), 69–86.

Nelson, William. *The Poetry of Edmund Spenser: A Study*. New York: Columbia University Press, 1963.

Novarr, David. "Gray Dissimulation: Ford and Milton." *PQ* 41 (1962), 500–504.

Ogilvie, R. M. *Latin and Greek: A History of the Influence of the Classics in English Life from 1600 to 1918*. Hamden, Conn.: Archon Books, 1964.

Osgood, Charles Grosvenor. *The Classical Mythology of Milton's English Poems*. New York: Henry Holt, 1900.

Otis, Brooks. *Ovid as an Epic Poet*. 2d rev. ed. Cambridge, Mass.: Harvard University Press, 1970.

Ovid. *The Art of Love and Other Poems.* Trans. J. H. Moxley. 2d ed., rev. by G. P. Goold. The Loeb Classical Library. Cambridge, Mass.: Harvard University Press, 1979.

———. *Fasti.* Trans. Sir James George Frazer. The Loeb Classical Library. Cambridge, Mass.: Harvard University Press, 1931.

———. *Heroides and Amores.* Trans. Grant Showerman. 2d ed., rev. by G. P. Goold. The Loeb Classical Library. Cambridge, Mass.: Harvard University Press, 1977.

———. *Metamorphoseon libris XV.* Ed. with commentary by J. Spanmueller (Pontanus). Antwerp, 1610.

———. *Metamorphoses.* 2 vols. Trans. Frank Justus Miller. 3d ed., rev. by G. P. Goold. The Loeb Classical Library. Cambridge, Mass.: Harvard University Press, 1977.

———. *Metamorphoses.* Trans. Rolfe Humphries. Bloomington: Indiana University Press, 1955.

———. *The "Metamorphoses" of Ovid.* Trans. A. E. Watts. Berkeley: University of California Press, 1954; rpt. San Francisco: North Point Press, 1980.

———. *Ovid's "Metamorphoses," Books 6–10.* Ed. with intro. and notes by William S. Anderson. Norman: University of Oklahoma Press, 1972.

———. *Ovid's "Metamorphosis" Englished, Mythologized, and Represented in Figures,* by George Sandys. Ed. Karl K. Hulley and Stanley T. Vandersall. Foreword by Douglas Bush. Lincoln, Neb.: University of Nebraska Press, 1970.

———. *P. Ovidii Nasonis. Metamorphoses.* Ed. William S. Anderson. Leipzig: Teubner, 1977.

———. *P. Ovidii Nasonis poete ingeniosissimi Metamorphoseos Libri XV. In eosdem libros Raphaelis Regii luculentissime enarrationes. Neque non Lactantii et Petri Lavinii commentarii non ante impressi.* Venice, 1527.

———. *Shakespeare's Ovid, Being Arthur Golding's Translation of the "Metamorphoses."* Ed. W. H. D. Rouse. London: De La More Press, 1904; rpt. Carbondale: Southern Illinois University Press, 1962.

———. *Tristia. Ex Ponto.* Trans. Arthur Leslie Wheeler. The Loeb Classical Library. Cambridge, Mass.: Harvard University Press, 1924; rpt. 1959.

"Ovide moralisé": Poeme du commencement du quatorzieme siecle. Ed. C. de Boer et al. Verhandeling der Koninklijke Akademie van Wetenschappen te Amsterdam. Amsterdam: Afdeeling Letterkunde, 1915–38.

Parker, William Riley. *Milton: A Biography.* 2 vols. Oxford: Clarendon Press, 1968.

Patrides, C. A. *Milton and the Christian Tradition.* Oxford: Clarendon Pesss, 1966.

———, ed. *Approaches to "Paradise Lost."* The York Tercentenary Lectures. London: Edward Arnold, 1968.

Pease, Donald. "Blake, Crane, Whitman, and Modernism: A Poetics of Pure Possibility." *PMLA* 96 (1981), 64–85.

Pigman, G. W. "Versions of Imitation in the Renaissance." *RenQ* 33 (1980), 1–32.

Bibliography

Pöschl, Viktor. *The Art of Virgil: Image and Symbol in the "Aeneid."* Trans. Gerda Seligson. Ann Arbor: University of Michigan Press, 1962.

Prince, F. T. *The Italian Element in Milton's Verse.* Oxford: Clarendon Press, 1954; rpt. 1969.

Puttenham, George. *The Arte of English Poesie.* Ed. Gladys Doidge Willcock and Alice Walker. Cambridge: Cambridge University Press, 1936.

Quintilian. *Institutio Oratoria.* Ed. H. E. Butler. The Loeb Classical Library. Cambridge, Mass.: Harvard University Press, 1920; rpt. 1963.

Radzinowicz, Mary Ann. "Man as a Probationer of Immortality." In *Approaches to "Paradise Lost,"* ed. C. A. Patrides, pp. 31–51. London: Edward Arnold, 1968.

——. *Toward "Samson Agonistes": The Growth of Milton's Mind.* Princeton: Princeton University Press, 1978.

Rajan, B. *"Paradise Lost" and the Seventeenth-Century Reader.* London: Chatto and Windus, 1947; rpt. Ann Arbor: University of Michigan Press, 1967.

Rand, E. K. "Milton in Rustication." *SP* 19 (1922), 109–35.

——. *Ovid and His Influence.* London, 1926; rpt. New York: Cooper Square Press, 1963.

Revard, Stella P. *The War in Heaven: "Paradise Lost" and the Tradition of Satan's Rebellion.* Ithaca, N.Y.: Cornell University Press, 1980.

Richardson, Janette. "Virgil and Milton Once Again." *CL* 14 (1962), 321–31.

Ricks, Christopher. *Milton's Grand Style.* Oxford: Clarendon Press, 1963.

Riggs, William G. *The Christian Poet in "Paradise Lost."* Berkeley: University of California Press, 1972.

Ringler, Richard N. "The Faunus Episode," *MP* 63 (1965), 12–19; rpt. in *Essential Articles for the Study of Edmund Spenser,* ed. A. C. Hamilton, pp. 289–98. Hamden, Conn.: Archon Books, 1972.

Roston, Murray. *Milton and the Baroque.* Pittsburgh: University of Pittsburgh Press, 1980.

Samuel, Irene. *Dante and Milton: The "Commedia" and "Paradise Lost."* Ithaca, N.Y.: Cornell University Press, 1966.

——. "Paradise Lost." In *Critical Approaches to Six Major English Works,* ed. R. M. Lumiansky and Herschel Baker, pp. 209–53. Philadelphia: University of Pennsylvania Press, 1968.

——. *Plato and Milton.* Ithaca, N.Y.: Cornell University Press, 1947.

Sasek, Lawrence A. "The Drama of *Paradise Lost,* Books XI and XII." In *Studies in English Renaissance Literature,* ed. W. F. McNeir, pp. 181–96. Baton Rouge: Louisiana State University Press, 1962; rpt. in *Milton: Modern Essays in Criticism,* ed. Arthur Barker, pp. 342–56. New York: Oxford University Press, 1965.

Scholes, Robert, and Robert Kellogg. *The Nature of Narrative.* New York: Oxford University Press, 1966; rpt. 1976.

Segal, Charles. *Landscape in Ovid's "Metamorphoses": A Study in the Transformation of a Literary Symbol.* Wiesbaden: Franz Steiner, 1969.

——. "Narrative Art in the *Metamorphoses.*" *CJ* 66 (1971), 331–37.

Bibliography

Seneca. *Medea*. Ed. C. D. N. Costa. Oxford: Clarendon Press, 1973.

Shawcross, John T. *With Mortal Voice: The Creation of "Paradise Lost."* Lexington: University of Kentucky Press, 1982.

Spencer, T. J. B. *"Paradise Lost:* The Anti-Epic." In *Approaches to "Paradise Lost,"* ed. C. A. Patrides, pp. 81–98. London: Edward Arnold, 1968.

Spenser, Edmund. *Edmund Spenser: "The Faerie Queene."* Ed. A. C. Hamilton. London: Longman, 1977.

Spingarn, J. E. *A History of Literary Criticism in the Renaissance.* New York: Columbia University Press, 1924; rpt. Westport, Conn.: Greenwood Press, 1976.

Starnes, DeWitt T., and Ernest William Talbert. *Classical Mythology and Legend in Renaissance Dictionaries.* Chapel Hill: University of North Carolina Press, 1955.

Steadman, John M. *Epic and Tragic Structure in "Paradise Lost."* Chicago: University of Chicago Press, 1976.

_____. *"Ethos and Dianoia:* Character and Rhetoric in *Paradise Lost."* In *Language and Style in Milton,* ed. R. D. Emma and John T. Shawcross, pp. 193–232. New York: Frederick Ungar, 1967.

_____. *Milton and the Renaissance Hero.* Oxford: Clarendon Press, 1967.

_____. *Milton's Epic Characters.* Chapel Hill: University of North Carolina Press, 1959; rpt. 1968.

_____. "Milton's Rhetoric: Satan and the 'Unjust Discourse.'" *MS* 1 (1969), 67–91.

_____. "Tantalus and the Dead Sea Apples." *JEGP* 64 (1965), 35–40.

Stein, Arnold. *Answerable Style: Essays on "Paradise Lost."* Minneapolis: University of Minnesota Press, 1953.

_____. *The Art of Presence: The Poet and "Paradise Lost."* Berkeley: University of California Press, 1977.

Summers, Joseph H. *The Muse's Method: An Introduction to "Paradise Lost."* Cambridge, Mass.: Harvard University Press, 1962.

Swaim, Kathleen M. "The Art of the Maze in Book IX of *Paradise Lost." SEL* 12 (1972), 129–40.

Tasso, Torquato. *Discourses on the Heroic Poem.* Trans. with notes by Mariella Cavalchini and Irene Samuel. Oxford: Clarendon Press, 1973.

Tillyard, E. M. W. *The English Epic and its Background.* London: Chatto and Windus, 1954.

Vinaver, Eugene. *The Rise of Romance.* Oxford: Clarendon Press, 1971.

Virgil. *The "Aeneid" of Virgil.* Ed. with intro. and notes by R. D. Williams. London: Macmillan, 1972; rpt. 1975.

_____. *The "Aeneid" of Virgil: A Verse Translation.* Trans. Allen Mandelbaum. New York: Bantam, 1972.

Voltaire. *An Essay upon the Civil Wars of France, Extracted from Curious Manuscripts, and also upon the Epick Poetry of the European Nations from Homer down to Milton.* 4th, corrected ed. London: N. Prevost, 1731.

Waldock, A. J. A. *"Paradise Lost" and Its Critics.* Cambridge: Cambridge University Press, 1947.

Bibliography

Watkins, W. B. C. *An Anatomy of Milton's Verse*. Baton Rouge: Louisiana State University Press, 1955.

Webber, Joan Malory. *Milton and His Epic Tradition*. Seattle: University of Washington Press, 1979.

Williams, Gordon. *Change and Decline: Roman Literature in the Early Empire*. Berkeley: University of California Press, 1978.

Williams, Kathleen. "Vision and Rhetoric: The Poet's Voice in *The Faerie Queene*." *ELH* 36 (1969), 131–44.

Wittreich, Joseph Anthony, Jr. *Angel of Apocalypse: Blake's Idea of Milton*. Madison: University of Wisconsin Press, 1975.

———. *Visionary Poetics: Milton's Tradition and His Legacy*. San Marino, Calif.: Huntington Library Press, 1979.

———, ed. *Milton and the Line of Vision*. Madison: University of Wisconsin Press, 1975.

———, ed. *The Romantics on Milton*. Cleveland: Case Western University Press, 1970.

Index

Library of Congress Cataloging in Publication Data

DuRocher, Richard J.
  Milton and Ovid.

  Bibliography: p.
  Includes index.
    1. Milton, John, 1608–1674. Paradise lost.   2. Ovid, 43 B.C.–17 or
18. Metamorphoses.   3. Milton, John, 1608–1674—Sources.   4. Ovid,
43 B.C.–17 or 18—Influence—Milton.   5. Metamorphosis in
literature.   I. Title.
PR3562.D84   1985   821'.4   85–47698
ISBN 0–8014–1812–7 (alk. paper)